# Forbidden Fictions

# Forbidden Fictions

**Pornography and Censorship in
Twentieth-Century French Literature**

**John Phillips**

**Pluto**  **Press**

**LONDON • STERLING, VIRGINIA**

First published 1999 by Pluto Press
345 Archway Road, London N6 5AA
and 22883 Quicksilver Drive,
Sterling, VA20166–2012, USA

British Library Cataloguing in Publication Data
A catalogue record for this book is available from the British
Library

ISBN 0 7453 1222 5 hbk

Library of Congress Cataloging in Publication Data
Phillips, John, 1950–
    Forbidden fictions: pornography and censorship in twentieth
-century French literature / John Phillips.
        p.   cm.
    Includes bibliographical references.
    ISBN 0–7453–1222–5 (hbk.)
    1. French literature—20th century—History and criticism.
2. Erotic literature, French—History and criticism.
3. Pornography—France. 4. Censorship—France. I. Title.
PQ673.P55   1999
840.9'3538'0904—dc21                                    98–45087
                                                            CIP

Designed and produced for Pluto Press by
Chase Production Services, Chadlington, OX7 3LN
Typeset from disk by Stanford DTP Services, Northampton
Printed in the EC by T.J. International Ltd, Padstow

# Contents

# Acknowledgements

A shorter version of Chapter 2 was read at a research seminar in the School of European and Language Studies of the University of North London in 1997. Chapters 3 and 5 are expanded versions of papers given in French at the conferences of the *Conseil International d'Études Francophones* in Charleston in 1995 and Québec in 1994, respectively, and subsequently published as 'Excès sexuels, excès textuels: Pierre Louÿs et l'écriture du débordement' in *Études Francophones*, vol. XIII, no. 2 (Autumn 1998) and '*Histoire d'O*: histoire d'un titre' in *Études Francophones*, vol. XI, no. 2 (Winter 1996). Parts of Chapter 5 also appeared in 'O, Really!', *French Studies Bulletin*, no. 55 (Summer 1995), pp. 15–17. I am grateful to both journals for permission to reproduce this material here. Chapter 4 grew from a paper given at Stetson University, Central Florida in March 1998. Chapters 7, 8 and the first part of Chapter 9 are based on unpublished papers delivered in French at CIEF conferences in Guadeloupe (1997), Moncton (1998) and Toulouse (1996), respectively.

I should like to thank, in no particular order, the University of North London for giving me a semester's sabbatical leave in 1998, without which the book would doubtless have remained unfinished for years, Olga Gomez, who read drafts of several chapters and made many helpful and characteristically perceptive observations, and finally, my ten-year old son, Sacha, for making me laugh, just when I was in danger of taking life too seriously.

# Note on Translations/Editions

All translations are mine, except where otherwise shown. In the case of the primary texts, English quotations are taken from published, English-language versions, currently available in the UK, except for *Récidive*, for which no English translation is in print. Page references following quotations are, therefore, to the French and English editions listed in the bibliography.

Chapter 6 analyses the unabridged version of *Emmanuelle*, which was not published in French until 1988. The extant English edition of the novel, first published by Grafton Books in 1975, is based on the earlier, abridged French version. Any page references following quotations in English are to this edition, whilst their absence indicates that the passage in question does not appear in the English edition and that the translation is, therefore, my own.

The analysis in Chapter 4 is of the first edition of *Histoire de l'œil*, upon which the Penguin translation is based.

# 1

# The Erotic Novel and Censorship in Twentieth-Century France

French culture has long been perceived by the English-speaking reader as somehow more 'erotic' than Anglo-Saxon culture. This impression is partly due to the large numbers of pornographic publications which have been imported from Paris since the sixteenth century, first into England and later into the United States, but also to the peculiarly French association of pornography and subversion, hence the fascination that the genre has held for well-known and highly regarded writers from Rabelais to Robbe-Grillet. The choice of modern French (as opposed to any other nation's) pornography as object of study is, therefore, justified by the unique existence of this historical tradition of literary erotica, invigorated in the eighteenth century by the enormous popularity of libertine writing and in the modern period by the Surrealists, and later by Roland Barthes and the *Tel Quel* group, all of whom vigorously opposed censorship and were responsible for an intellectual fascination with the Marquis de Sade, which has had considerable influence on this century's artistic and cultural output.

In the context of such a plethora of erotic works produced by France over the last four hundred years,[1] this study, therefore, has two modest aims: to introduce a limited number of modern French erotic texts to the anglophone reader, and to help open up the long neglected field of erotic and pornographic fiction to serious and objective study.

If pornography has become one of the most hotly debated academic subjects of the 1990s, it is partly because it encompasses many different discourses – feminist discourses about the representation of women, Marxist discourses about cultural commodification, postmodern discourses about the identity of human culture and the human individual, and discourses about representation itself. And of course,

1

pornography is provocative but sexy, controversial yet thrilling, even if for some, the thrill is less about sex than about power, the victory over the monster that others dare not even contemplate lest they recognise themselves in its image, or the satisfaction derived from defending the same monster against those who fear it because they don't understand it. As the nine works chosen for analysis will hopefully demonstrate, textual pornography is the most reader-centred of genres and it is this reader-orientation which makes the genre not only artistically innovative, but also socially subversive and, consequently, threatening to a political *status quo* founded on a conservative moral consensus.

This is a study of what we might agree to call 'literary' erotica, in order to distinguish it from the popular erotic novel as a separate genre, although the boundaries between the two are by no means clear, especially in the contemporary period. Pornography in general might be said to contain many elements characteristic of so-called popular fiction (for instance, erotic themes, violence, travel to exotic places, the extended use of colloquial, even vulgar language). Indeed, the tendency of the pornographic text to cross generic and cultural boundaries is part of its subversive character, unsettling the conventions and expectations associated with social and cultural stereotypes. However, if the novels discussed in this volume have a claim to be part of the literary canon, it is chiefly because they have a sophistication of form which makes them interesting on a textual as well as on a sexual level. On the other hand, the exclusion of pornography which lacks such formal properties can in no way be taken to imply that such writing is less socially or morally acceptable. As we shall see later, the notion of 'artistic value', so widely employed to defend erotic and obscene writing in the court cases of the 1950s and 1960s, is no longer relevant in a debate about freedom and responsibility.

Even within the category of so-called 'literary' pornography, a severely limited choice had to be made, dictated mainly by the need to introduce English-speaking readers to some of the acknowledged landmarks of modern French eroticism as well as to some exciting examples of 'transgressive' writing. The nine novels discussed in this volume are representative of the highly transgressive character of twentieth-century French pornography, dealing as they do with masturbation, voyeurism, fellatio, cunnilingus, masochism, paedophilia, buggery, coprophilia, lesbianism (from a male point of view), troilism, multiple rape, bestiality, sadistic violence and murder. Regrettably, many pornographic works that others might consider masterpieces of literature, such as Louis Aragon's *Le Con d'Irène*, Jean de Berg's *L'Image*, Pierre Guyotat's *Éden, Éden, Éden*, Pierre Klossowski's *Les Lois de l'hospitalité* or Bernard Noël's *Le Château de Cène*, do not have a place here; this is because, with the exception of Guyotat's apocalyptic novel, which is largely unreadable for all but the most conscientious of readers, they do not, in my view, represent a turning point in the evolution of modern French erotic literature.[2]

Individual works apart, I have also excluded discussion of a whole category of erotic fiction, lesbian erotica. This is an important sub-genre of the erotic, including the work of many well-known and highly regarded authors – Colette, Violette Leduc, Monique Wittig and Hélène Cixous, for instance, have made significant contributions to erotic writing by and for lesbians in France. It is, in my view, however, a form of eroticism best commented on by female critics.[3]

The novels which have been selected for discussion are, in almost equal number, by male and female writers (five by men, four by women, the additional male-authored work being by the gay activist, Tony Duvert). Four of these texts (*Les Onze Mille Verges*, *Trois Filles de leur mère*, *Histoire de l'œil*, and *Histoire d'O*) figure in the list of the twelve most pornographic French works of the century, drawn up by the writer and critic, André Pieyre de Mandiargues.[4]

In this introductory chapter, I shall first attempt to define the terms 'erotic', 'pornographic' and 'obscene' in the French context in particular, but also in relation to the wider debate on sexual representation and censorship presently going on in the English-speaking world. I shall then briefly summarise the evolution of French erotic writing in this century and the censoring forces which have attempted to suppress it before examining the main arguments currently advanced for and against censorship. The chapter will end with a brief résumé of subsequent chapters and some concluding observations.

## Definitions

'Pornography,' Alain Robbe-Grillet once remarked, 'is what other people find erotic.'[5] Robbe-Grillet's remark captures perfectly the subjectivity of any distinction between erotica and pornography and suggests the difficulty of precise definition. Others make a virtue out of this difficulty, preferring to abandon the attempt to define altogether. This seems to be Catherine Itzin's position, when she approvingly cites Supreme Court Justice Potter Stewart's infamous remark, 'I can't define pornography, but I know what it is when I see it.'[6] Such disregard for scientific objectivity, surprising in a serious academic like Itzin, is hardly desirable in a debate generating so much emotion that clear thinking and the proper definition of terms is especially important, whatever the difficulties involved. Let me, therefore, at least attempt my own definition of 'pornography' and 'erotica', but first it is necessary to consider the etymological and cultural history of these terms and of the associated notion of obscenity.

In antiquity, the word 'pornographos' bore little relation to our contemporary notion of pornography as writing or images aiming to arouse sexually, since it merely denoted a type of biography, 'the lives of the courtesans', which was not necessarily obscene in content.[7] In fact, it was not until the nineteenth century that the dictionary definition of the word was widened to include 'the expression or suggestion of obscene or unchaste subjects in literature or art'[8] and began, therefore, to assume a pejorative meaning.

The etymology of the word 'obscenity', by contrast, is dubious. Its modern definition of 'indecent' or 'lewd' is preceded by the archaic meaning of 'repulsive' or 'filthy' (*OED*). Some recent commentators have suggested that the word originally meant 'off the scene', in other words, referring to actions in the classical theatre which were too shocking to take place 'on stage' in full view of the audience.[9] What all of these definitions have in common is their subjective basis, for what is 'repulsive' or 'shocking' to some will not be so to others. Moreover, when used in a sexual context, the word reveals a profoundly negative attitude to the sexual functions and to sexual pleasure. For Susan Sontag,

It's just these assumptions that are challenged by the French tradition represented by Sade, Lautréamont, Bataille, and the authors of *Story of O* and *The Image*. Their assumption seems to be that 'the obscene' is a primal notion of human consciousness, something much more profound than the backwash of a sick society's aversion to the body.[10]

Like 'pornography', 'obscenity' has therefore acquired a negative charge in a Western culture, conditioned by the puritanism of Christianity, a negativity which legal definitions have reinforced.

Concepts of obscenity are central to anti-pornography legislation in Britain and the USA, as well as in France. In Britain, the law currently defines obscenity as 'anything that may deprave or corrupt persons who are likely to read, see or hear the matter contained or embodied in it'.[11] In the USA, the so-called 'Miller Test' is still the predominant legal definition of obscenity. According to this test, which originated in a 1973 case tried before the American Supreme Court, *Miller* v. *California*, there are three criteria: 1) does a work as a whole appeal to 'prurient interest'?; 2) does it depict or describe sexual conduct in a 'patently offensive way'?; 3) does it lack 'serious literary, artistic, political or scientific value'?[12] A recent ruling by the Canadian Supreme Court, masterminded by anti-pornography campaigners Catherine MacKinnon and Andrea Dworkin, defines obscenity according to the harm it does to women's pursuit of equality.[13]

These definitions of obscenity are dangerously vague, since they all depend upon the inescapable subjectivity and cultural relativity of other terms, such as 'indecent', 'deprave', 'corrupt', 'prurient', 'offensive', 'value', 'harm', 'equality', embedded in them. In the French law of the last two centuries, the concept of *bonnes mœurs* (which roughly translates as 'public decency') is equally vague and culturally relative, as the history of censorship clearly shows – how many of us would consider Flaubert's *Madame Bovary* or the racier pieces in Baudelaire's best known collection of poems, *Les Fleurs du Mal* (*The Flowers of Evil*), a threat to public morals now?

To distinguish between pornography and erotica, as Robbe-Grillet implies, is equally unhelpful in a debate about social or moral acceptability. Some sort of consensus grew up earlier in the century that, while pornography merely aims to arouse sexually, erotica stimulates the sensibilities and the imagination as much as sexual desire. The difference here is clearly perceived on an artistic level, and has absolutely nothing to do with sex. Eroticism, says Angela Carter, is simply the 'pornography of the elite'.[14]

In 1978, Gloria Steinem's militant feminist perspective articulated quite a different distinction between the two terms: 'Erotica is about sexuality, but pornography is about power and sex-as-weapon', she declared.[15] Many anti-censorship feminists, however, such as Gayle Rubin, Ellen Willis and Ann Snitow have rightly attacked this distinction as based on a utopian notion of 'good sex' as a 'ladylike activity', excluding the important role played by infantilism and aggression in adult sexual fantasy.[16]

Such distinctions valorise erotica against pornography, associating the former with high and the latter with low culture, and we have seen how subjective they are. To differentiate between them in terms of value also implicitly condones the denigration, if not censorship, of the pornographic. In my own analysis, therefore, I propose a distinction that is purely descriptive and, therefore, free of moral or qualitative judgments. I shall continue to employ the term 'erotic' in its accepted, denotative sense of 'concerning (sexual) love', simply to describe either the thematic content of a work (or of passages within it) or the responses of a reader, whilst implying nothing about the work's principal aims. On the other hand, 'pornographic' will, in this volume, describe passages or texts which contain explicit sexual material aimed at producing a particular effect of sexual arousal.

All of the texts discussed in the following chapters may, under these definitions, be described as 'erotic'. Most, though not all, may also be said to contain 'pornographic' elements, while having, at the same time, other, mainly literary, qualities which make them important examples of the erotic genre and worthy of our attention as students of literature. The terms 'pornography' and 'pornographic' will, however, in no sense be used pejoratively. The signifier 'pornography', which has been so demonised by puritanical and politically correct discourses, will, in the process, be recuperated as a morally neutral term. In thus attempting to rehabilitate the term 'pornography' I am consciously following the lead taken by Judith Butler, who has advocated the 'restaging' of injurious speech rather than censoring it:

> Butler is effectively protesting against the brand of feminism advocated by Catherine MacKinnon and Andrea Dworkin, activists who want to protect women against verbal and physical abuse through legislation and the state. [...] But according to Butler, [banning pornography] only represses the problem without confronting it. MacKinnon has under-estimated 'the power people have to change language and to be changed by language [...] I'd like pornography as a genre redefined. I'm not even sure I would want to call it pornography. I think there needs to be a shame-free exploration of sexuality in art'.[17]

In these definitions, pornography becomes as positively coded as erotica and neither needs to be justified on grounds of artistic merit (although many pornographic and erotic texts do possess such merit). Indeed, I would suggest that the pornographic character of a text can itself be regarded as a quality: writing that sexually arouses, making a passive reader an active participant in the imaginative process, is, after all, a skilfully performative use of language. For the psychoanalyst, Robert Stoller, 'Sexual excitation [...] has an aesthetics which is as complex, coded and meaning-laden as other forms of narrative, theatre or art.'[18]

## Literary Eroticism in Twentieth-Century France

At the end of the eighteenth century, the century of Sade and of *libertinage*, of the collapse of both Monarchy and Church in the French Revolution, eroticism in France appeared to go underground. The despotic measures introduced by Robespierre during the Terror marked the beginning of a long period of sexual repression. The adoption of the Napoleonic code and, later, the return of the monarchy, encouraged a general decline in the production of pornographic literature.[19] Sex took refuge in the mushrooming medico-legal discourses of the period,[20] peeping out only occasionally from the pages of a literature policed more than that of any other century, and was largely avoided and displaced throughout the nineteenth century as a subject of mainstream literature by the convention of romantic love. By the end of the century, however, more and more educated French readers were consuming Laclos and Sade in secret and there was a renewed interest in Sade as a literary and philosophical ancestor, particularly among the writers and poets of what was known as the Decadent period (c. 1870–1900).

For Jean-Jacques Pauvert, the real turning point came around 1905, when the generation of young writers, led by the symbolist poet Guillaume Apollinaire, began to express themselves.[21] Pauvert argues that the last *fin de siècle* saw profound changes in attitudes, influenced by important new work in the sciences and in philosophy: Freud published his *Interpretation of Dreams* in 1899 and his *Three Essays on Sexuality* in 1905, destroying forever the notion of childhood innocence, while Henri Bergson, Max Planck, Niels Bohr and Albert Einstein all shook the foundations of a logical positivism which had dominated scientific thinking for most of the previous century. A new, modern spirit was abroad, it was a spirit of uncertainty and disillusion with the old values of religion and the old ruling dynasties.

Born in 1880 and dying in 1918, victim of the Paris influenza epidemic, Apollinaire symbolised in both his life and his work this passage from the absolute certainties of the nineteenth century to the new doubts and relativities of the twentieth. During his short life, he did perhaps more to hasten the advent of an *esprit nouveau* and, especially, to promote the reading of erotic works than any other writer of the period.[22] *Les Onze Mille Verges ou les Amours d'un hospodar*, which appeared secretly in 1907, was of its time. Not only did it reflect topical events (the victory of the Japanese over the Russians at Port-Arthur in 1904–5), but it was, for some, Apollinaire's masterpiece, bursting with a plurality of meanings and full of a playfulness that make it one of the first erotic novels of the modern age.

In spite of its many qualities, *Les Onze Mille Verges* is, of course, typical of most erotic output up until the mid-twentieth century in being authored by a man and thoroughly male-centred. In this, Apollinaire's erotic imagination merely reflects the structures and prejudices of the patriarchal society in which he lived. It is also noticeably Sadean in influence and characteristic of the genre as a whole in that it represents homosexual acts (sodomy, male-to-male fellatio) as interesting diversions rather than as substitutes for heterosexual activities. In Pierre Louÿs's *Trois Filles de leur mère* (1926), female homosexuality is similarly presented from a heterosexual male perspective, offering voyeuristic objects for the male reader. Like Apollinaire, Louÿs follows a tradition stretching back to the eighteenth century, when an entirely male-authored erotic genre favoured the inclusion, for voyeuristic purposes, of scenes of lesbian lovemaking.[23] Both of these works suffered the fate of all obscene erotica of the period of being restricted to private circulation among friends and acquaintances or to 'under-the-counter' sales, and did not appear in legal editions until 1970.

The transgressive fictions of Georges Bataille, together with his profoundly intellectual theories of the erotic, dominate the mid-century in France and, in a sense, look backwards as well as forwards: both the extreme obscenity and the sado-masochistic contents of his fiction owe much to Sade, while the theoretical basis of his eroticism, in particular his presentation of the human subject as disintegrated, his belief in the essential autonomy of the text and the generally unsystematic nature of his philosophical method, seem to prefigure the plural discourses of postmodernism and its textualisation of the subject and the world. As Bataille's first and probably best known erotic fiction, the thoroughly obscene, yet artistically innovative, *Histoire de l'œil* (1928) has, of all his works, attracted the most critical attention.

Bataille continued to write pornographic fiction until his death in 1962. Eight years earlier, the first French pornographic novel of the century written by a woman had made its appearance. *Histoire d'O* was published in 1954 by Pauline Réage, a pseudonym for Dominique Aury. Frappier-Mazur rightly considers this text to represent the penultimate stage in the evolution of erotic writings by women in that it depicts male domination and female subjection from the victim's point of view for the first time.[24]

While Réage's book was thoroughly traditional, even classical in form, Emmanuelle Arsan's *Emmanuelle*, written only four years later, though not officially published until 1967, could not have been written before the end of the 1950s. Arsan's novel is certainly very 'literary' in form (a fact that might surprise those readers familiar only with the film and its sequels), but its optimistic, life-affirming conception of eroticism and its portrayal of female sexual autonomy are completely alien to the morbid and guilt-ridden eroticism of Bataille. For André Pieyre de Mandiargues, *Emmanuelle*, like *Les Onze Mille Verges*, represents nothing less than a new spirit of eroticism,[25] and for Jean-Jacques Pauvert, the novel marks the beginning of a new, permissive era, 'the Emmanuelle era' which lasted until 1985, the year when AIDS came to full public attention in France.[26]

It is during this permissive era that Tony Duvert and other homosexual French writers (for example, Jean Demélier, Renaud Camus and Dominique Fernandez) publish their explicitly homoerotic works, openly projecting homosexuality in a positive light for the first time. *Récidive*, which was originally published by Duvert in 1967, is one of the first examples in France of the pornographic novel written specifically for the homosexual reader. This is a unique period, during which sexual discourses are relatively free of legal or moral constraints, reflecting the sexual freedoms enjoyed in Western society as a whole; it is a time when Duvert can actively champion the sexual rights of the child in his essays and fictions without becoming the target of a hysterical witchhunt and when Alain Robbe-Grillet, the leader of the New Novel movement in France, can make films and write novels in which very young females are depicted as objects of male sexual violence without any overt sense of moral condemnation on the author's part. Robbe-Grillet's *Projet pour une révolution à New York* (1970) is both typical of the author's preoccupation with little girls as erotic objects and its most direct and most daring expression.

With AIDS in the mid-1980s, however, comes a new puritanism, which calls for abstention from uncontrolled pleasure and advocates chastity as the only condom. In America, pro-censorship forces organised by Dworkin and MacKinnon begin to push for legislation to ban all pornography. (In 1983, they achieved their first legal victory with an anti-pornography law passed by the Minneapolis

City Council.) The 1980s is also the decade when political correctness emerges from US university campuses, threatening artistic freedoms. Admittedly, the pro-censorship and political correctness lobbies appear to have had little direct impact on French political and cultural life – there is, significantly, no equivalent of Dworkin or MacKinnon in France – but as we shall see later, censorship finds other ways of justifying its continued presence in French society.

Among feminism's many positive achievements is the emergence, from the 1970s onwards, of a female eroticism, written, like *Histoire d'O* and *Emmanuelle*, from a female viewpoint but, unlike Réage's novel, addressing the growing economic and sexual independence of women and shunning the phallocentric sexual imagery that characterises the style of Emmanuelle Arsan. The political and social revolution of 1968 is also a clear turning point for women's erotica:

> In France, the link with the 1968 'events' seems unmistakable. 1968 launched the women's movement which, despite many feminists' hostility to erotica, has inspired more women to 'write themselves' in their own words, hence an unprecedented upsurge of erotic novels whose tone is altogether new.[27]

Though it is true that some female writers of the erotic have continued to ape their male counterparts, producing a pornographic literature for the male reader, the 1970s, 1980s and 1990s have seen the emergence of a large number of French women authors, writing about women's sexuality with women readers in mind. The two writers whose first novels are discussed in the last chapter of the book, Élisabeth Barillé and Marie Darrieussecq, exemplify this trend, as do many others, whose work is not represented here.[28] What all of these women writers have in common is a tendency to situate the erotic firmly in the context of relationships between men and women, and between women and women. For Frappier-Mazur, this prioritising of relational values extends to female bonding which is often indistinguishable from erotic love:

> In this respect, women's erotic novels simply actualise the unconscious or unavowed sexual component of romantic

female friendships. A common occurrence in the lives of women through the beginning of the twentieth century, these friendships were considered asexual and usually did not arouse any blame or suspicion.[29]

As Barillé's heroine declares with an ironic wink, meant as much for the reader as for her female friend, 'Comme est douce la complicité féminine!' ('Female complicity is so sweet!')[30]

If the heroines of these narratives enjoy fleeting erotic encounters, as many do,[31] they are far less promiscuous than their counterparts in either the heterosexual or the homosexual erotic literature of the 1960s and 1970s (as typified by *Emmanuelle* on the one hand and *Récidive* on the other). Erotic fantasy is often seen as a substitute for real sexual experience. Increasingly feminine in inspiration, erotic fiction in general thus mirrors a real decrease, from the mid-1980s onwards, in the promiscuity of both hetero- and homosexuals, mainly owing to the AIDS epidemic, but perhaps also to the increasingly right-wing rhetoric of political leaders in France as in Britain and America championing 'family values' and backing them up with legislation designed to reinforce conventional Judeo-Christian morality. In this sense, much contemporary erotic writing can be said to be promoting a sexual responsibility which frequently takes the form of serial monogamy. *Corps de jeune fille* (1986) is as much about love as it is about sex. In *Truismes* (1996), the female narrator's prostitution is generally seen to have disastrous consequences and gives way, in the second half of the novel, to a focus on eroticism within the context of romantic relationships (though it should be stressed that there is no hint of judgementalism with regard to *any* of the narrator's sexual conduct; she is presented as the innocent, indeed guileless, victim of an exploitative consumerism).[32]

If we are to discern the main trends affecting the erotic and pornographic genre in France during the course of this century, four distinct changes stand out above all else. Firstly, and most importantly, the male-centredness of the genre gradually lessens as female authors begin to write and publish erotic works dealing with female sexuality, pseudonymously to begin with (Dominique Aury writing as Pauline Réage, for example, while the real identity of Emmanuelle Arsan is still unknown to all except her publisher) and eventually as openly as their male counterparts.

Secondly, by the 1960s, gay and lesbian works,[33] written by and for gay men and women, began to appear more openly in France. One of the best known and most talented of this wave of homosexual writers was Tony Duvert.

Thirdly, from the 1970s onwards, French erotic fiction increasingly becomes a part (and some would say a very lucrative part) of mainstream literary production and we can witness a gradual erosion of generic boundaries.[34] Frappier-Mazur notes that new 'erotic' stories by women 'are distinguished from mainstream literature only by the predominance they give to erotic episodes: they bypass the formulaic and ritualized model and read as less specialized than erotic novels by, for instance, Robbe-Grillet or Mandiargues'.[35] The two novels which form the subject of Chapter 9 exemplify this trend well: to label either *Corps de jeune fille* or *Truismes* as 'pornographic fiction' (in a reductive and pejorative rather than a merely descriptive sense), as some critics have done, is to ignore the complexity of a writing, informed in both cases by a plurality of discourses and addressing the representation of love and sexuality in a manner which firmly establishes both as bestselling novels with a broad appeal to the general (especially female) reader. Frappier-Mazur's survey of women's recent erotic writing suggests that this blurring of borderlines between genres is indeed largely due to the increased influence of women writers in this area.[36]

Fourthly, and lastly, direct forms of book censorship have virtually disappeared in France, though, as we shall now see, they have to some significant degree been replaced by indirect, less overt, more insidious forms of censorship. This change has had some impact on the themes and forms of French erotic writing.

## Censorship in France: a Brief History

The Paris of this century, if not of earlier ones, is associated in the popular imagination with liberal attitudes to pornography, an association which does have a basis in fact. British, Irish and American writers of the modern period, whose work contained erotic elements, found a haven in Paris, the 'city of culture and tolerance'.[37] Indeed, Maurice Girodias's Paris-based Olympia Press (and its earlier avatars, Obelisk Press and Éditions du Chêne) made a great deal of money in the 1930s, 1940s and 1950s, publishing in English what are now regarded as classics of the modern erotic canon.[38]

It is certainly true, generally speaking, that for most of the century there has been a great deal less censorship in France than in Britain or in the United States. Until the late 1950s, Britain's draconian obscenity laws were the most restrictive in the world, whilst in 1950s' America, during the McCarthy era, the publication of erotic works could be construed as communist subversion.[39] When one begins to examine the detailed history of censorship in France, however, things appear a little more complicated.

Books have been considered dangerous in France, as in other European countries, since the early days of printing in the fifteenth century when the Catholic Church realised the power of the medium and the need to watch out for dangerous material. Robert Netz sees the burning of Martin Luther's 'heretical' writings in 1523 as the beginning of a long history of book censorship in France.[40] Until the eighteenth century, this censorship was both religious and political in motivation, with the king controlling the publication of all works by the end of the sixteenth century, though by far the largest number of prosecutions were for books attacking the Church.[41] By the eighteenth century, such controls had become severe, with a form of pre-censorship exercised by numerous royal censors, and the galleys or even the death penalty threatening authors and printers who flouted the laws. In 1759, 40 per cent of prisoners held in the Bastille were there for book-related crimes![42]

This situation, nevertheless, gave rise to a flourishing 'under-the-counter' trade in banned books, most of which came into the country from abroad. These included anti-Catholic and anti-Monarchy pamphlets (or 'libelles') and pornographic tales of lascivious monks and nuns, which began to make their appearance at the beginning of the eighteenth century. Much of this 'pornography' was satirical in nature, aimed at both the Church and the Monarchy.[43] As Robert Darnton points out, however, eighteenth-century Frenchmen did not distinguish a genre of pure pornography from other types of fiction, the notion of pornography itself not appearing until the nineteenth century.[44] Hence, the term 'philosophical books' was used by booksellers to denote material of any kind that fell into the forbidden category. Because of the increasing uses of obscenity to subvert the *ancien régime* in the third quarter of the eighteenth century, it is arguable that the pornographic, indistinguishable from other forbidden discourses, played a significant role in creating a climate favourable for revolution.[45]

In 1789, following the Revolution, the National Assembly abolished all censorship, but it was not long before the return of even more repressive controls: in 1793, it was decreed by the Terror's ruling Committee of Public Safety that any author or printer of works inciting opposition to the *status quo* would be sentenced to death.[46] This set the tone for the whole of the next century, from Napoleon to the Third Republic. In particular, the law of 17 May 1819 introduced a very important article (article 8), extended in scope and severity in 1822, which was to form the basis of print censorship until 1881 and, indeed, would be reactivated in 1958, upon de Gaulle's return to power. This article allowed for the imposition of heavy fines and up to five years' imprisonment for 'any offence against religious and public morals, or against public decency', including mockery of the State religion.[47] It is this law that was used to prosecute Baudelaire's *Les Fleurs du Mal* and Flaubert's *Madame Bovary* in 1857. Baudelaire was fined 300 francs and ordered to remove six poems from the collection. Flaubert was acquitted, though the judge insisted that the novel was blameworthy in that it did not fulfil literature's mission of 'elevating the mind and purifying our morals'.[48]

Altogether, 24 writers were tried in the nineteenth century on the grounds that their work offended against 'public decency'.[49] Two main fears underlay this vague and changeable concept of public morality: that 'immoral' works were a threat to public order and social stability, and that 'innocence' must be protected.[50] Although article 8 was replaced in 1881 by a law which declared the press to be free and all references to religious morality and absolutes such as public morality, God or the State had disappeared, 'offence against public decency' remained the basic principle of censorship of the written

word and the thinking behind it lingered on to influence the
direction of and provide justification for censoring legislation
in the twentieth century. Moreover, Catholicism continued to
exercise a repressive influence outside French law, by means
of Rome's 'Index of Prohibited Works'.[51] At the end of the
nineteenth century there was some public concern, encouraged
by the Church and other guardians of morality, that a 'wave
of pornography' threatened to undermine social values – 'plus
ça change ...'! – consequently, regional 'leagues' or committees
were set up to keep an eye on bookshops and take action
against the authors and publishers of obscene literature.[52]
The actions of these anti-obscenity leagues drove erotic
literature underground by reinforcing a repressive legislation
that affected, not just pornography, but all writings about
sex, including technical works about contraception.[53]

Throughout the twentieth century, as indicated earlier, the
defence of *bonnes mœurs* has remained the basis of all
censorship laws in France, although both World Wars and the
Algerian War of 1955–62 also saw extensive political
censorship. In laws of the postwar period, the protection of
youth, above all, has been the overriding aim. For instance, in
1949 it became illegal to expose minors under 18 to
publications of a 'licentious or pornographic nature'. In 1958,
on General de Gaulle's election to the presidency, the scope
of this provision was widened considerably, to the point of
forbidding display of such material 'in any place whatever' and
advertising for it 'in any form whatever'. Many comic books
were suppressed under this law and, at the very least, authors
and editors were obliged to exercise self-censorship.[54]

The period between the end of the war and the end of the
1960s could be considered a period of extreme censorship. The
principle of the protection of youth, together with the defence
of public morality, have been the basis of all prosecutions of
adult fiction during this period, Maurice Girodias's Olympia
Press becoming a particular focus of attention for the
authorities under this legislation. Henry Miller's *Tropic of
Capricorn* and *Tropic of Cancer* were banned for 'offence against
public decency in the medium of print'. After 'L'Affaire Miller'
came 'L'Affaire Lolita', with the prevention of the publication
of Nabokov's novel; Olympia Press's English-language editions
of Sade's *La Philosophie dans le boudoir* (*Philosophy in the*

*Bedroom*), Apollinaire's *Les Onze Mille Verges* (published as *The Debauched Hospodar*) and Bataille's *Histoire de l'œil* (published as *A Tale of Satisfied Desire* by Pierre Angélique) all came under scrutiny by the government authorities. In the 1950s, the *Brigade Mondaine* (or 'Vice Squad') made frequent visits to the Olympia Press's offices, taking books away and issuing banning orders and lawsuits, which Girodias swiftly contested.[55] Meanwhile, Jean-Jacques Pauvert was famously prosecuted from 1954 to 1958 for publishing Sade's complete works. During this period, he was heavily fined and the works were ordered to be confiscated and destroyed. *Les Onze Mille Verges*, which had reappeared in 1948 under a false Dutch provenance, was repeatedly prosecuted until the 1960s, and when it was finally published openly by Régine Deforges in 1970, it had to include a warning that it should be 'kept out of the hands of minors'. *Histoire de l'œil* and other works by Bataille were also the object of numerous prosecutions at this time.[56]

What, then, of literary censorship in France since the 1960s? A 1970 edition of *Magazine littéraire*[57] announced on its front cover that there was no censorship in France – 'Il n'y a pas de censure en France.' Yet, in the very same year, Pierre Guyotat's *Éden, Éden, Éden*, an obscene novel apparently set in the Algerian War, was the subject of an order banning all advertising of the book and its sale to minors. Jérôme Lindon, head of the Éditions de Minuit, launched a petition against the ban, which was signed by many well-known writers, including Jean-Paul Sartre and Louis Aragon.[58] Since that date, despite a drop in the number of book prosecutions following the defeat of de Gaulle, books continue to be seized, and their editors threatened with fines and prison sentences. In 1975, *Histoire d'O* was seized in Brussels' bookstores, having been banned in Belgium since 1965, and in 1977 the publisher, François Maspero, declared that 21 of his books had been banned since 1969.[59]

The book and press censorship provisions of the new Penal Code, which came into force on 1 March 1994, have been welcomed by some as the most liberal that France has ever known; yet, Jean-Jacques Pauvert regards one article of the Code (article L 227-24) as a 'masterpiece of censorship' because of its vagueness. The article makes it illegal to manufacture, transport or broadcast by whatever means [...] any message of violent or pornographic character or the nature of which seriously injures human dignity [...]⁶⁰

As Pauvert observes with regard to this 'catch-all' piece of repressive legislation, 'The effectiveness of any censorship law increases [...] with the vagueness of its terms.'⁶¹

Where Pauvert still sees the pernicious effects of direct manifestations of censorship in law, Maurice Girodias places the emphasis on indirect and more subtle forms of control. In his autobiography, *Une Journée sur la terre*, Girodias draws depressing conclusions concerning the evolution of censorship in recent years, seeing the State's control of individual sexuality become increasingly sophisticated:

> Whereas under the IVth Republic, de Gaulle and Pompidou, control was exercised through application of the obscenity laws which remained on the statute books until their abolition by Giscard d'Estaing, the Socialist record since 1981 has been scarcely less uninspiring, even if the State now employs the innovation of soft-porn on the TV as a means of conditioning sexuality into approved channels.⁶²

For Girodias, as for Philippe Sollers, censorship in contemporary France is no longer the political and moral censorship of the nineteenth century, but a manipulation of thinking. In the contemporary French media, the erotic is controlled, sanitised, reduced to banality, so that it has ceased to be effective as a weapon of subversion.⁶³ This is probably the best reason to reject political correctness in its most extreme and most pernicious form, that is, the policing of the human imaginary, whether manifested in the language of literature or in the language of every day.⁶⁴ The imagination needs spaces in which to play, which are out of reach of both the censor and the prejudices generated by culturally relative notions of what is and is not morally or socially acceptable.

As I said earlier, the anti-pornography movement, led by Andrea Dworkin and Catherine MacKinnon in the USA, and less prominently by Catherine Itzin in the UK, has made little or no progress in France, though the issues they raise are, of course, of universal relevance. These pro-censorship feminists base their arguments on the notion that pornography is simply part of the generalised oppression of women by patriarchy, so that what they see as the sexism of pornography and its objectification of women's bodies both reflects and influences the treatment of women in the real world. For MacKinnon, pornography is not just an offensive use of language, but springs from or leads to real actions, while Dworkin appears to regard not only representations of heterosexual intercourse but the 'thing itself' as rape.[65] Their campaigns to introduce censoring legislation in the US and in Canada have therefore been based on the principle that pornography causes actual harm. Now, this is not the place to debate their arguments in the kind of detail that would be required to do justice to the issues involved – such a debate would fill another book. Readers should, nevertheless, be aware that there is a considerable body of opposition to their views, both within the feminist movement and outside it.[66] My own position is unequivocally in the anti-censorship camp, for a number of reasons which I shall briefly summarise:

- The debate on the relationship between pornography and violence is highly topical, both in the UK and in the USA. The question central to this debate, crudely put, is, 'Can pornography lead the consumer of it to commit violent sex crimes against women and children?' Now, people are undoubtedly influenced by what they read (and see) – my definition of pornography as material which aims principally to excite the reader sexually and the hypothesis, referred to earlier, that libertine literature in the eighteenth century helped bring about the French Revolution both imply that writing can, in certain circumstances, influence individual behaviour. But to believe that this process obeys a simple cause and effect law, unconstrained by individual conscience and outside of any ethical or moral context, is to deny the complexity of all cultural phenomena, including the pornographic, and of human interaction with those phenomena. In fact, not only is there no evidence of any kind of any direct causal link between violence and pornography, but a serious body of research suggests that exposure to some types of pornography actually reduces aggressivity in males.[67] The banning of pornographic matter will not, therefore, reduce levels of real violence against women and children, because, as the most reliable scientific studies confirm, pornography is less likely to induce violent behaviour than the Bible or the Koran. Indeed, the fantasy spaces of pornography, like those of religion, are the best place for extreme behaviour.

- Censorship legislation enacted in the USA and in Canada has been seen to restrict rather than to extend women's rights; indeed, the introduction of censoring laws always has negative effects on intellectual and artistic freedoms and on the civil liberties of all minority groups. Not surprisingly, many of those in the pro-censorship lobby are motivated by a blind hostility to heterosexual sex (extreme militant lesbians) or by a puritanical hatred of sex in general (the moral and Christian right).

- Pornography has an important cathartic role in a culture still sufficiently imbued with Christianity's repulsion for the body to repress the erotic side of human experience, unless it is contained and controlled within sanitising societal norms.

- To ban pornography on the sole grounds that it is sexist and objectifies women is to ignore the existence of gay and lesbian or SM pornography. Voyeurism and objectification are, in any event, endemic in our scopophilic culture. Far from being aberrant or undesirable, some types of objectification are unavoidable and even necessary aspects of human behaviour. It goes without saying that the objectification that drives all physical attraction is indispensable to human reproduction and, therefore, survival. We all, men and women, constantly objectify in both a sexual and a non-sexual sense. If women have not done so in the past, is it not because they were prevented by their social conditioning rather than by lack of any 'natural inclination'? As we have seen, the evolution of French pornographic writing in this century is marked, above all, by an increasing involvement of women in the genre and by a concomitant decrease in its traditionally sexist and phallocentric character.

- As an outlaw discourse, pornography has a crucial potential for transgression, both at a political and a personal level. We have seen that French literary pornography in particular has played a positive role since the eighteenth century as the most subversive and the most reader-centred of all genres.[68] Pornography is a 'limit' genre, provoking, subverting, giving birth to new forms and new ideas.

## Chapter Contents

All the following chapters deal essentially with the formal properties of the nine texts chosen for analysis, properties which make our responses to those texts more complex than to commercial pornography of no literary value.

Analysing Guillaume Apollinaire's *Les Onze Mille Verges*, Pierre Louÿs's *Trois Filles de leur mère* and Alain Robbe-Grillet's *Projet pour une révolution à New York*, Chapters 2, 3 and 7 draw attention to the strongly intertextual, self-referential and parodic character of the genre.

Chapter 4 (on Georges Bataille's *Histoire de l'œil*), Chapter 6 (on Emmanuelle Arsan's *Emmanuelle*) and Chapter 8 (on Tony Duvert's *Récidive*) bring the critical gaze back to the representational elements of erotic writing, asking to what extent these elements are acceptable to the contemporary reader from the point of view of a sexual politics.

Like Chapter 6, Chapters 5 and 9 focus on women's writing, but from different points of view: while Chapter 5 is primarily concerned with the thematic and linguistic structures of *Histoire d'O* in relation to the sexual identity of both text and female protagonist, Chapter 9 considers how the female-centred eroticism of two contemporary novels – Élisabeth Barillé's *Corps de jeune fille* and Marie Darrieussecq's *Truismes* – may be said to renew a male erotic tradition and in what ways these novels reflect current debates on political correctness and women's sexual roles.

## Concluding Remarks

In spite of a certain idealised vision of Paris as the Mecca of sexual freedom, even a cursory reading of the history of censorship in France suggests that, though perhaps comparing favourably in this area with the even more puritanical Anglo-Saxon world, the country of Robespierre and Napoleon, of Madame de Gaulle and the Brigade Mondaine, has a long tradition of rigid controls in publishing and, though these may have lessened in the postwar period, we can still find striking instances of their damaging effects. Maurice Girodias, the head of the Olympia Press in Paris, was a spectacular casualty of the illiberal forces of Gaullist France: 'By the mid-1960s, he had collected four to six years in suspended prison sentences, $80,000 in fines and an eighty-year ban on all publishing activity.'[69] More recently, the 'loi Gayssot' of 13 July 1990 expressly forbids the denial of 'crimes against humanity' committed during the Second World War. However well-intentioned this law may be, Jean-Jacques Pauvert points out the obvious dangers associated with the banning of all but an 'official' version of history.[70]

While a persuasive case can be made that, in this century in particular, censor and censored have at times enjoyed a parasitical and 'mutually perpetuating' relationship, with prosecuted books attracting considerably more public interest,[71] censorship has also caused undeniable harm, both directly in terms of the penalties imposed and indirectly in leading to the pre-censorship or self-censorship of authors and publishers anxious to avoid scandal or prosecution (an effect of censorship, which is obviously difficult if not impossible to measure).

Michel Foucault famously questioned the very existence of a repressive censorship in Western culture. In his *Histoires de la sexualité*,[72] Foucault launched a vigorous attack on the hypothesis that sex has been repressed at all, arguing instead that the last three centuries have in fact seen an 'explosion of discourses' on the subject. He is undoubtedly right to claim that since the nineteenth century the medico-legal study of what came to be known as 'sexuality' (which for Foucault is a cultural fabrication) has functioned as a substitute for the lost erotic arts, that in other words, the 'scientia sexualis', have become our 'ars erotica'. Manuals and guides to sexual behaviour have indeed taken the place of the *Kama Sutra* in our postwar culture, authorising us to talk about (and read about) sex in a legitimate way. The repackaging of sex by medicine and psychiatry which began in the nineteenth century was an attempt to control, through discourse, forms of behaviour whose very uncontrollability threatened the stability of bourgeois society, founded on the anti-sex ideology of Christianity. However, Foucault underplays the fact that, until the middle of this century at least, such discourses were the preserve of a small, educated elite – the workers and peasants of a society with no developed mass media had better things to do than read Krafft-Ebing or Havelock Ellis (if they could read at all). The multiplication of discourses on sex that Foucault talks about was limited to those who exercised power to keep others in ignorance. In fact, those who read psychiatric studies of sexual deviations were also most likely to make up the equally limited readership of erotic and pornographic writing.

For Foucault, *Les Bijoux indiscrets* (*The Indiscreet Jewels*), Diderot's exotic eighteenth-century tale of speaking vaginas, is emblematic of modern discourses about sexuality. When the Sultan, Mangogul, receives a magic ring from the genie, Cucufa, he only has to point it at a woman in his court and her 'bijou' or 'sex' is compelled to confess its experiences. In his selective reading of the tale, however, Foucault ignores both the repression of the sexual that the jewel metaphor represents (metaphors substitute one thing for another, in this case, jewels for vaginas) and the controlling power of the ring itself, an obvious metaphor for the control of knowledge by an elite.

For the vast majority of a Western population, whose moral values were largely derived from a particularly rigid and often literal-minded version of Judeo-Christianity, sex was a taboo subject until the explosive growth of the media and the development of mass education that followed the Second World War.[73] Nor have we entirely rid ourselves in the modern era of the 'taboo' status of discourses on sex, a notion that is central to Georges Bataille's thinking about the erotic. We have seen how, both in France and in the USA and Britain, direct and indirect censorship have played a significant role in ensuring that discourses about sex were limited to the tiny minority thought capable of remaining uncorrupted by them (white, male, middle- and upper-class professionals). Writing about sex may well continue to have something of a taboo status in our culture – how else can pornography retain its transgressive force? – but any such status must not be allowed to legitimate repression. One of the main challenges for the future of erotic writing must surely be to protect it from the forces of censorship and repression, while if possible preserving its subversive potential. If erotica and pornography have a social mission at the end of the millennium, is it not, precisely, to subvert the ideological control of sex by any one interest group, whether political or religious, phallocratic or feminist?

# 2

# Pornography, Poetry, Parody: Guillaume Apollinaire's *Les Onze Mille Verges*

It was not until 1970 that the first legal edition of the pornographic novel, *Les Onze Mille Verges*, bearing the name of Guillaume Apollinaire, was published. The heirs to his estate had finally admitted the existence of the book, written over 60 years earlier, and which has been described as the most explicit and violent erotic novel ever written in French. As Jean-Jacques Pauvert observes, there was no immediate public outcry, although only two years previously, in 1968, the *Commission de protection de l'enfance et de la jeunesse* had attempted to prosecute Pauvert himself for illicit publication of the work, having found it to contain 'une accumulation des vices les plus variés, l'érotisme, la pornographie et les perversions de tous genres y voisinant avec la scatologie et le sadisme' ('an accumulation of the most varied vices, with eroticism, pornography and perversions of all kinds mixed in with scatology and sadism').[1] This is, indeed, a fair description of the book's subject matter, although it omits its humorous and parodic context.

Critics are divided about the exact date of first publication, though Jean-Jacques Pauvert persuasively argues that both this novel and the equally pornographic *Les Exploits d'un jeune Don Juan* were completed by Apollinaire in 1908.[2] In addition to the novels, Apollinaire edited a collection of erotic writings by others[3], notably Arétin, Baffo, Nerciat, Leland (the author of *Fanny Hill*) and Sade. In the introduction to his Sade anthology,[4] he rightly predicted that, though neglected by the nineteenth century, Sade would come to dominate the twentieth. Indeed, it was this edition of extracts from a number of Sade's tamer writings that kindled the enthusiasm for Sade of many of his Surrealist friends. In addition to his own erotic output and his work of editing the erotic writings of others,

Apollinaire compiled a catalogue of all the pornographic works in *La Bibliothèque Nationale*.[5]

Despite this clear fascination with the genre, Apollinaire's work in this area has generally been despised by critics, judged to contain no literary value and reduced to the level of a mercenary pursuit.[6] For Pauvert, however, it was in his 'enfers' that Apollinaire's love of life and freedom found its strongest expression, although evidence of this interest in the obscene can be found in many of his less explicitly erotic texts, including the poetry.[7] Rather than being the creations of a dishonest, puerile and therefore less well-developed poetic sensibility, as most commentators have maintained, the pornographic writings form an integral part of Apollinaire's œuvre. The poet's surrealist friends, notably André Breton, Louis Aragon and Robert Desnos, recognised this at once. For Desnos, for example, Apollinaire was not so much a great erotic writer as a great modern poet, a midwife at the birth of Cubism and champion of the new, there being no fundamental distinction to make between his poetic and his pornographic writings: '*Les Onze Mille Verges* sont un livre moderne, et avec *Calligrammes* le chef-d'œuvre d'Apollinaire' ('*Les Onze Mille Verges* is a modern book, and together with *Calligrammes*, Apollinaire's masterpiece').[8]

His eroticism was a positive manifestation of the spirit of playful innovation that characterised the intellectual life of Paris in the early years of this century. The most innovative painter of his generation, Pablo Picasso, thought that *Les Onze Mille Verges* was the finest book he had ever read. It was Aragon, however, who saw more clearly than any other that Apollinaire's sexualisation of poetry was not only radically modern but intensely creative: 'Une conscience aussi claire des liens de la poésie et de la sexualité, une conscience de profanateur et de poète, voilà ce qui met Apollinaire à un point singulier de l'histoire' ('A clear awareness of the links between poetry and sexuality, the awareness of a profaner and of a poet, is what places Apollinaire at a conspicuous point in history').[9] Of all Apollinaire's writings, *Les Onze Mille Verges* is the best example of this marriage of poetic creativity and modernist subversion.

Apollinaire's encyclopedic knowledge of the history of pornography, his fascination with obscenity and his ludic tendencies[10] all help to explain why *Les Onze Mille Verges* reads as a parody of the Sadean text rather than as a classic of the pornographic genre, as some have described it. Frans Amelinckx rightly insists on the novel's parodic purposes:

> Apollinaire deliberately sets out to violate the conventions of the genre by introducing even more exaggerated performances, situations and characters. The whole tone is parodic and plays on different registers.[11]

To argue, therefore, as Michael Perkins does,[12] that Apollinaire's novel suffers from a lack of characterisation and a haphazard plot is to miss the point – all parody unavoidably debases its literary model by exaggerating its principal features. Sade's narratives are, in any case, not noted for their plot construction or their psychological exploration of character, but *Les Onze Mille Verges* draws particular attention to these literary weaknesses by caricaturing what is already caricatural. For Peter Michelson, 'It is as if the reader were watching Sadean narrative sped up to 64 frames per second.'[13] Given that Sade's fictions are already cartoon-like in many respects, this accelerated version of the Sadean picaresque is grotesque in the extreme. Perversions are combined or follow upon each other at such a rate that the effect is inescapably comic and one cannot help thinking that the writer has thrown down a gauntlet, in this case, to cram all the main Sadean 'passions' into a narrative, less than one hundred pages long. Along the way, Apollinaire finds time to include a number of bawdy poems, to make witty allusions to friends and contemporaries, and to pay homage to the libertine tradition of eighteenth-century France.

As the title implies, the narrative is itself based upon a challenge. *Les Onze Mille Verges* plays on the ambiguity of *verge* which can mean 'birch-rod' (and therefore carries sado-masochistic connotations) or 'penis'. Early on in the story, the central character, Prince Mony Vibescu, a Romanian aristocrat and libertine of the turn of the century, compounds this ambiguity in the title when he boasts of his sexual prowess to his future mistress, the aptly named Culculine d'Ancône:[14] 'Si je vous tenais dans un lit, vingt fois de suite je vous prouverais ma passion. Que les onze mille vierges ou même onze mille verges me châtient si je mens!' (p. 23) ('If I were holding you in a bed, I'd prove my passion for you twenty times over. May the eleven thousand virgins or even eleven thousand rods chastise me if I lie!' (p. 19)). 'Verges' or 'rods' is thus here mixed with its paronym, 'vierges' or 'virgins', which in this context is a reference to the medieval Breton legend of Saint Ursula and her eleven thousand virgin followers, martyred in Cologne while on a pilgrimage to Rome for refusing to yield their maidenhood to barbarian Huns. Mony's wager, together with his oblique allusions to saintly celibacy and holy pilgrimage, structure the entire narrative as the outrageously priapic prince inverts the legend's valorisation of virginity by embarking on a sexual pilgrimage, first to Paris and finally back to Eastern Europe and the war between Russia and Japan. Eventually, the prince is court-martialled by the Japanese for murder and is sentenced to run the gauntlet of an army of eleven thousand men. Mony reflects on the events which have led him to this pass and recalls his boast to Culculine: 'Il n'avait pas baisé vingt fois de suite, et le jour était arrivé où onze mille verges allaient le châtier.' (p. 123) ('He had not fucked twenty times in a row, and the day had arrived when eleven thousand rods were going to chastise him.' (p. 98)). In a further inversion of the Saint Ursula legend, his death will therefore be a direct consequence of his sexual inadequacy rather than his chastity, of his failure to keep his word, not to God but to Eros.

My aim in this brief survey of Apollinaire's Sadean novel is not principally to analyse its considerable humour – this has been done already[15] – but to consider in what other ways *Les Onze Mille Verges* might be said to be worthy of the modern reader's attention. In doing so, I shall focus upon the imagery of the text, which I shall show to function not only on poetic, but also on parodic and intertextual levels.

Just as Perkins misses the point in arguing that the plot and characterisation do not conform to conventional standards of realism, it would equally be inappropriate to refuse to read this novel because of the obscenity and violence. As a parody of the French Sadean tradition, *Les Onze Mille Verges* is above all a metatext and it is primarily its intertextual elements that keep the novel outside reality and in the domain of fiction and metafiction.

*Les Onze Mille Verges* is a text that, like all parody, undermines its target (in this case, Sade) and this process of subversion requires the complicity of a reader, who is acquainted with both Sade and Apollinaire and therefore sensitive and sympathetic to the author's parodic aims. At the same time, Apollinaire's agenda is complicated on the one hand by an underlying fascination with Sade, which makes the parody an affectionate one, and on the other by a mischievious tendency to ironise his own poetic project and that of his Surrealist circle. The absence in Apollinaire's text of anything like Sade's extended pseudo-philosophical diatribes focuses the reader's attention on a ludic treatment of Sadean sexuality, which in Sade is already caricatural, though of course such a focus was also a direct challenge by the poet to contemporary standards of decency.

The paragraph which describes Mony's death reflects in many ways the ambivalence of Apollinaire's representation of the Sadean. We recall that, in spite of Sade's tongue-in-cheek claims that in his works vice was always punished, this was never the case in those novels, notably *Justine* and *Histoire de Juliette*, which he denied having written. Apollinaire's execution of his own anti-hero is, therefore, an ironic reminder both of Sade's hypocrisy as author and of his insistence as narrator and through the mouths of his libertine protagonists on the sublime indifference of nature to human concepts of virtue, vice or natural justice:

Au deux millième coup, Mony rendit l'âme. Le soleil était radieux. Les chants des oiseaux mandchous rendaient plus gaie la matinée pimpante. La sentence s'exécuta et les derniers soldats frappèrent leur coup de baguette sur une loque informe, sorte de chair à saucisse où l'on ne distinguait plus rien, sauf le visage qui avait été soigneusement respecté et où les yeux vitreux grands ouverts semblaient contempler la majesté divine dans l'au-delà. (p. 124)

At the two thousandth blow, Mony gave up the ghost. The sun was dazzling. The songs of the Manchurian birds made the spring morning even more bright and gay. The full sentence was executed and the last soldiers delivered their single cane-stroke upon a shapeless mass, a sort of raw sausagemeat, none of it any longer recognizable save for the face, which had been sedulously respected and wherein the glassy eyes staring wide seemed to contemplate divine majesty in the world beyond. (p. 98)

Commenting upon this paragraph, Michelson succinctly identifies the complexity of the network of relationships between text, reader and Sadean subject matter:

Here [Apollinaire] parodies, in order, the benign idealization of nature, the body itself, and by implication materialist positivism, the symbolist romance of death, and simultaneously his own post-symbolist project of the fourth dimension. In the process of satirizing competing ideologies, Apollinaire put Sade back on the poetic agenda. It certainly was a reminder to Breton, for whom Sade was to be a surrealist touchstone.[16]

A thorough acquaintance with Sade is therefore essential for any competent reading of the text's parodic elements. In addition to scenes of extreme necrophilia and bestiality, the cutting off of the head of the sodomised victim to tighten the anus and so increase sexual pleasure, the instruction to a father to sodomise his own daughter and, of course, the brutal whipping of an unfortunate German waitress are all recognisably Sadean. In practically every case, however, Apollinaire frames the Sadean within a distinctly humorous *mise en scène*. The bestiality evoked does not stop at dogs, but involves cats, horses, birds, tigers, fish and even octopuses! A cossack, for instance, warms his hands in a mare's vagina. In the sodomy scene, the horror of decapitation is somewhat attenuated by the sodomiser's comically and incongruously casual gesture, described in the line that immediately follows: 'Le général décula ensuite et s'essuya la queue avec son mouchoir.' (p. 93) ('The general then withdrew from the arsehole and wiped his tool with his handkerchief.' (p. 74)). The German waitress is not simply whipped, but artistically branded in a manner that ironically recalls the word-pictures invented by Apollinaire himself (his book *Calligrammes* was published in 1918):

Le Tatar était un artiste et les coups qu'il frappait se réunissaient pour former un dessin calligraphique. Sur le bas du dos, au-dessus des fesses, le mot putain apparut bientôt distinctement. (p. 97)

The Tartar was an artist and the blows he was inflicting were joining up to form a calligraphic design. On the base of the back, above the buttocks, there soon appeared distinctly the word *whore*. (p. 77)

## Textual Imagery

Arguably the silliest, crudest and certainly the most misogynistic use of bawdiness in the novel, however, involves the story of a madwoman who imagines herself transformed into a latrine. This rather too clever metaphorical conceit unfortunately has the ring of literal truth for many female readers, victims of male abuse, but the passage is worth quoting as an example of the author's verbal ingenuity:

[...] elle se croyait changée en tinette, monsieur, et décrivait des culs imaginaires qui chiaient dans elle. Il fallut l'enfermer le jour qu'elle se figura que la fosse était pleine. Elle devint dangereuse et demandait à grands cris les vidangeurs pour la vider. Je l'écoutais péniblement. Elle me reconnaissait.

– Mon fils, disait-elle, tu n'aimes plus ta mère, tu fréquentes d'autres cabinets. Assieds-toi sur moi et chie à ton aise.

*Où peut-on mieux chier qu'en le sein de sa mère?*

Et puis, mon fils, ne l'oublie pas, la fosse est pleine. Hier, un marchand de bière qui est venu chier dans moi avait la colique. Je déborde, je n'en puis plus. Il faut absolument faire venir les vidangeurs. (p. 110)

[...] she believed she'd been turned into a latrine, monsieur, and she would describe imaginary arses that shat in her. She had to be locked up the day she supposed the trench was full. She became dangerous and used to yell loudly for the cesspit emptiers to drain her. I'd listen to her with distress. She would recognise me.

– My son, she'd say, you don't love your mother any more, you visit other privies. Sit on me and shit in comfort. *Where better to shit than in one's mother's breast?*
And son, don't forget, the hole's full. Yesterday a publican who came and shat in me had an attack of colic. I'm overflowing, I can't take any more. You absolutely must fetch the sewermen. (pp. 87–8)

In spite of their somewhat juvenile tone, this and other images in the novel provide the key to the complexity of relationships between reader, text and intertext, alluded to earlier. I want to suggest that Apollinaire's use of imagery in the novel serves a number of associated purposes. Firstly and most obviously, the images are predominantly comic and this comedy has the effect of defusing their erotic potential. Secondly, they intensify the capacity of humour to reach out to the reader by requiring recognition of a shared intertextual ground. Thirdly, there is a self-consciousness in their use which suggests a playful self-questioning, both in relation to the Surrealist poetic agenda at the time of writing and to Apollinaire's own poetic methods. Fourthly and lastly, while commonplaces tend to circumscribe meaning by leading the reader down familiar and often well-worn paths, Apollinaire's extraordinary and incongruous imagery produces a shock effect, disseminating meaning along chains of highly individualistic associations. The shocked or surprised reader is thus stimulated into a train of thought emerging from his/her own sensory experience.[17] The seeming incompatibility of the second and last of these effects further underlines the complexity of Apollinaire's project in writing this novel. I now propose to analyse these separate though related effects by examining three types of images identified according to shared semantic characteristics.

Before doing so, a general observation needs to be made which bears in particular upon the first and third of the above. Most of the images in this text are similes rather than metaphors. Unlike the metaphor, the simile, Paul Ricœur insists, preserves a distance between the two things compared: 'Aucun transfert de signification n'a lieu; tous les mots gardent leur sens et les représentations elles-mêmes restent distinctes et coexistent avec un degré presque égal d'intensité.'[18] ('No transferral of meaning takes place; all the words keep their meaning and the representations themselves remain distinct and coexist with an almost equal degree of intensity.') I would argue that this distance and the fragmented, discontinuous view of the world that the simile generates reinforce the comic sense of incongruity that is generally characteristic of Apollinaire's comparisons. As we read the similes (arguably among the most visible of all poetic or rhetorical devices) which punctuate this prose narrative at regular intervals, we are also constantly made aware that the narrative voice is that of a poet and this self-consciousness adds a certain irony to the comic effect.

There is a further sense in which the use of both similes and metaphors creates a distance from the real. Pierre Guyotat avoids similes, because he wants to express the world directly. His avoidance of images is linked to what he perceives as an ever-narrowing gap, in his writing, between imagination and reality:

> [...] il suffit de désigner les choses, de les donner à voir telles qu'elles sont [...] Il y a de moins en moins d'images dans ce que j'écris, parce que je découvre un accord toujours plus grand entre ce que j'imagine et la réalité dont je suis le contemporain.[19]

> [...] it is enough to designate things, to show them as they are [...] There are fewer and fewer images in what I write, because I see an ever greater harmony between what I imagine and my contemporary reality.

Following both Ricœur and Guyotat, we can say that the metaphor and the simile are expressive of a distancing from reality, brought about by the intrusion of imagination. As we shall see, Apollinaire's imagery constantly refers to the mundane on the one hand and the comically surreal on the other, thus paradoxically carrying the reader away from the horrors or obscenities that the imagery is intended to convey.

A good example of this effect can be found in the scene of horrible violence and necrophilia involving Mony and his sidekick, Cornaboeux, on the Orient Express. After an act of necrophilic buggery, Cornaboeux has inserted his entire arm into the dead servant, Mariette's, vagina: 'Au moment de la jouissance il avait déjà tiré deux mètres d'entrailles et s'en était entouré la taille comme d'une ceinture de sauvetage.' (p. 55) ('At the moment of climax he had already pulled out two metres of entrails and had wrapped them around his waist like a lifebelt.' (p. 44)). The grotesque 'lifebelt' image is highly ironic, given the context of death and disembowelling. Here, as so often elsewhere, the reader is disorientated, pushed and pulled between the obscene and the banal, between the horrific and the comic. The novel's images function above all to vitiate the pornographic elements, not merely because they are amusing (most are, some are simply bizarre) but because they interfere with the arousal of erotic and/or sadistic responses in the reader.

The intertextual positioning of the narrative and its status as parody written for a specific group of readers help to determine a number of its most striking images.

Alexine, one of the two prostitutes Mony takes up with, 'apparaissait, dans son charmant déshabillé rose, aussi délicate et aussi mutine qu'une marquise friponne de l'avant-dernier siècle' (pp. 24–5) ('appeared, in her charming pink négligée, as delicate and as impish as a saucy marquise of the century before last' (p. 20)). Laclos's Marquise de Merteuil? Sade's aristocratic female libertines? In any event, the image clearly alludes to the dominant female figures of eighteenth-century *libertinage*.

In a less obviously sexual context, the following passage, from the episode in which Mony and Cornaboeux witness the siege of Port-Arthur by the Japanese, is strongly reminiscent of Voltaire's battlefield scenes in *Candide*, right down to the incongruous juxtapositions which typify Voltaire's deadpan comic style:

Quelques boulets de canon passèrent en sifflant au-dessus de leur tête, ils enjambèrent une femme qui gisait coupée en deux par un boulet et arrivèrent ainsi devant *Les Délices du Petit Père*. (p. 74)

Several cannon-balls whistled past above their heads; they strode over a sprawling woman cut in half by a projectile and thus arrived outside *Les Délices du Petit Père*. (pp. 59–60)

The principle of comic incongruity is particularly successful in the description of the view from the carriage window, which functions as caesura in the middle of the Orient Express scene:

Et comme on passait sur un pont, le prince se mit à la portière pour contempler le panorama romantique du Rhin qui déployait ses splendeurs verdoyantes et se déroulait en larges méandres jusqu'à l'horizon. Il était quatre heures du matin, des vaches paissaient dans les prés, des enfants dansaient déjà sous des tilleuls germaniques. Une musique de fifres, monotone et mortuaire, annonçait la présence d'un régiment prussien et la mélopée se mêlait tristement au bruit de ferraille du pont et à l'accompagnement sourd du train en marche. Des villages heureux animaient les rives dominées par les burgs centenaires et les vignes rhénanes étalaient à l'infini leur mosaïque régulière et précieuse. (p. 56)

And as they were crossing a bridge, the prince went to the window to contemplate the romantic panorama of the Rhine which was unfolding its verdant splendours and unwinding in wide meanders as far as the horizon. It was four o'clock in the morning, cows were grazing in the meadows, children already dancing under German linden trees. The music of fifes, monotonous and dirgeful, heralded the presence of a Prussian regiment, and the strains mingled sadly with the iron clank of the bridge and the muffled accompaniment of the moving train. Contented villages enlivened the riverbanks dominated by age-old donjons and the Rhenish vines displayed ad infinitum their regular and precious mosaic. (p. 45)

Sandwiched between acts of extreme sadism and uncontrolled violence, this exaggerated Romantic idyll reads both as a merciless Sadean parody of Rousseau's sentimental view of nature and of the natural goodness of man on the one hand and as an ironising of the poet's own poetic sensibility on the other: this Rhineland landscape bears a close physical and emotional resemblance to the scenes evoked in Apollinaire's Rhenish suite, composed of nine 'Rhénanes' or Rhenish songs, all written from September 1901 to May 1902, and all heavy with a personally inspired melancolia. In these three cases, then, the novel's implied reader must be well acquainted with both eighteenth-century literature and philosophy and with Apollinaire's own poetic writings to be able to share the joke.

Many of the obscene images in this novel have a culinary basis and, as such, provide further intertextual echoes. There is nothing new in comparing the enjoyment of sex with that of food or in viewing the female body in particular as something to be eaten. Marina Yaguello reminds us that many metaphors of the French language situate women as food and therefore as merchandise to be consumed by men,[20] and there is a long tradition in pornography linking culinary and sexual over-indulgence. The Sadean text provides particularly good examples of such links. Roland Barthes tells us that Sade's libertines engage in their gargantuan feasts with a pleasure which has nothing to do with transgression,[21] but their appetite for food is clearly as excessive as their appetite for sex. Barthes also suggests that detailed description of food in Sade's fiction constitutes an *excess* of meaning which he describes as 'la marque même du romanesque' ('the very mark of the novelistic').[22] The indirect links in Sade between food, sexual violence and excess undergo a parodic inversion in *Les Onze Mille Verges*, which Apollinaire's 'educated' reader could not fail to recognise.

Unlike Sadean libertines, Apollinaire's protagonists seem to have no time for eating, since all their free time is devoted to a sexual activity of one kind or another, which is frequently evoked in culinary terms. Thus, while in Sade food is enjoyed as food, Apollinaire's characters enjoy sex as food. Food has, in other words, become a figure for *jouissance*. Alexine *Mangetout*, bears a name which clearly encapsulates this synonymity of culinary and sexual self-indulgence.[23] For the most part, food imagery is used to evoke the appetising qualities of the female body, though the male organ, too, is occasionally seen as a tasty morsel. The female anal orifice is 'rond comme une pastille' (p. 17) ('round as a pastille' (p. 14)), but elsewhere in the text, the same image is also employed to convey the delectability of a penis: 'Je vis le gros membre entrer dans un con velu qui l'avala comme une pastille' (p. 119) ('I saw the great member enter a hairy cunt that swallowed it like a pastille' (p. 94)).

The novelty or incongruity of many such images is frequently humorous. Breasts are as white as cream cheese ('petits suisses') (p. 49), translated as 'creamiest cheese' (p. 40), and a girl's bottom 'semblait un beau melon qui aurait poussé au soleil de minuit, tant il était blanc et plein' (p. 18) ('so white and full that it resembled a fine melon which might have ripened under the midnight sun' (p. 15)). When the same bottom is spanked, 'on eût dit de ces fesses qu'elles étaient faites de crème mêlée de framboises' (ibid.) ('it might have been said of these thighs that they were made of cream with raspberries stirred in' (p. 15)). The pleasing accuracy of these visual images, painted by a poet with an eye for the detail of colour, tone or texture, is characteristic of Apollinaire's use of imagery, as much in this novel as in his poetry.

The comic 'watermelon' image is repeated a few lines later and this time the image works to convey the texture rather than the colour of the girl's behind: 'Ses mains tenaient fermement ce gros cul ferme comme une pastèque dure et pulpeuse.' (p. 19) ('His hands firmly grasped that big arse swelling like a hard yet pulpy watermelon.' (p. 15)) Feet, too, are compared in taste with dishes as disparate as ham and raspberries: 'Il reconnut que le pied droit avait le goût de framboise. La langue lécheuse fouilla ensuite les plis du pied gauche auquel Mony trouva une saveur qui rappelait celle du jambon de Mayence.' (p. 66) ('He found out that the right foot tasted of raspberry. The licking tongue next truffled into the creases of the left foot, whereon Mony located a flavour reminiscent of Mainz ham.' (p. 53)) Quite apart from the comic incongruity of such comparisons, they also presuppose a reader who has experience of both fine cuisine and toe-sucking!

In an ironic reversal of Sade's repeated insistence on the excessive character of the sexual enjoyment of the protagonists, which is a function of their equally excessive physical qualities and dimensions, Apollinaire's 'food' imagery tends to have the opposite effect, ridiculing in particular the size and appearance of the penis: Mony's erect penis is 'rouge comme une grosse prune' (p. 36) ('red as a plump plum' (p. 30)), La Chaloupe's organ is so thin that Culculine calls it a 'cure-dent' (p. 40) ('toothpick' (p. 32)), and Mony and Cornaboeux engage in mutual fellatio like two little boys sucking sticks of barley sugar: 'Tous deux suçaient goulûment leurs sucres d'orge respectifs' (p. 60) ('Both were gluttonously sucking their respective sugarsticks' (p. 49)).

It is, in fact, worth looking in some detail at the sorts of images used in the text to evoke the male and female genitals. Like those which fall into the culinary category, many of these are, quite simply, visually amusing and all bear the stamp of Apollinaire's genius for poetic invention. Images for body parts are reassuringly and comically humanising. The penis is a doll or orphan, waiting to be cuddled by its mummy ('ce gros poupon qui veut se réchauffer dans le sein de sa maman' (pp. 67–8)), while breasts, when they're not tasty dishes, are lace handkerchiefs ('un mouchoir de batiste' (p. 52)). Ida, the daughter of the dragoman of the Austro-Hungarian embassy, possesses a clitoris, which, à la Sade, serves the same penetrative function as the penis – 'Le clitoris en érection de Wanda pénétra bientôt entre les fesses satinées dans lesquelles elle alla et vint comme un homme' (p. 71) ('Wanda's erected clitoris soon penetrated the satin buttocks between which she worked to and fro like a man' (p. 57)) – but which is modestly only as long as a little finger – 'long comme le petit doigt' (p. 70). Less believably, Volmar, Sade's clitoridean woman par excellence, has a clitoris three inches long![24]

In true Sadean fashion, it is the female posterior, above all, that Apollinaire favours in his descriptions of the body and again the imagery used to evoke it is visually comic. The 'cul' or 'arse' is a 'lune si vaine' (p. 49) ('moon, so vain' (p. 40)) or a 'lune(s) ivre(s)' (p. 125) ('drunken moon(s)' (p. 99)). The depiction of the female bottom as a face recurs several times in the text, suggesting an underlying, perhaps unconscious, need to individualise and humanise sex, in total opposition to Sade's tendency to represent the body as dehumanised and machine-like. At the same time, these facial images inject the eroticised body with a de-eroticising dose of Chaucerean comedy: 'Il faut absolument que je le fasse rougir, ton gros visage postérieur,' says Mony to Culculine's sister, Helen, 'Tiens, il n'est pas fâché, quand tu le remues un peu, on dirait qu'il rigole' (p. 67) ('I absolutely must make your big bumface blush. Hey, he's not angry, and when you joggle him a bit he looks quite jolly' (p. 54)). Elsewhere, the anus is 'comme un œil de cyclope entre deux globes charnus, blancs et frais'

(p. 32) ('like a Cyclops eye between two cool white fleshy globes' (p. 26)) and the delicate pink skin just inside it 'ressemble à une lèvre retroussée' (p. 35) ('akin to a curled lip' (p. 29)).

The vagina, too, has facial characteristics. Pubic hair, for instance, is 'a beard', 'une délicieuse barbe blonde bien frisée' (p. 19) ('a delicious, very curly blond beard' (p. 19)), 'la barbe du con' (p. 40), translated as 'thatch' (p. 32) but meaning literally 'the beard of the cunt' – ostensibly positive images which may nevertheless conceal unconscious negative attitudes towards the feminine.[25] The same could hardly be said, however, of the depiction of an eight-year-old girl's hairless vagina as a newborn chick's open beak, 'une petite fente imberbe et rose comme l'intérieur du bec ouvert d'un geai qui vient de naître' (p. 59) ('a small hairless slit pink as the interior of the open beak of a newborn nuthatch' (p. 47)). This disturbing image appears to eroticise a child, incongruously mixing connotations of immaturity ('a newborn bird') and sexual availability ('open beak/slit'), yet it is also strikingly original and visually amusing, qualities which perhaps help to focus the reader's attention less on the signified than on the signifier.

## The Erotic Carnaval

Apollinaire's humorous appropriation of the Sadean, which is largely dependent on his exaggerated and burlesque use of imagery as we have seen, produces a fictionality even greater than Sade's, increasing the self-referentiality and amusing dimension of a text which talks about itself. The result is a work rich in discourses: in addition to the Sadean, the historical-political,[26] the poetic, the Voltairean, a bawdy tradition dating back to the *commedia del arte* and Boccaccio and, not least, a Surrealist taste, on the one hand for bizarreries and on the other for parodic humour. These discourses are predominant, resonating throughout the novel's imagery, subjugating the erotic to the comic, the parodic, the poetic, reaching out to a reader who, by virtue of his/her culture, willingly becomes the writer's accomplice.

Indeed, this plurality of discourses, ambiguities of language and of genre, and the strong intertextual elements of

Apollinaire's narrative invite us to apply to it the carnavalesque model of reading developed by Mikhaïl Bakhtin.[27] The terms most often associated with Bakhtin – 'carnaval', 'dialogism', 'heteroglossia' and 'polyphony' – all point to the essential basis of his thought: that language is always a dialogue with a plural 'other', made up of a listener, a totality of previous language use and of present use. In literary discourse, all these different languages are structured to play off each other and the result is frequently ironic or parodic, as in *Les Onze Mille Verges*. The polyphony of Apollinaire's text, to which the title of this chapter attempts to draw attention, is allied to a dialogue with other which occurs both within and outside the text. The poetic, parodic and pornographic discourses that interweave and speak to each other *intra*diegetically[28] are also directed to a past and present *extra*textual world, consisting of the Sadean and the Surrealist, the Bawdy and the Boccaccian, the Poetic and the Picaresque. The 'Orient Express' episode provides us perhaps with the best example of such polyphony, a visual representation of dialogic contrasts, as the Romantic idyll outside the train contrasts sharply with the scenes of Gothic horror and Sadean obscenity within. In 'Discourse in the Novel', Bakhtin discusses the issue of rewriting or what he calls 're-accentuation':

> The process of re-accentuation is enormously significant in the history of literature. Every age re-accentuates in its own way the works of its most immediate past. The historical life of classic works is in fact the uninterrupted process of their social and ideological re-accentuation.[29]

Discussing the concept of 'intertextuality' which she takes from Bakhtin, Julia Kristeva points out that *any* text 'is constructed as a mosaic of quotations; any text is the absorption and transformation of another'.[30] Nevertheless, some texts are more transparently intertextual than others and *Les Onze Mille Verges* belongs to this category.

*Les Onze Mille Verges* appears to correspond to the Bakhtinian definition of the carnavalesque in every other salient respect. For Kristeva, 'Carnavalesque discourse breaks through the laws of a language censored by grammar and semantics and, at the same time, is a social and political protest. There is no equivalence, but rather, identity between challenging official linguistic codes and challenging official law.'[31] There is, then, in carnaval, an opening up and breaking down of the received order which expresses itself linguistically. This dynamic challenge to the law takes the form of a transgression of authoritative voices, an opposition to authoritarian, literary language, undermined in Apollinaire's text by parody and by juxtaposition of conventional speech, especially cliché, with the irreverent and base discourses of the obscene.

For Bakhtin, who refers to the Freudian unconscious as a model, these are the origins of a revolutionary ideology: a challenge to the law of repression in the unconscious is also a challenge to the political *status quo*. The laughter generated by Apollinaire's use of the obscene is equally subversive, since like the carnaval, it challenges God, authority and the ethical and social law. The Bakhtinian refusal of any kind of unifying transcendance is particularly manifest in his focus on the fragmentation of the body, which is joyously celebrated in Apollinaire as in Rabelais. We have seen how in *Les Onze Mille Verges*, body parts are both literally and metaphorically devoured with delight, in spite of or even because of their grotesqueness, grotesque because unfinished, open, a non-Cartesian body of orifices, falling to bits. The structural dyad of sexuality and death which also plays an essential role in carnaval is perhaps most evident in the necrophilia of Apollinaire's text, a figure of life overcoming death by feeding parasitically upon it.

The bawdy and sadistic elements of *Les Onze Mille Verges* are certainly transgressively pornographic, but they also represent an inversion of conventional authoritative structures which is fundamentally political. Other inversions in the text have a similar function as avatars of a revolutionary ideology. In addition to the poetic and parodic inversions of conventional pornographic objectives, the text also frequently inverts master/servant, if not gender roles (the novel's principal paradigm of such an inversion is the act of sodomy of Mony the aristocrat by Cornaboeux the petty criminal). We have seen, too, that there is inversion of the animal and the vegetable in a whole series of images which transform the bodies of men and women into culinary feasts. Such transgressive strategies are essentially those of what Jean Mainil has termed 'l'érotisme carnavalesque':

> En quoi consiste ce carnaval de la chair et de l'érotique? Le carnaval est, Bakhtine l'a montré ainsi que bien d'autres, avant tout un renversement. Renversement des règnes animal et végétal et plus métaphoriquement, mais intimement lié au premier, le renversement des rôles où, l'espace d'une transgression, les esclaves deviennent maîtres.[32]

> What does this carnaval of flesh and eroticism consist of? Bakhtin has shown, as have many others, that carnaval is above all an inversion. Inversion of the animal and vegetable kingdoms and more metaphorically, but intimately linked to it, the inversion of roles, whereby in a transgressive space, slaves can become masters.

The images in Apollinaire's novel which reverse the poles of the physical body (the facial, humanising images of the genitals and posterior) are similarly characteristic of the Bahktinian carnaval:

> La métaphorisation du corps a lieu à partir de ses pôles inférieurs et elle prend la forme de 'permutations constantes du haut et du bas ('la roue'), de la face et du derrière.'[33]

> The metaphorisation of the body starts at the lower end and takes the form of 'continual exchanges between the top and bottom ('the wheel'), between the face and the posterior.'

The carnaval is fundamentally hedonistic but, as the single day in the year when servant becomes master and peasant becomes monarch, the carnaval is also an implicitly violent event in that it enjoins us to overturn hierarchies. Readers of Apollinaire's carnavalesque eroticism are thus invited to ignore conventional hierarchical distinctions between registers and genres, to become the willing accomplices of a poet-pornographer, whose taste for pleasure in a transgression of poetic, social, moral, ethical, religious and even physical boundaries is revolutionary on both literary and ideological levels.

# 3

# Sexual and Textual Excess: Pierre Louÿs's *Trois Filles de leur mère*

Like the man who wrote them, the novels, stories and poems of Pierre Louÿs (1870–1925) overflow with an irrepressible and childlike *joie de vivre* and, in the case of both man and work, the dominant trait is excess. The extreme emotions of a romantic adolescence, the practical jokes of a young poet and, later, an extravagant self-indulgence, whether in the consumption of cigarettes or in the socially less acceptable tastes of the libertine, all of these excesses in Louÿs's life and character are reflected in his writing, both in the critically acclaimed published canon and in the erotic works which he composed in secret throughout his life and which remained unpublished during that time.

His are excesses, however, which bear little resemblance to those of Sade or Bataille. The passions and perversions of his work are sketched with a candid innocence, without any awareness of transgression. Louÿs certainly appears preoccupied with sexual themes to an obsessive degree, but there is no evidence in his writing of the underlying guilt that is so frequently the price of such obsession. This spirit of uninhibited eroticism informs the writing at both its thematic and formal levels, generating a text in which obscenity is, above all, a linguistic game played with the reader.

While it is true that Louÿs is by no means the first writer of the genre to innovate at the level of form,[1] he made an important contribution to the inventiveness of French pornography and in certain respects went much further than his literary and generic antecedents. Louÿs's erotic fiction may well be the most obscene writing of his day, but its irrepressible humour also makes it curiously *un*erotic, which is why it might be argued that he was not a pornographer in the sense we established for this term in Chapter 1.[2]

The novel, *Trois Filles de leur mère*, was just one among the numerous obscene works written by Louÿs and published secretly after his death.[3] I shall, therefore, briefly consider the themes of this obscene *œuvre* in general, before focusing on the qualities that make *Trois Filles de leur mère* its most interesting example.

All of Louÿs's work in the genre, none of which is ever mentioned in literary histories, reflects the characteristic obsessions of its author, especially his passion for women of all ages. For Jean-Paul Goujon, four main themes inform Louÿs's erotic interest in the female body – incest, scatology (or coprophilia), sapphism and sodomy.[4] To this list, we can also add a particular interest in little girls, although the Louÿs case in no way conforms to the stereotype described by Stephen Heath:

> The point of the little girl is her existence before womanhood, supposedly before sexual life, before the critical moment 'when the stream and river meet' as C. L. Dodgson (Lewis Carroll) could put it: investment in an untroubling image of female beauty, avoiding any reality of women and men [...]'[5]

The *fillette* of Louÿs's fiction is not the creature of pre-pubescent innocence that we might expect, the Lolita that fascinates Humbert Humbert *because* of her girlishness, so much as the self-assured and street-wise Zazie,[6] the child who always gets the better of the adults around her, and who is far more depraved than they are. As Goujon observes,

> Chez Louÿs, l'enfant est pleinement conscient du sexe, qui semble être l'unique jeu à sa portée, et même sa grande affaire: la seule activité où il excelle vraiment. Étrange renversement, où les enfants usurpent la place des adultes et finissent même par leur tenir la dragée haute.[7]

In Louÿs's work, children are fully conscious of sex, which seems to be the only game available to them, and even their domain: the only activity in which they really excel. A strange inversion, according to which children usurp the

place of adults and even end up making them dance to
their tune.

The *gamines* of *Trois Filles de leur mère*, so typically Louÿsian,
far from being the sweet, innocent things beloved of the
paedophile, are simply younger and smaller versions of their
prostitute mother – 'three daughters that take after their
mother', as the French title has it.

Lesbianism, too, obsessed Louÿs. Indeed, many of his works
focus on this activity (apart from *Trois Filles de leur mère*,
*Aphrodite* and *Les Chansons de Bilitis* are the best novelistic
examples, though there are also short stories about girls in
convent schools, indulging in sapphic pleasures). For Goujon,
this preoccupation with sapphism goes beyond the obvious
voyeurism of a male writer to express a real fascination with
female sexuality, as something autonomous and independent
of men.[8]

*Trois Filles de leur mère* certainly contains all of Louÿs's
favourite sexual themes and preoccupations and, in this
respect, is typical of his work in the genre, but as a brilliant
stylistic and formal exercise, this novel stands out from the rest
of the author's obscene composition, deserving more attention
than it has hitherto received from the critical establishment.

The original edition of the novel appeared without any
information concerning the place or date of publication and
circulation was restricted to the author's friends. Only the
initials, P. L., were printed on the cover. However, in the
watermark of the paper, the author's name can be read spelt
backwards: Syuol Erreip. According to Pascal Pia, it appeared
in 1926 and was distributed by Gaillandre booksellers,
although Goujon dates the writing of the novel around 1913.[9]
A very small number of copies were printed and they were not
for sale to the general public.

It is possible that the characters, if not the events, of the
novel had their basis in real experience, as claimed in the
author's 'Avis à la lectrice' ('Foreword addressed to the female
reader'), which is regrettably omitted from the English
translation : 'Ce petit livre n'est pas un roman. C'est une
histoire vraie jusqu'aux moindres détails. Je n'ai rien changé,
ni le portrait de la mère et des trois jeunes filles, ni leurs âges,
ni les circonstances.' ('This little book is not a novel. It is a true

story in every detail. I have changed nothing, neither the portrait of the mother and of the three young girls, nor their ages, nor the circumstances.'). Some have speculated that the story was based on Louÿs's experiences with the three daughters of the well-known Parnassian poet, Hérédia, one of whom, Louise, was his wife until 1913, the assumed date of the novel's composition. Whatever the truth of this speculation, the novel's power does not depend on its possible autobiographical source, but on the marriage of a shocking obscenity with a masterful narrative style.

The novel concerns a family of four prostitutes, ranging from the 30-year-old mother, Teresa, to the ten-year-old baby of the family, Lili. The narrator is a young man of 20 who lives in the same building and who is visited in turn by Teresa, Lili, and by Lili's two sisters, Mauricette, aged 14 and Charlotte, aged 20.

On the face of it, the novel owes much to a long pornographic tradition dating back to the sixteenth century and also, perhaps, to more recent influences. The crude realism of his erotic descriptions and of the dialogue of his characters suggests the influence of the Naturalists (Zola, Huysmans, Maupassant, the Goncourts). The language is vulgar, the actions described are without a doubt obscene. Among the latter, a marked preference for sodomy is reminiscent of Sade, as is the sexist and masculinised portrayal of female sexuality: women 'get hard' and ejaculate; prostitutes like their work because they need to be degraded, vilified; even rape is not so bad and 'Faire jouir les femmes pour les faire taire,' the narrator confides in us, 'est un principe connu de toute antiquité.' (p. 74) ('Making women come in order to shut them up is a principle known and used thoughout antiquity' (p. 60)). The account of Charlotte's education in sexual matters, especially with regard to her introduction to sodomy between the ages of ten and thirteen, and the instruction of the youngest daughter by her mother merely repeat a theme privileged by the genre in the seventeenth and eighteenth centuries.

The narrator plays the part of an innocent young man, ravished by profligate young women. Flirtatious and seductive, their irresistible nature leads them to corrupt any man they come across,[10] whilst he is a reticent actor in scenes of debauchery intiated by them: 'Je raconte cela pour retarder un peu la fin de cette horrible scène qui m'est pénible à écrire' (p.

98) ('I'm telling this to try to put off the end of this horrible narrative a little' (p. 79)); 'Il m'est plus que pénible, vraiment, de raconter la scène suivante avec détails. Je ne le puis. Elle me fait honte. Je n'avais à aucun degré le vice que Mauricette me demandait de satisfaire' (p. 155) ('It's really more than painful for me to relate the following scene in detail. In fact, I cannot. It makes me ashamed of myself. I did not have the first instinct for the vice that Mauricette wanted me to satisfy.' (p. 127)). The 'vice' in question is the 'English vice', masochism which, for Andrea Dworkin, is attributed to women by men to justify the violence committed against them in a phallocratic society.[11]

These are, admittedly, some of the most salient characteristics of the pornographic genre. However, the obvious exaggeration of conventions which are instantly recognisable as being characteristic of pornography makes *Trois Filles de leur mère* parodic rather than pornographic.[12] The narrative voice is frequently heavy with irony; indeed, the expression overall goes much further than the superficially obscene to become a parody of it. For example, in the repetitions and permutations of the following extract, in which the signifieds are completely overshadowed by the weight of the signifiers, there is an insistence which suggests that the language is here engaged in ridiculing its own vulgarity:

[Mauricette to her mother]:«Ne me touche pas! je t'emmerde! je t'emmerde! et je foutrai le camp cette nuit! Je t'emmerde, sale vache! sale grue! sale gousse! sale enculée! sale maquerelle! sale putain! Tu ne veux pas qu'on t'appelle comme ça? Putain! Putain! Putain! Putain! Putain! Putain! Putain! Putain! Putain! Putain! Putain! Putain! Putain! Putain! Putain! Putain! Fille de putain! Mère de putains, gousse de putains, branleuse de putains. Je ne suis pas une putain, moi, je suis une pucelle! Tu as laissé vendre ton pucelage par ta putain de mère, mais moi je ne suis pas une andouille comme toi! je ne te laisse pas vendre mon pucelage, je le donne! Tiens, regarde-le, sale maquerelle! regarde-le, ma garce! tu en voulais cent louis, tu n'en auras pas cent sous! tu n'en auras que du foutre et du sang dans la gueule!» (p. 161)

'Don't touch me! Shit on you! Shit on you! I'm getting out
of this dump tonight! I shit on you, you dirty bitch! Dirty
beast! Dirty fairy! Dirty slut! Dirty fucker! Dirty whore! You
don't like to be called that, do you? Good! Whore! Whore!
Whore! Whore! Whore! Whore! Whore! Whore! Whore!
Whore! Whore! Whore! Whore! Whore! Whore! Whore!
Whore! Daughter of a whore! Mother of whores! Whore
licker! Whore smeller! I'm no whore like you! I'm a virgin!
You let your whore of a mother sell your cherry, but I'm not
a strumpet like you! I'm not going to let my cherry be sold,
I'm going to give it away! Look! Look there, dirty trollop!
Look, my fine bitch! You wanted a hundred louis for it,
didn't you? Well, you're not even going to get a hundred
sous! The only thing you're going to get is blood and come
in your filthy trap!' (pp. 132–3)

Elsewhere, the very objectification and fetishisation of women
is specifically mocked: '«Quand je vous demande à voir un
con» dit Lili à sa sœur aînée, Charlotte, «c'est pas de vous tout
entière que je parle.» (p. 200) ('"When I ask to see a cunt I'm
talking about part of you, not all of you."' (pp. 164–5))

Mauricette's masochism is so extreme that it becomes unreal
and grotesque, the biting irony of her exclamation '"Jamais
personne ne m'a fait aussi mal que toi!"' (p. 155) ('"No one ever
hurt me as much as you did!"' (p. 127)) serving to defuse
everything that precedes it.

The instruction of the daughters is also so caricatural that
we laugh with recognition. There are striking inversions: the
least naïve of all the characters turns out to be the youngest,
Lili, while it is the women who instruct the male narrator in
the arts of lovemaking, thus reversing the convention of the
genre, according to which women are sexually awakened and
educated by men. The women of this story are prostitutes, an
ancient stereotype of all women, admittedly, but this
superficial distribution of roles is actually undermined by the
effective prostitution of the narrator himself, who is obliged
to perform a number of unusual sexual acts for his female
visitors. Moreover, there is never any question of payment for
the services rendered (although, as we have just observed,
there are no fixed positions), *jouissance* being the only
remuneration enjoyed by all parties. This *jouissance* is far

more often that of the female characters than that of the male narrator.

*Trois Filles de leur mère* can therefore be said to enrich the long tradition of innovation and inventiveness in the genre in a number of ways. At the level of content, Louÿs seems to wish to shock the female reader[13] by taking the genre's thematic conventions to new extremes – in combining incest, coprophilia, paedophilia and even zoophilia, Louÿs appears determined to outdo the most obscene of all French writers, Sade, himself. And yet, there are two major differences between a Louÿsian and a Sadean erotics.

Firstly, not only is there no direct representation of cruelty or violence in the Louÿsian text, but such representations become on more than one occasion the target of a sarcasm which deflates any sadistic potential. We are invited to share the narrator's incomprehension of Mauricette's somewhat extreme masochism, for example:

[Mauricette to the narrator:] «Prends-moi le bout des seins entre tes dents et serre! je te le donnerai, mon pucelage de devant pour que tu me fasses mal avec ta queue, pour que tu le crèves et qu'il y ait du sang. Maintenant que j'ai bu ton foutre, je suis à toi. Serre-moi dans tes bras, je vais jouir. Serre-moi de toutes tes forces. Casse-moi...»

Décidément, pensai-je à part moi, Lili est la seule raisonnable. Les trois autres sont toquées. (pp. 144–5)

'Take the ends of my breasts between your teeth and bite! And I'll give you my cherry from in front so that you can hurt me some more with your prick, so that you can rip it, so that I'll bleed. Now that I have drunk your come, I'm yours. Hold me tight, I'm going to come. Hold me with all your might. Crush me. Break me...'

Decidedly, I thought to myself, Lili is the only sane one in this mélange. The other three are crazy. (p. 118)

Secondly, the pleasure of transgression, which in Sade seems to depend on a respectful awareness that sin exists, takes on quite a different character in Louÿs's writing. Sade's Juliette derives much of her pleasure from her fundamental belief in the moral and religious rules that she infringes, a belief which is difficult to reconcile with her creator's aggressive atheism. The Sadean character must take sin seriously to be able to enjoy the sacrileges that (s)he commits.[14] There is none of this in Louÿs. Any mention of religion in his writing is designed to create comic effects. The pleasure which both author and reader derive from these passages is a far more facetious than transgressive one:

> Si cette comparaison n'était pas irrévérencieuse, je dirais: une petite fille qui aime à sucer les hommes a l'air d'une première communiante à genoux devant la sainte table; on dirait qu'elle attend une nourriture sacrée, au sein d'un mystère incompréhensible où le dieu de l'Amour va se donner à elle. (p. 39)

> If the comparison is not irreverent, I would like to say that a young girl who likes to suck men is like a child on her knees in front of the holy altar at her first communion. She seems to be awaiting some sacred nourishment from the bosom of an incomprehensible mystery, something the God of Love is going to give her. (pp. 29–30)

Charlotte was about to make her first communion. On the morning of the ceremony, when the communicant is required to fast, one of her clients

> est venu à sept heures et il a voulu que je le suce pour que j'aie du foutre dans l'estomac... Maman disait que dans ces conditions-là ce n'était pas la peine de faire ma première communion; mais il a donné cent francs et alors... (p. 65)

> came at seven o'clock and wanted me to suck him so that I should have some come in my stomach ... Mother said that under those conditions it was hardly worth bothering to have a first communion, but he had given a hundred francs and... (p. 53)

Here, as elsewhere, the little girl takes pleasure in shocking her listener, just like any child telling a dirty joke to grown-ups. With Sade, the pleasure derives from the very act of transgression itself, whilst the Louÿsian text foregrounds the narrator's (and therefore, the virtual reader's) scandalised reactions: 'Elle me vit palir [...] "Je t'en prie, tais-toi! Cette histoire est pire que tout!"' (p. 86) ('She saw me grow pale [...] "For God's sake, shut up! This is worse than anything you've said!"' (pp. 69–70)). In this text, the awareness of sin, of transgression and of the reprobation of a piously Catholic society thus serves a social irony as well as at times an infantile brand of humour.

The humour also has the effect of distancing the narrative from the real world and thus of removing its erotic charge.[15] Much of this humour springs from a tendency to exaggerate the reality which the story claims to reproduce faithfully.[16] Charlotte's account to the narrator of the conception of her youngest sister, Lili, for example – Charlotte 'a fait une fille à sa mère, à l'âge de neuf ans, et avec son cul!' (p. 59) ('I gave my mother a daughter when I was only nine years old, and with my ass!' (p. 48)) – is one of those comical because vulgar and incredible tales, operating well outside the bounds of realism:

> «On lui a mis le derrière sur un oreiller, le con grand ouvert. Moi, j'avais mon petit cul plein de foutre [...] Je me suis accroupie ...j'ai fait ce qu'elle disait ... et comme elle ne croyait guère qu'on pouvait faire un gosse comme ça, elle a été sur son bidet deux heures après.» (p. 59)

> 'She put her behind up on one of the pillows with her cunt spread wide. You can believe how full my little arse was with come. So I squatted, did what she told me, and since she didn't really think that she could become pregnant like that she didn't go to the bidet until two hours later.' (p. 47)

With a final wink of complicity to the eavesdropping reader, this tall tale's 'strange but true' status is underlined in conclusion by its leg-pulling child narrator: 'Et je te jure sur la tête de maman que c'est vrai!' (p. 59) ('And I swear to you on my mother's head that it's true!' (p. 48)).

Such exaggeration extends to practically all of the sexual activities described in the novel. The acrobatic skills which many of these call upon are more likely to stir the reader's admiration rather than his or her desires. The mother's account of her childhood is typical in this regard:

> «Comme maman et ses sœurs étaient acrobates et disloquées, chacune d'elles pouvait se bouffer le chat elle-même et surtout ce qu'elles faisaient souvent, c'était de se plier en deux pour aller sucer les couilles des hommes qui les enculaient [...]» (pp. 103–4)

> 'Mother and her sisters were all acrobats and double-jointed to boot, and each one of them could suck her own pussy if she wanted. But what they did most often was to bend themselves double and suck the balls of a man who was buttfucking them [...]' (p. 84)

These activities are more reminiscent of the gay obscenity of Rabelais or Voltaire than of the 'limit texts' of the Marquis de Sade. Teresa's rubbing spicy mustard into Mauricette's anus is a scene from Boccaccio, not Bataille.

Almost every page of this text contains examples of a verbal comedy which deflect the reader's attention from content to form. We laugh at literary jokes,

> En criant ce «Tiens! ah! tiens!», Teresa ignorait sans doute qu'elle introduisait une prosopopée dans son discours, mais il n'est pas nécessaire de connaître par leurs noms les figures de rhétorique pour les mettre comme Bourdaloue au service de la persuasion. (p. 160)

> In crying out her 'and then...! Ah! Then!' Teresa had no doubt been unaware that she was introducing a prosopia into her discourse, but it isn't necessary to know the terms of rhetoric by their names in order to, like Bourdaloue, press them into the service of persuasion. (p. 132)

at puerile wordplays,

> – Suivez-vous un traitement [pour la virginité]?
> – Oui, monsieur. Des massages. Avec le bout du doigt.»
> (p. 180)

'Are you taking any treatment for [your virginity]'?
'Oh, yes! Massages. With the end of my finger.' (p. 148)

– Je vous confie une enfant de dix ans pour lui apprendre
le français, l'histoire, la géographie, les langues vivantes, et
voilà quelles langues vous lui enseignez? (p. 201)

'I put a child of fourteen into your charge for you to teach
her history, geography, mathematics, and foreign tongues
and that's the sort of tongue you show her how to use?'
(p. 166)[17]

at sarcastic asides,

– Veux-tu jouer comme ça? ou me répondre zut chaque
fois que je te fais une proposition?... Je dis «zut» parce que
je suis putain. Si j'étais une jeune fille du monde, je dirais
que tu me réponds merde. (p. 154)

'Don't you want to play? You just want to say no every time
I try to do something with you? I use the word "no" because
I'm a whore. If I were a society girl I'd say "shit"' (p. 126)

Louÿs's writing overflows with a cheerful obscenity which
amuses rather than excites, an obscenity framed with an irony
which constantly takes us beyond it. In the following
exchange, which illustrates this technique well, the shock
effect created by a long list of obscene signifiers is suddenly
neutralised or marginalised by a literal but comic punchline:

– Ben, dit Lili [en mettant la langue dans le derrière de
Mauricette], ça sent le foutre, la gousse, le caca, la putain,
la moutarde, la guimauve, la queue, le jus de chat, la peau
d'Espagne, le caoutchouc du godmiché, les suppositoires, le
fond de bidet, le rouge pour les lèvres, la serviette à cul, la
vaseline, l'amidon, le musc, les chiottes de bordel et des
saloperies que je n'ose pas dire.
– Que je n'ose pas dire! répéta Ricette. Merci! oh! merci! Viens
que je te foute une claque. (pp. 189–90)

'Well,' began Lili [putting her tongue into Mauricette's
bottom], 'it smells of come, garlic, cocoa,[18] whores, mustard,

marshmallow, pricks, pussy juice, Spanish fly, dildo rubber, suppositories, the bottom of a bidet, lipstick, towels, vaseline, starch, musk, bordello shit-houses, and bitcheries I don't even dare mention.'

'That you don't dare mention!' repeated Ricette. 'Oh, thanks! Come here and let me give you a slap in the head.' (p. 156)

The reader who responds physically to the text is more likely to be laughing than lusting. Yet, *Trois Filles de leur mère* is not a simple parody either, since the construction of the text is founded on plurality and excess at all levels: the parodic exploitation of existing forms (autobiographical narrative, personal diary, 'books that are read with one hand'[19]), a bold use of vulgar expressions and a complete lack of sexual inhibitions are combined with a textual polyphony generated by the multiplication of narrative voices and the active role which the reader is encouraged to play. I shall consider separately these two latter aspects of the novel's form, which are the most playful and the most innovatory traits of Louÿs's entire erotic *œuvre*.

In *Trois Filles de leur mère*, the combination of a multiple focalisation with the *mise en scène* of both narrative and sexual activity generates a text which, in its fragmentation and its metatextuality, resembles some modern and even postmodern texts. To the first-level narrative of an extradiegetic and homodiegetic fictional author and male protagonist are added four second-level metadiegetic narratives[20] those of the mother and of each of her three daughters. It is here, above all, that Louÿs innovates: in the complex play of relations woven between fictional narrator (as character), the four female characters (as narrators), and the virtual reader which the text constructs as co-narrator and confidant(e) with whom we can all identify, regardless of gender or sexuality.[21]

The relationship between the narrator and his narratees is, indeed, fairly complex, marked by a complicity which is, in turns, mocking, ironic, moralising, waggish, didactic and sometimes even downright malicious. Like the narrators, the narratees are multiple. Firstly, there is the female reader, who is addressed by the wry 'Foreword addressed to the female reader'. However, this female reader often changes sex in the course of the narrative: at one time, the narrator undeniably addresses a male reader, at another young girls, and there are times when both sexes are addressed simultaneously. Whatever the reader's gender, (s)he is sometimes impatient – '(...) il faudrait avoir connu les deux jeunes filles ... Elles offraient une série de contrastes que vous n'auriez pas la patience d'entendre si j'avais celle de vous les dire.' (pp. 151–2) ('... But you have to know the two girls. There was to be found in them a series of contrasts that you wouldn't have the patience to listen to if I had it to write them down.' (p. 124)) – sympathetic and/or antipathetic to the narrator's actions – 'Je partage mes lecteurs en deux groupes. Les uns me reprochent d'avoir donné auparavant une douzaine de bourrades sur l'épaule gauche de Teresa [...] l'autre groupe de lecteurs n'a pas encore compris pourquoi, si j'ai déjà battu cette femme, j'hésite à la flanquer cette fois, hors de mon lit.' (pp. 119–20) ('I therefore split my readers into two groups: the ones who will have already criticized me for having beaten Teresa a dozen times on the shoulder [...] my other group of readers have not yet understood why, if I had already beaten this woman, I hesitated to throw her this time out of my bed.' (p. 97)) – a friend with whom the narrator shares a writer's joke – 'En quelques mots elle fit savoir ce qu'elle m'offrait de voluptés, ce qu'elle attendait de ma persévérance, et le rôle que jouerait Lili. Je ne vous le dis pas; ce n'est point par dissimulation; c'est parce que vous le lirez à la page suivante.' (p. 131) ('She proceeded to tell me what she was now going to offer in the way of pleasures, what awaited my perseverance, and the role that Lili would play. I won't tell you now what they were, not in order to hide them, but because you will read them on the next page.' (p. 107)) – argumentative – 'J'aimais mieux cela. Pas vous. Mais moi.' (p. 179) ('That was more like it. Not for you, I suppose, but for me.' (p. 148)) – naïve – 'Apprenez donc, lecteur ingénu [...]' (p. 196) ('Listen carefully then, young reader, and take heed.' (p. 161)) – worldly-wise and versed in child psychology – 'J'en appelle d'abord à ceux qui ont vécu en Orient et ensuite à vous, qui me lisez, si la psychologie des petites filles ne vous est pas trop mal connue.' (p. 200) ('I appeal first of all to those who have lived in the Orient and second of all to you, if you know anything about adolescent psychology, for support.' (p. 165)) – moralising – 'Concevez l'âge de Mauricette, sa précocité, son ardeur ... Imaginez par-dessus tout le sentiment illimité qu'elle devait avoir de son sacrifice! et combien ... Mais pourquoi vous le dire? Vous ne m'avez déjà que trop condamné!' (p. 145) ('Recall Mauricette's age, her precocity, her ardour ... Imagine above this base the unlimited sentiment which she must have had for the sacrifice she wanted to make! And how much ... But why say any more? I've already written enough to hang myself in the eyes of my readers.' (p. 119)) – snobbish – 'Si vous ne connaissez les actrices que par les conversations de fumoir, n'en dites rien.' (p. 26) ('If the only way you know actresses is through smoking-room conversations, don't say any more.' (p. 19)) – or quite simply, young or, at least, young at heart – 'Je dormis neuf heures et me réveillai avec un irrésistible désir de ... Terminez la phrase si vous êtes jeune ou si vous vous souvenez de l'avoir été.' (p. 100) ('I slept soundly for nine hours and awoke with an irresistible desire to ... Finish the sentence if you are young or if you ever have been.' (p. 81)).

The narrator dialogues so frequently with this reader that, even though extradiegetic, (s)he is almost omnipresent. This, then, is an active reader who is already inscribed into the formal construction of the novel. However, we are not dealing with a reader who is simply *reactive*, like the male reader who, according to Sade, may 'perdre du foutre' ('lose some spunk') as he reads,[22] whilst remaining all the while outside the text in the real world, but a reader who is encouraged to cross the line between fiction and reality to look over the narrator's shoulder and share his responsibility for a narrative that is plural in origin: 'Teresa nue ressemblait à un mezzo d'opéra. Vous alliez dire: à une fille de bordel? Pas du tout. Vous murmurez c'est la même chose? Non. C'est le jour et la nuit.' (p. 26) ('Nude, Teresa ressembled an operatic mezzo. A whore, in other words, you will say. But I answer, not at all. You murmur that it is much the same thing? No. Not unless night and day are the same.' (p. 19)). The use of the first person plural involves this reader directly in the production of the narrative: 'Bref, très probablement *vous* avez oublié que *nous* avons laissé Mauricette en délire [...]' (p. 152; my emphasis) ('To resume, *you* have probably forgotten by this time that *we* left Mauricette in a state bordering on delirium [...]' (pp. 124–5)).

In addition to the virtual readers, all the characters of the novel also adopt the role of narratee at given moments. The narrator himself listens to the embedded narratives of the three girls, thus becoming an intradiegetic narratee with whom the real reader can identify or not, as (s)he wishes. This is, after all, a reasonable (or perhaps falsely modest?) individual, who pales at the idea of a young girl sucking a horse's penis or who is frankly repulsed by Charlotte's account of oral sex with other animals and shocked by her coprophilic propositions.

This narratee serves to reproduce instantly the responses expected of a reader who is appropriately excited.[23] At the same time, and unlike the traditional erotic narrative, the authenticity of these responses is undermined by their ironic representation. Charlotte, for example, becomes the addressee of her own narrative, by immediately putting into practice what she is describing: 'Elle retomba sur le lit, aussi faible et brisée que si elle venait de revivre son récit.' (p. 85) ('She fell back on the bed weak and exhausted, as if she had just relived her story.' (p. 68)). Similar *mises en abyme*[24] of the reading of erotic literature are identifiable elsewhere in the text: "Tu veux que je te dise? Ça m'excite presque autant d'y penser près de toi que si tu me le faisais." (p. 146) ("You want me to say it? It excites me almost as much to think it when I'm next to you as to have you do it to me." (p. 120)) says Mauricette, standing in for the female reader. But it is above all in the final scene of the novel that such ironies are most striking, in a long dénouement, in which the voyeurism of the reader is staged in a Rabelaisian playlet, put on by the three daughters. In this outrageously obscene farce, all the characters in turn adopt the position of the virtual reader: "Quelle éducation!' exclaims Lili, the youngest of the three, affecting high indignation, 'en se tournant vers les spectateurs.' (p. 206) ("What an education!' sighed Lili turning toward us.' (p. 169)). The active participation which the erotic narrative demands of its male addressee is here inverted and therefore parodied when Teresa, the mother, abandons her spectator role to join in the action: 'Teresa en peignoir traversa la chambre à grands pas, *prit le rôle de la mère* [...]' (p. 201; my emphasis) ('Teresa in a dressing-gown suddenly crossed the room with great strides *in the role of Lili's mother* [...]' (p. 166)). At this point, the text becomes self-consciously theatrical, the girls' playlet the *mise en scène* of a *mise en scène*. There is even an interval. These frequent sardonic allusions to the erotic writing and reading process place the emphasis on the manner of narration at the expense of what is narrated. The consequence of this is that, by reproducing brilliantly and comically the pornographic *effect*, the text by contrast loses its own erotic charge. This narrative constantly reminds us that, even if the events related are supposed to be true (a claim which is, anyway, characteristic of the genre), we are dealing with a story with pages and chapters, a first person narrator who admits his incompetence and readers who keep interrupting to have their say.

This heightened awareness of the activity of narration and therefore of the fictional status of what is narrated is increased by the disapproving attitude of the narrator towards his own narrative, for which he eventually refuses to accept any responsability:

> Ayez la bonté de ne pas croire que j'invente ce théâtre enfantin. Si vous jugez que mon style n'est pas celui d'un primaire, faites-moi la grâce de supposer que ces dialogues de courtisanes ne sont pas le fruit de mes veilles. (p.191)

> Please be kind enough not to think that I am making up these childish programmes. If you can accept my style as not being that of a primer, have the grace also not to think that these dialogues are the fruit of my imagination. (p. 157)

If not the narrator, then who else penned these lines but the self-mocking author, well known for fooling the literary establishment by passing his own inventions off as authentic originals?[25] The conceit of a narrator, dissociating himself from his own narrative, invites us to place the blame squarely where it belongs – with the coyly winking and irrepressibly schoolboyish prankster and revered writer of fiction. Knowing that the novel would have been read at the time of its publication only by a very limited coterie of friends and devotees, we cannot help but read this passage as a literary joke, shared by author and friends.

The tendency of the text to refer to itself in jest suggests a fictional status, which contradicts the (auto)biographicality, implied in the novel's Foreword. Nevertheless, this ambivalence constitutes a slippage of identity, from which the narrator and the narratee also suffer. The multiplicity of narrators discourages identification with a singular fixed narrative voice and, like the intradiegetic narrators and narratees, the real readers are cast adrift, their sexual and psychological identities, as we have seen, constantly challenged. This confusion of narrative identities tends to undermine the conventional reading contract of the pornographic genre and the *effet de réel* (reality effect), which is so necessary to the pleasure of the male reader, is consequently threatened. We are more accustomed to encountering such slippages in the postmodern text than in a novel of *La Belle Époque*.

## Conclusion

At the end of this discussion, let us return to the dominant word in my title, 'excess', and its various meanings in relation to Louÿs's text: stylistic excess, thematic excess and above all, a pornographic excess which takes us beyond the pornographic genre itself. In de-eroticising the text by means of humour and parodic *mise en scène*, Louÿs challenges the conventional pre-occupation of the pornographic text with bodily *jouissance*. *Trois Filles de leur mère* plays on this reductive characteristic of the genre to offer the reader a pleasure which is more textual than sexual. All of Pierre Louÿs's works express the desire to translate the body into language and to contain it in words, which are the author's real love object. The Louÿsian text overflows with language (obscenity, humour, polyphony) on to a body whose *jouissance* is as verbal as it is physical. Far from being a dissipation or a loss (one of the negative meanings of 'excess'), this verbal 'spilling over' is both positive and creative, an excess in the sense of a ludic multiplicity. In undermining accepted definitions of the pornographic through the staging of consciously theatrical and undeniably linguistic events, *Trois Filles de leur mère* displays a skilful manipulation of literary form worthy of the *nouveau roman*.

# 4

# Masochism and Fetishism: Georges Bataille's *Histoire de l'œil*

Introducing the Gallimard edition of Georges Bataille's complete works, Michel Foucault declares him to be one of the most important writers of the century.[1] It is certainly true that his work covers an impressively wide area: during the course of his life (1897–1962), Bataille wrote studies in sociology, anthropology, economics, philosophy, art and literary criticism as well as novels and poems, and it is difficult to appreciate his work fully without some knowledge of the whole range of his writing. His first book, the short novel, *Histoire de l'œil* was published secretly by René Bonnel in 1928, under the pseudonym, Lord Auch, a rather puerile wordplay, combining an English term for Christ, 'Lord', with an abbreviation for 'aux chiottes', a vulgar expression, meaning 'to the shithouse'.[2] Further editions appeared in 1940 and 1941, giving Burgos and Seville as places of publication, respectively, although all three editions were actually published in Paris. It was not until 1967 that an edition bearing the author's name appeared, five years after his death.[3]

As a public librarian and therefore a French civil servant, it would have been difficult for Bataille to acknowledge the authorship of this or any of his other pornographic fictions[4] during his lifetime. Indeed, as Michael Richardson points out, Bataille went out of his way to distance himself from his fictional writing, not only by the use of pseudonyms but by the use of different narrative voices.[5] At a practical level, of course, he was clearly anxious to avoid prosecution, although Richardson suggests that he also had a 'sense of shame' about his pornographic writings which was at the root of his self-censorship; a feeling that his novels were somehow 'indefensible'. It is tempting to relate the guilt that Bataille obviously felt as a writer to the guilt and anxiety experienced by so many of his characters.

Paradoxically, the student-led liberalising revolution of the year that followed the publication of the first acknowledged edition of *Histoire de l'œil* encouraged a more direct form of censorship. In 1968, several school–student committees distributed pamphlets railing against the decadence of bourgeois, capitalist society, as represented by the works of Georges Bataille and especially by *Histoire de l'œil*, which they called upon to be banned.[6]

Around the same time, however, the French avant-garde elevated Bataille's work to near cult status, regarding the now dead author, mainly thanks to *Histoire de l'œil*, as an anti-establishment hero. As Susan Suleiman points out,[7] many of the other leading French cultural heroes of the 1960s and 1970s (Barthes, Kristeva, Sollers, Foucault, Blanchot) wrote about him at length. To this list of French intellectuals, Suleiman rightly adds the name of Susan Sontag, whose seminal essay on literary pornography, 'The Pornographic Imagination', drew the attention of Anglo-American readers to Bataille, praising his work as 'the chamber music of pornographic literature', with *Histoire de l'œil* 'the most accomplished artistically of all the pornographic prose fictions I've read'.[8] This interest in Bataille among Parisian intellectuals, however, did not spread outside France until the 1980s, when a sudden fashion for his work is perhaps attributable, as Richardson suggests,[9] to the rise of postmodernist criticism. There are a number of reasons for this neglect, not least a repulsion among Anglo-Saxon scholars for the pornographic and sacrilegious elements of the fictional writing. The author's personal reputation as, at best, a maverick[10] intellectual with eccentric and eclectic interests (cave paintings, numismatism, mysticism, shamanism) and, at worst, an unbalanced erotomaniac with suicidal tendencies and a taste for human sacrifice[11] doubtless contributed to this unwillingness among the academic community in the UK and the USA to make Bataille part of the twentieth-century canon.

Superficially, at least, the texts appear no less idiosyncratic than their author, portraying a twilight world of *fin de siècle* decadence, peopled by self-indulgent, upper-middle class manic depressives, who throw frequent convulsions for no apparent reason other than alcoholic or narcotic inebriation or sexual frenzy. As Bataille argues in his major theoretical work on eroticism, *L'Érotisme*, work and violence are incompatible,[12] so it is hardly surprising that the sexually violent world of his fiction is inhabited predominantly by the leisured classes. In the pages of Bataille's novels, *la Belle Époque* lingers on.

The themes to which Bataille incessantly and obsessively returns might also be considered rebarbative by many readers. All of his fiction can be said to enact in extreme fashion and graphic detail the links between sex and death, and the irresistible need for humans to transgress, theorised later in *L'Érotisme*. As for the wider reading public, Bataille's highly abstract narrative style has always been considered too 'difficult', even 'incomprehensible', to achieve any real degree of popularity outside university circles. Most critical work on Bataille to date has simply compounded the problem.

If we except Sontag, whose analysis is necessarily cursory in the context of a wider discussion of avant-garde pornography in a single article, it is possible, as Susan Suleiman does,[13] to make three main criticisms of this critical corpus.

Firstly, surprisingly few critics have accorded particular attention to Georges Bataille's fictional work (as opposed to his theoretical writings). Philippe Sollers's influential essay on Bataille, 'Le toit',[14] for instance, is notable for making no reference whatsoever to the fiction.

Secondly, those who have analysed the fiction in any detail have taken the theory as their starting point, viewing the fiction as 'putting the theory into practice'.[15] This approach has the effect of elevating the theory above the fiction, conspiring with the 'pornography' label further to downgrade it. It also encourages us to view the fiction in terms of the theory, to see it as mere illustration thereof, which can lead to a forcing of the argument and to the creation of blindspots.

Thirdly, those whose approach, like Roland Barthes's,[16] *has* been resolutely textual, have typically focused on the workings of the signifier, reading Bataille's texts as transgressive at the level of form rather than content, and in so doing have tended to avoid discussion of the latter. Surprisingly little attention, therefore, seems to have been paid to the identity of a sexual subject in the text beyond the more superficial evocations of sado-masochistic themes (Susan Suleiman's work on the novel is an honourable exception). This concentration on form was for a very long time part of a more general trend, in defence of pornography from an aesthetic viewpoint, evacuating the sexual content, 'averting the gaze' from the naked body in the text.

In the discussion of *Histoire de l'œil* that follows, I shall try to avoid these pitfalls. Although applying another body of theory, psychoanalysis, to Bataille's text, I shall avoid prioritising his own theory over the fiction, taking the latter as starting point at all times, whilst, of course, referring to the author's theoretical ideas where appropriate. I shall also follow Suleiman in bringing the critical gaze back to the representational elements of the text. These elements are, in any event, inseparable from the metaphorical and symbolic levels. Having reviewed the theoretical consensus of psychoanalysis on masochism, I shall argue that the sexual subject of the narrative is mainly (though not exclusively) a masochistic subject, governed not by the Father's but by the Mother's Law; that, as in the fictions of Sacher-Masoch, the masculine is expelled in favour of the feminine–maternal and the masochistic subject is thus reborn under the sign of the Mother; that the fetishising in the writing of female urination may be seen as evidence of a 'phallic mother' fantasy, associated with an underlying desire to erase sexual difference, and that this erasure of difference is both transgressive and potentially liberating for women as well as for men.

There is a ubiquity of suffering in Bataille's fiction which has led many to describe it as 'sadomasochistic'. The use of this portmanteau term, of course, implies the Freudian perspective, according to which sadism and masochism are not separate perversions afflicting different 'types' but the active and passive forms of a single perversion or, in other words, cohabiting tendencies within the same individual.[17] Freud's view of masochism as simply the other side of the sadistic coin has dominated psychoanalytic theory and practice for most of this century. According to this conventional analysis, the masochist first passes through a sadistic stage, during which he puts himself in his father's place, wishing to possess his power and virility. Then, a creeping feeling of guilt, combined with a fear of castration as punishment by the father for usurping his position, leads the subject to move from an active to a passive role, to take the place of the mother and to offer himself submissively to the father.

Unlike Freud, the contemporary philosopher Gilles Deleuze sees masochism and sadism as entirely separate. There is a huge difference, Deleuze argues, between a sadist who derives pleasure from controlling and hurting an unwilling victim and a masochist who willingly enters into a pleasure–pain contract with a dominant partner. While conceding that the father is dominant in sadism, Deleuze was the first to argue against explaining masochism in terms of a father complex.[18] Deleuze suggests that, rather than being the 'reverse side' of a 'father-identified' sadism, masochism has its roots in the symbiotic relationship between the male child and the oral mother of the pregenital stage. As Linda Williams so succinctly puts it, 'Deleuze thus views masochism as a kind of plot carried out between mother and son to replace the father with the mother as the figure of power.'[19]

Arguing from the problematic perspective of female identification with masochism, which Deleuze ignores in his analysis, Williams is rather more sympathetic to the view put forward by Parveen Adams that there is, in the female spectator of SM films, an oscillation between male and female subject positions so that 'she does not necessarily identify only and exclusively with the woman who is beaten; she may also, simultaneously, identify with the beater or with the less involved spectator who simply looks on. And even if she does identify only with the tortured woman, she might identify alternately or simultaneously with her pleasure and/or her pain.'[20]

This view of how a female spectator may respond to the masochistic scenario is a persuasive one in my view and clearly influences the broader question of sadism and masochism as related or separate positions.

We now need to ask whether we can identify a sexual/textual subject in *Histoire de l'œil*, and to what extent this subject bears out the Deleuze hypothesis, following which we shall return to the issue of reader identification in the conclusion.

## Analysis of the Text

There is, undoubtedly, a strong element of sadism in *Histoire de l'œil*: in the treatment of the virginal and sexually repressed

Marcelle by the amoral adolescent male narrator and his equally delinquent, 15-year-old girlfriend, Simone, in the behaviour of the aristocratic English libertine, Sir Edward, but above all, in Simone's sexual obsessions. On the other hand, this sadistic element is of secondary importance in what is, in my view, a narrative orientated towards the masochistic reader.

Sir Edward's acts of sadism are strictly limited to the procurement of 'entertainment' for his young disciples in debauchery: he shuts a young whore up in a pigsty so that she is trampled underfoot by the sows; at the *corrida* in Madrid, he serves up bulls' testicles to Simone at her request; most memorably, he is an active accomplice in the sexual torture and murder of a Spanish curate in his own sacristy, instructing Simone, who is eager but inexperienced in homicide, how to strangulate the young cleric so that he will ejaculate into her as he dies. Sir Edward's role, however, is largely symbolic. He is the foreign 'other' upon whom guilt for depravity and corruption can, to some degree, be projected, the English lord who has almost become a stock character in nineteenth- and twentieth-century French pornography (Sir Stephen in *Histoire d'O*, for instance, or the aristocratically named Quentin in *Emmanuelle*), a reminder to the French reader of the decadence of the *ancien régime*. He functions on a realist level largely as a facilitator – it is his wealth, we are told, which enables the young couple to flee France after the death of Marcelle (sexual guilt and a deranged state of mind, induced largely by the corrupting influence of her young companions, finally drive her to commit suicide). The unpleasantness of an inquiry is thus avoided and they are able to continue their life of debauchery in Spain. In catering for Simone's sadistic tastes, he also relieves the narrator of much of the responsibility in this regard. (Unlike his female companion, the narrator is essentially a masochist, as we shall see shortly.) Sir Edward is a stereotype of the genre, with even less psychological depth than the other characters; his function in the narrative is severely limited and his sadism relatively unexplored, a dim reflection of that of Simone.

On the face of it, Simone delights in the pain and humiliation of others: this is her dominant trait, dictating her behaviour throughout the novel. It is Simone who directs the orgies, in which she and the narrator take part, instructing and challenging others: she embarrasses a young boy, for example, by stripping him in public; she imagines the narrator smearing Marcelle's face with his come, 'pour qu'il fume' (p. 26) ('till it sizzles' (p. 22)), thus revelling in the visual and graphic soiling of her innocence; later, when Marcelle hangs herself, Simone urinates on her dead body; she is sexually excited by the death of both bull and bullfighter at the *corrida* in Madrid; finally, and most tellingly, in a scene which might have been conceived by Sade himself, she takes enormous pleasure in the humiliation, torture and death of a Spanish priest.

Yet, in all of this, what matters is not Simone's point of view, but that of the narrator, whose perspective we are invited to share. As the feelings of all the characters are presented to us by this first-person male narrator, it is reasonable to view him as the principal sexual subject of the writing – a mobile subject, certainly, whose identification with others allows for the crossing of gender and, to some degree, sadistic–masochistic boundaries, but arguably the main focus of sexual experience. Simone's 'sadism' is, in other words, what Deleuze calls the 'pseudo-sadism of masochism',[21] a sadism staged by a 'cold and cruel woman' for the benefit of a male subject (the narrator), who has contracted with her for this to happen. Both whore and priest are anonymous victims of crimes enacted before a masochistic male onlooker. As the priest is strangled to death, it seems to me that in the narrator's physical discomfort there is the suggestion of a perverse, masochistic identification with the victim as he takes the dead man's place:

Je m'allongeai auprès d'elle pour la violer et la foutre à mon tour, mais je ne pouvais que la serrer dans mes bras et lui baiser la bouche à cause d'une étrange paralysie intérieure profondément causée par mon amour pour la jeune fille et la mort de l'innommable. Je n'ai jamais été aussi content. (pp. 66–7)

I stretched out at her side to rape and fuck her in turn, but all I could do was squeeze her in my arms and kiss her mouth, because of a strange inward paralysis ultimately caused by my love for the girl and the death of the unspeakable creature. I have never been so content. (p. 65)

As with Sir Edward, Simone's sexual cruelty is largely symbolic. No details are given of the whore's trampling by the sows, and the murder of the priest is far more erotic than violent, perverse sexuality being foregrounded in this scene as against sadistic aggression. As in other orgiastic scenes in the novel, the focus is not so much on the *process* of violence, but on its erotic *effects*, on male erections and ejaculations, and on Simone's and the narrator's sexual pleasure. Even the gouging out of the priest's eye, which Simone proceeds to slip into her vulva, is an essentially symbolic act, whose significance, as Barthes has shown, depends on its position in a network of images of eggs, eyes and testicles.[22]

That Simone acts as Deleuze's 'stern, cruel mother',[23] with whom the masochistic male narrator has contracted, is, I suggest, borne out by a more detailed analysis of the *récit*'s sexual contents. It is Marcelle's sexual guilt and humiliation which seal the bond between them. To pursue the legal metaphor, Marcelle is the 'consideration' for their contract, since it is across her body (both alive and dead) that the masochistic scenario is enacted. Each 'gives' Marcelle to the other, in return for sexual excitement, but it is the narrator, not Simone, who identifies with Marcelle, projecting his own masochism on to her. Both the narrator and Marcelle are, I would suggest, repressed masochists, who need a trigger for their masochism to surface – Simone for the former, and Simone and the narrator for the latter – but the narrator sees his own masochism reflected in Marcelle: he shows no initiative whatsoever, sexual or non-sexual, at any time and is content to follow Simone's lead in all the situations of the narrative, so his description of Marcelle as someone who 'manquait exceptionnellement de volonté' (p. 19) ('who had an unusual lack of willpower' (p. 15)) is not a little ironic. There are further clues pointing to the narrator's unconscious identification with Marcelle: when Marcelle loses her reason, he contemplates suicide with his father's revolver, as if it was Simone, the girl he supposedly loved, and not Marcelle who had suffered the breakdown; when they next have sex, Simone tells him that he 'smells of Marcelle'; most tellingly, in the text's closing lines, he sees Marcelle's eye in Simone's vagina, a symbolic vision of Marcelle the victim as cement for his erotic bond with Simone and evidence of his sympathetic identification with her:

> Il me semblait même que mes yeux me sortaient de la tête comme s'ils étaient érectiles à force d'horreur; je vis exactement, dans le vagin velu de *Simone*, l'œil bleu pâle de *Marcelle* qui me regardait en pleurant des larmes d'urine. Des traînées de foutre dans le poil fumant achevaient de donner à cette vision lunaire un caractère de tristesse désastreuse. (p. 69, the emphasis is the author's).

> I even felt as if my eyes were bulging from my head, erectile with horror; in *Simone's* hairy vagina, I saw the wan blue eye of *Marcelle*, gazing at me through tears of urine. Streaks of come in the steaming hair helped give that dreamy vision a disastrous sadness. (p. 67)

Apart from this projective identification with Marcelle, Simone's and the narrator's relationship has many more of the specific characteristics which, for Deleuze, typify the masochistic contract.

There is, firstly, a strong sense of anxiety in their relationship which Deleuze claims is a marked feature of the contract.[24] The narrator emphasises this feeling in the opening lines of the narrative: 'J'ai été élevé très seul et aussi loin que je me rappelle, j'étais angoissé par tout ce qui est sexuel.' (p. 13) ('I grew up very much alone, and as far back as I recall I was frightened of anything sexual.' (p. 9) and this anxiety is repeatedly foregrounded when he and Simone are together. Marcelle, too, is in a state of almost permanent anxiousness.

Secondly, the Deleuze masochist is punished *before* he is rewarded, giving him the right to the forbidden satisfaction of desire. Suffering, in this scenario, is not the cause of pleasure, as it is for the sadist, but the precondition for it. The reward of sexual pleasure is, in other words, delayed as much as possible:

> [...] la forme du masochisme est l'attente [...] Le masochiste attend le plaisir comme quelque chose qui est essentielle-ment en retard, et s'attend à la douleur comme à une condition qui rend possible enfin (physiquement et

moralement) la venue du plaisir. Il recule donc le plaisir tout
le temps nécessaire pour qu'une douleur elle-même attendue
le rende permis.[25]

[...] the nature of masochism is waiting [...] The masochist
waits for pleasure as for something that is essentially delayed,
and expects pain as the condition that finally makes the
arrival of pleasure (physically and morally) possible. He
therefore puts the pleasure off for as long as is necessary for
the pain, which is itself expected, to make it permissible.

The general pattern of the Bataille narrator's relationship to
pleasure is that suffering precedes it. This is the case, not only
of *Histoire de l'œil*, but also of most of Bataille's narratives. Significantly, the narrator and Simone are not able to have full
sexual intercourse until Marcelle has killed herself. The pain
of her loss, experienced by him, which is also an identificatory
pain, extends into and becomes mingled with the physical
pain of Simone's deflowerment:

Je coupai la corde, mais elle était bien morte. Nous l'avons
installé sur le tapis. Simone vit que je bandais et commença
à me branler. Je m'étendis moi-même aussi sur le tapis,
mais il était impossible de faire autrement; Simone étant
encore vierge, je la baisai pour la première fois auprès du
cadavre. Cela nous fit très mal à tous les deux mais nous
étions contents justement parce que ça faisait mal. (p. 46)

I cut the rope, but she was quite dead. We laid her out on
the carpet. Simone saw I was getting a hard-on and she
started tossing me off. I too stretched out on the carpet. It
was impossible to do otherwise; Simone was still a virgin,
and I fucked her for the first time, next to the corpse. It was
very painful for both of us, but we were glad precisely
because it *was* painful. (p. 43, translator's emphasis)

Thirdly, and most importantly, there is, for Deleuze, a
strong element of fetishism in masochism.[26] Now, Simone's
and the narrator's sexuality is nothing if not fetishistic. This
fetishism takes a liquid form. Liquids dominate the imagery
of the narrative, from the saucer of milk into which Simone

lowers her vagina in the opening pages (milk for the pussy) to the many emissions of urine, semen and vomit (for instance, in the orgy which drives Marcelle over the edge of insanity) to the vitreous liquids of eggs and eyes which, for Roland Barthes, constitute one of the text's structural metaphorical chains.[27] Of all these liquids, urine is the one we encounter most often. Apart from Simone's obsession with eggs, eyes and testicles, both she and the narrator are strongly excited by urination – their own and that of others. Indeed, the eroticism of the novel is, above all, I would suggest, urethal.[28]

Urination also plays an extremely important structural and symbolic role. Acts of urination leading to or accompanying orgasm both open and close the text. 'Est-ce que tu ne peux pas faire pipi en l'air jusqu'au cul?' ('Can't you pee up to my cunt?') Simone asks the narrator near the beginning,

> – Oui, répondis-je, mais comme tu es là, ça va forcément retomber sur ta robe et sur ta figure.
> – Pourquoi pas? conclut-elle; et je fis comme elle avait dit, mais à peine l'avais-je fait que je l'inondai à nouveau, cette fois de beau foutre blanc. (p. 15)

> 'Yes,' I answered, 'but with you like this, it'll get on your dress and your face.'
> 'So what,' she concluded. And I did as she said, but no sooner was I done than I flooded her again, this time with fine white come. (p. 11)

As the narrative draws to a close, after the rape and murder of a priest by Simone, the narrator gazes thoughtfully on Simone's hairy vulva, which is streaked with come and beneath which urine is streaming forth. The language dies away into silence, evacuated with the dying stream of urine: 'L'urine brûlante ruisselait sous l'œil sur la cuisse la plus basse...' (p. 69) ('The burning urine streamed out from under the eye down to the thighs below...' (p. 67)).

Surprisingly, although many critics, like Roland Barthes, have focused upon the egg/eye/sun imagery in their analysis of the text's formal aspects, none of them, including Barthes, appears to have noticed that all this imagery, even that evoking the cruel sunlight of Spain, leads to urine. The death of a bullfighter in Madrid is accompanied, both by the simultaneous insertion by Simone of a bull's testicle into her vagina, as the matador's eye falls out of its socket, and by 'une sorte de liquéfaction urinaire du ciel' (p. 57) ('a sort of urinary liquefaction of the sky' (p. 54)). The astral and the urinary are directly linked in another key passage. After Simone and the narrator have 'liberated' the psychotic Marcelle from the insane asylum in which she had been incarcerated on her breakdown, Simone wets herself from sexual ecstasy (whether it is with urine or female ejaculate is not clear) and the narrator himself simultaneously comes into his pants. He then lies in the grass, gazing up at the Milky Way, 'étrange trouée de sperme astral et d'urine céleste à travers la voûte crânienne formée par le cercle des constellations' (p. 44) ('that strange breach of astral sperm and heavenly urine across the cranial vault formed by the ring of constellations' (p. 42)).

What Barthes and others seem to have missed is that, unlike the more properly sadistic images discussed below, these urinary images are not just to be read on a symbolic level, but are also signifiers of a urethal eroticism that underpins and defines the sexual relationship between Simone, Marcelle and the narrator. Even the smell of urine is erotic for them. After the slaughter of the bull at the *corrida*, the narrator and Simone have violent sex in a stinking toilet. The emphasis here is on the power of the repulsive to excite, strongly suggesting a link between urine and masochism. The passage is worth quoting at length:

> Elle me prit par la main sans mot dire et me conduisit dans une cour extérieure de l'arène extrêmement sale où il y avait une odeur d'urine chevaline et humaine suffocante étant donné la grande chaleur. Je pris, moi, Simone par le cul et Simone saisit à travers la culotte ma verge en colère. Nous entrâmes ainsi dans des chiottes puantes où des mouches sordides tourbillonnaient dans un rayon de soleil, et où, resté debout, je pus mettre à nu le cul de la jeune fille, enfoncer dans sa chair couleur de sang et baveuse, d'abord mes doigts, puis le membre viril lui-même, qui entra dans cette caverne de sang pendant que je branlais son cul en y pénétrant profondément avec le médius osseux. En même

temps aussi les révoltes de nos bouches se collaient dans un orage de salive. (pp. 53–4)

> She took my hand wordlessly and led me to an outer courtyard of the filthy arena, where the stench of equine and human urine was suffocating because of the great heat. I grabbed Simone's cunt, and she seized my furious cock through my trousers. We stepped into a stinking shithouse, where sordid flies whirled about in a sunbeam. Standing here, I exposed Simone's cunt, and into her blood-red, slobbery flesh I stuck my fingers, then my penis, which entered that cavern of blood while I tossed off her arse, thrusting my bony middle finger deep inside. At the same time, the roofs of our mouths cleaved together in a storm of saliva. (p. 51)

To what extent are the masochistic undertones of this passage typical of the functioning of urinary eroticism in this text?

Whether masochistic or sadistic in character, the erotic charge carried by urination in *Histoire de l'œil* depends, as so graphically illustrated above, on its association with degradation of self or other and as such is essentially the product of a *transgressive* act. Bataille has himself written at great length on the importance of transgression in all truly erotic activity. In a discussion of the links between reproduction and death in *L'Érotisme*, Bataille reminds us that, long before Freud, Saint Augustine himself was only too aware of the proximity of the sexual organs to the processes of bodily evacuation: 'Inter faeces et urinam nascimur,' he declared, ('We are born between faeces and urine').[29] For Bataille, the taboo and its transgression are two sides of the same coin: as taboo substances that remind us of degeneration and death, urine and faeces are repugnant, but like all taboos, they are also fascinating, because they represent the challenge of transgression:

> Pour aller au bout de l'extase où nous nous perdons dans la jouissance, nous devons toujours en poser l'immédiate limite: c'est l'horreur. [...] il n'est pas de forme de répugnance dont je ne discerne l'affinité avec le désir.[30]

To enjoy to the utmost the ecstasy in which we lose ourselves in orgasm, we must always know what the borderline is: it is horror. [...] there is no form of repugnance that does not have an affinity with desire.

Hence, like the white tablecloth that Simone takes a sexual pleasure in soiling, it is because Marcelle represents purity that she invites defilement: thus, Simone fantasises about the narrator smearing Marcelle's face with his come. Marcelle's urination acts as a trigger for her orgasms and for that of others for the simple reason that the most pure, virginal innocence has been transgressed in public by a grossly impure substance with strong sexual associations. In the orgy scene which finally drives Marcelle mad, she shuts herself up in a wardrobe to masturbate, a powerful image of her unsuccessful attempt to contain her desires and to hide her shame. Her orgasm is accompanied by uncontrollable urination:

> Et soudain il arriva une chose incroyable, un étrange bruit d'eau suivi de l'apparition d'un filet puis d'un ruissellement au bas de la porte de l'armoire: la malheureuse Marcelle pissait dans son armoire en se branlant. Mais l'éclat de rire absolument ivre qui suivit dégénéra rapidement en une débauche de chutes de corps, de jambes et de culs en l'air, de jupes mouillées et de foutre. Les rires se produisaient comme des hoquets idiots et involontaires, mais ne réussissaient qu'à peine à interrompre une ruée brutale vers les culs et les verges. Et pourtant, bientôt, on entendit la triste Marcelle sangloter seule et de plus en plus fort dans la pissotière de fortune qui lui servait maintenant de prison.
> (pp. 20–1)

And all at once, something incredible happened, a strange swish of water, followed by a trickle and a stream from under the wardrobe door: poor Marcelle was pissing in her wardrobe while masturbating. But the explosion of totally drunken guffaws that ensued rapidly degenerated into a debauche of tumbling bodies, lofty legs and arses, wet skirts and come. Guffaws emerged like foolish and involuntary hiccups but scarcely managed to interrupt a brutal onslaught on cunts and cocks. And yet soon we could hear Marcelle dismally sobbing alone, louder and louder, in the makeshift pissoir that was now her prison. (p. 17)

The powerfully transgressive nature of urine is also underscored in the scene in which the priest is tortured and murdered. In an act that is doubly transgressive, because both unnatural and sacrilegious, he is made to urinate into a chalice and drink from it. He does so 'avec une sorte d'extase immonde' (p. 64) ('with a well-nigh filthy ecstasy' (p. 62)), an ecstasy, therefore, with strong masochistic origins, and comes – on to hosts – immediately afterwards. In both of these scenes, as elsewhere in Bataille's fiction, urination and orgasm are linked activities. This link is encapsulated linguistically on the last page of the narrative, when Simone succumbs to a final 'urinary *spasm*' (my emphasis).

In these and other scenes of urinary eroticism in *Histoire de l'œil*, the question of whether the transgression is of a sadistic or masochistic nature is, self-evidently, I think, crucial to any assessment of the novel's sexual politics.[31] It seems significant, therefore, that in most of these scenes, the narrative perspective is with the masochistic object, rather than with the sadistic agent of urination.

It is true that some of the transgressive urination in the novel has a sadistic character – Simone's pissing 'comme une chienne' ('like a bitch') in the priest's sacristy, for example, or her pissing on her own mother, perhaps the most graphic examples of acts of urination that are both transgressive and sadistic. Yet, the sexual significance of such acts is rendered more complex by the narrator's perception of them and his tendency to identify erotically and masochistically with the object. Not surprisingly, therefore, most of the urination in the novel is by females – by Simone, by Marcelle, even by female animals, such as the mortally wounded mare, gouged by a bull at the corrida: 'En particulier, [son cœur] palpitait quand la vessie crevée lâchait sa masse d'urine de jument, qui arrivait d'un seul coup sur le sable en faisant floc' (p. 50) ('Simone's heart throbbed fastest when the exploding bladder dropped its mass of mare's urine on the sand in one quick plop' (p. 47)). The male narrator does also himself urinate erotically on occasions, but this is always either at Simone's request ('piss on my cunt', etc.) or in sympathetic response to *her* urination.

Simone is not exclusively sadistic any more than the narrator is exclusively masochistic, both occasionally displaying characteristics of the reverse tendency. On the whole, however, their behaviour tends more towards one pole than the other. At the same time, since the erotic charge that urination carries is always directly linked to transgression and both narrator and reader (and sometimes even Simone) are indirectly invited to identify with the transgressed, this charge more frequently has a masochistic than a sadistic character. Marcelle is the most obvious specific instance of this, but this is also true in a more general sense.

Only Simone's urination, therefore, can be said to be sadistic, yet this is more the theatrical or symbolic sadism of male masochistic fantasy than sadism proper. In both the 'corrida' and the 'priest' scenes, our attention is undeniably drawn to the symbolic rather than the referential use of language, to the functioning of the signifier and away from the signifieds of sadism and cruelty, which explains in part why earlier commentators focused their attention on form rather than content. Indeed, priest and bull victims are *linguistically* linked by the symbolism of eggs/sun/balls/eyes and by the word 'monstre' applied to both of them. Even Simone's shockingly taboo-breaking act of urinating on Marcelle's corpse has a symbolic rather than a truly sadistic significance, a gesture of contempt for death itself. I would argue, however, that the main symbolic significance of female urination in *Histoire de l'œil* is castration, which, as we shall see shortly, has its unconscious origins in the author's own 'primal scene'.

As well as being responsible for most of the urination, it is only the females who kill in the novel: Marcelle kills herself, sows kill the prostitute and, of course, Simone kills the priest. Rather than making sense on a realist level, I would argue that these killings are essentially symbolic castrations, enacted in the first instance for the masochistic male narrator and in the second instance for the masochistic male reader. (I shall return shortly to the connection between castration and masochism.)

The text is full of castration imagery, most of which surrounds the behaviour of Simone. Like some latter-day Salome, it is she who demands the bull's raw testicles to be served up to her on a plate at the bullfight in Madrid. It is she who rapes, tortures and finally murders the priest, the 'man in skirts', to use Dworkin's phrase,[32] a man, therefore, who is feminised by his dress, by his rather supine acceptance of a 'victim-martyr' status (he scarcely puts up any resistance) and, symbolically, by Simone's violent sexual assaults, in particular her demand that an eye be cut out from the dead priest's skull and then inserted into her vagina.[33]

That Simone is a 'femme castratrice' is, of course, strongly suggested by her sexual obsession with spherical objects and by what she does with them. Early on in the narrative, when she takes pleasure in smashing eggs (testicles?) in the toilet and urinating on them, she tells the narrator that the word 'urinate' ('uriner') makes her think of '*buriner, les yeux, avec un rasoir, quelque chose de rouge, le soleil*' (p. 38) ('*terminate*, the eyes, with a razor, something red, the sun' (p. 34)). All of these associations suggest castration, from the more obvious razor and the colour red (which is, of course, the colour of blood and of the sun), to the Freudian reading of the act of blinding as symbolic castration, to the word 'buriner' itself, which means 'to engrave', an action of cutting with a knife.[34] Moreover, the word 'burnes', which it closely resembles, is a slang word for testicles.[35] Eggs remind her of calves' eyes and breaking eggs of bursting eyeballs. She adds that a stream of urine is, for her, 'un coup de feu vu comme une lumière' (p. 38) ('a gunshot seen as a light' (p. 34)) and she asks the narrator to shoot eggs with his revolver. This passage is, in fact, so self-consciously metatextual in defining and analysing the narrative's key images as perhaps to make us wary of accepting the author's own self-reading uncritically (this is also true of the autobiographical account of his father's illness, recounted in an essay appended to the novel, which I shall consider shortly). Nevertheless, on the face of it at least, there is a clear connection here for Simone, not only between urination and castration, but between urination and phallus-as-gun-as-phallus. Simone, it seems, sees herself not only as a castrating woman, but also as a phallic woman. The stream of urine, in other words, endows her with the phallus which she symbolically removes from both narrator and priest.

If this is so, it is of course because the male narrator and, potentially, the male reader are masochistically excited by the dominant, phallic woman and simultaneously threatened and reassured by the castrator-with-phallus.[36] An analogy here with hard-core pornographic films might prove instructive. For Linda Williams, a fully visible male ejaculation, or what is known in the business as the 'money-shot', is an essential component of every hard-core movie. Williams sees the money-shot as a fetishistic figure of female lack, reassuring men, calming their castration anxieties.[37] All fetishes are, for Freud, a substitute for the phallus that the female has lost and, as such, a means of calming male castration fear.[38] Female ejaculation serves similar purposes in pornographic films. Firstly, it provides the visible evidence of female pleasure that, according to Williams, hard core strives to provide. Secondly, and most interestingly in relation to Bataille, like the male ejaculation, it reassures the male who fears castration. Now it seems to me that female urination is, in part, a substitute for female ejaculation. Indeed, the erotic performance artist, Annie Sprinkle intentionally blurs the boundaries between the two, presenting the former as the latter.[39] Sprinkle's approach could be seen as an attempt to give female urination the same symbolic and erotic power as male ejaculation. In this perspective, female urination in Bataille's text serves the same function as female ejaculation in hard-core cinema, which is to neutralise male fear of castration by endowing the woman with an imaginary phallus, to make visible what is otherwise invisible. Like the penis, the vulva must be seen and urination in the text is erotically associated with this process of making the female genitals more visible:

Simone à force d'éclater avait légèrement pissé le long de ses jambes et un petit filet d'eau avait coulé sur la plaque de cuivre.

Nous constatons de plus un autre effet de cet accident: l'étoffe légère de la robe étant mouillée avait adhéré au corps et comme elle était ainsi tout à fait transparente le joli ventre et les cuisses de Simone étaient révélés d'une façon particulièrement impudique, noirs entre les rubans rouges de la ceinture. (p. 59)

In our mirth, Simone had lightly pissed down her leg, and a tiny trickle of water had landed on the brass.

We noted a further effect of her accident: the thin dress, being wet, stuck to her body, and since the cloth was now fully transparent, Simone's attractive belly and thighs were revealed with particular lewdness, a dark patch between the red ribbons of her garter belt. (p. 56)

Male fascination with female urination must, in part at least, be attributable to an unconscious desire for the phallic woman. The stream of urine – 'filet d'eau' – directed at the man's face or genitals (favourite scenarios in porn movies, as in *Histoire de l'œil*) thus becomes a penile shaft, pushing at the male orifices in imaginary penetration (as in the male penetration of women in fellatio and coitus), and urination comes to stand in, as it were, for female ejaculation with which, moreover, it is frequently confused in hard-core movies.

In the masochistic scenario theorised by Deleuze, the masochist contracts with his 'ideal woman' to undergo a process of rebirth at her hands.[40] This is precisely what happens to the narrator in the imagery of the novel: under Simone's influence, he is symbolically reborn under the sign of the feminine, the Moon, the Mother's Law, in opposition to the sign of the masculine, the Father's Law, as symbolised in the text by the Spanish sun: 'je n'aimais que ce qui est classé comme "sale",' he declares, 'J'associe la lune au sang du vagin des mères, des sœurs, c'est-à-dire aux menstrues à l'odeur écœurante, etc...' (p. 45) ('I cared only for what is classified as "dirty" [...] I associate the moon with the vaginal blood of mothers, sisters, that is, the menstrua with their sickening stench ...' (p. 42)). The process of rebirth, which Deleuze sees as the crucifixion of Christ by the Virgin,[41] is symbolically enacted in the strangulation of the priest by Simone. Thus, the priest, who is Christ's representative on earth, dies, but the ejaculation of his sperm into Simone seems to imply the possibility of a (re)birth under the sign of the Mother alone. This 'rebirth' takes both narrator and Simone beyond death, so that, when Marcelle dies, Simone's act of urinating on Marcelle's body is, as I suggested earlier, a symbolic challenge to the conventional norms of respect for the dead:

Marcelle nous appartenait à un tel point dans notre isolement que nous n'avons pas vu que c'était une morte comme les autres. [...] les impulsions contradictoires qui

disposaient de nous dans cette circonstance se neutrali-
saient en nous laissant aveugles et, pour ainsi dire, situés très
loin de ce que nous touchions, dans un monde où les gestes
n'ont aucune portée, comme des voix dans un espace qui
ne serait absolument pas sonore. (p. 47)

Marcelle belonged to us so deeply in our isolation that we
could not see her as just another corpse. [...] the contradictory impulses overtaking us in this circumstance neutralized
one another, leaving us blind and, as it were, very remote
from anything we touched, in a world where gestures have
no carrying power, like voices in a space that is absolutely
soundless. (p. 44)

Erotic urination thus serves to blur distinctions between
masculine and feminine, between active and passive forms of
sexuality, between life and death, to erase both sexual
difference and the difference between sex and death. Simone
is Deleuze's 'stern, cruel mother', who expels the Father and
establishes her Law under the masochistic contract: 'Dans le
cas du masochisme, toute la loi est reportée sur la mère, qui
expulse le père de la sphère symbolique'.[42] ('In the case of
masochism, the whole of the law is represented by the mother,
who expels the father from the symbolic realm.')

It is, for Deleuze, the image of the Father in himself that the
masochist gets humiliated and beaten.[43] Like the narrator of
*Histoire de l'œil*, the Deleuzian masochist experiences strong
feelings of sexual anxiety and guilt. It is not that the masochist
experiences guilt because of a crime committed against the
Father, as Freud argued, but that, as Deleuze puts it, it is the
Father's likeness in him that he experiences as a sin and which
must be atoned for.[44] In *Histoire de l'œil*, then, it is, above all,
in the humiliation and torture of the priest that the 'Father'
is symbolically expelled, as the priest is feminised in front of
the masochistic male narrator/reader. The priest's function as
father figure is, after all, underlined at the beginning of this
scene, as Simone pretends to confess her sins to him in the
confessional, a wayward daughter, apparently submitting to
the 'father's' spiritual (and sexual) law but, in masturbating in
front of him, actually transgressing it.

Given the importance of urination in this and other texts by Bataille, we must now ask whether it is in the account of his own father's urination that the unconscious origins of the text's masochism can be found. In 'Coïncidences', a brief essay published by the author alongside his narrative, Bataille himself offers autobiographical data of a strongly erotic and oedipal nature for the origins of all the symbolic objects of *Histoire de l'œil*. Among this data, two vivid memories from his youth stand out.

The first involves his syphylitic father, who, blinded and paralysed by his illness, had great difficulty urinating. Bataille recalls watching his father trying to urinate and rolling his unseeing eyes, so that the eyeballs virtually disappeared. It is the whites of his father's eyes which are, he claims, directly associated with the egg and eye imagery of the novel, which we have seen to be intimately linked, in turn, with urination. This memory has been considered a 'primal scene', which fixated in the young Bataille's psyche an intimate association between, on the one hand, urine and the penile orifice and, on the other, blindness, which, since Freud, we read as an unconscious metaphor for castration. The bullfight in *Histoire de l'œil* can be read as a re-enactment of the primal scene, in which the sun/bull are the blinding/blinded father, killed by the oedipal son (bullfighter). Simone, who looks on and symbolically 'comes' through her nose (her phallus?), as she suffers a nosebleed at the moment of the bull's death, is thus the focus of sexual desire, arousal, ejaculation and blood, mirroring the piercing of the bull by the fighter.[45] As we have seen, the ritual's climax occurs not in the stadium but in the toilet stinking of urine, in which the narrator and Simone have sex immediately afterwards.

The second of these memories found in 'Coïncidences' concerns Bataille's mother, who has begun to lose her sanity and to attempt to take her own life. On one such occasion, the author remembers scouring the neighbourhood for her and eventually finding her, dripping with water, after trying to drown herself in the stream near their home. The language he uses to describe his mother's appearance is telling: 'Elle était mouillée jusqu'à la ceinture, la jupe *pissant* l'eau de la rivière' (p. 78, my emphasis) ('She was drenched up to her belt, the skirt was pissing the creek water' (p. 74)).

Urination, or urethal imagery, dominates the author's strongest memories of both his parents and, in each case, the memory carries a powerful erotic charge. At the same time, Bataille emphasises a change in attitude towards his father from affection to unconscious aversion, a change which, significantly, occurred at puberty. Clearly, we are being invited by the author to read *Histoire de l'œil,* and perhaps his other works of fiction, as oedipally inspired. Now, admittedly, our lack of innocence as postmodern readers may make us more reluctant than Bataille's contemporaries to accept this authorial reading without some scepticism. The author, as Roland Barthes famously argued, is not to be taken as the text's only source. Yet, the author's determination in this essay to provide a psychoanalysis of his own textual unconscious does not preclude the existence in the text – a text that includes 'Coïncidences' – of an unconscious level that eluded him. It is, I would suggest, the very link between urination and masochism, fixated in the young Bataille by the sight of his syphilitic father apparently enjoying the act of urination, which forms the unconscious element of a text which attempts to impose on the reader a straightforwardly oedipal interpretation.[46] This link, in turn, supports the Deleuzian reading which I have conducted of *Histoire de l'œil* as an essentially masochistic narrative, presenting negative images of a 'dethroned' masculine and ambivalence towards a feminine that is simultaneously eroticised but also demonised. Simone is the object of the narrator's love and desire, but also a dangerously self-gratifying subject. Like the whores who, we assume, gave Bataille's father syphylis and blinded or metaphorically castrated him, she castrates males (the bull literally, the priest symbolically), yet in so doing, sexually excites the male narrator. Simone is, therefore, the good/bad mother, for whom the narrator/son feels a guilty desire.[47]

Urination is therefore an eroticised act in the fiction, because it is unconsciously associated for the writer with what he perceived as the pain–pleasure nexus of his father's syphilis, so it becomes linked to orgasm in the network of white eggs/eyes/sperm of the fiction.[48]

One final point which, I think, supports this reading: in the author's autobiographical essay, we note that the power to urinate metaphorically passes from father to mother, who is finally seen 'pissing water from the stream', just as for the Deleuzian masochist the Law passes metaphorically and symbolically from castrated Father to Phallic Mother. The Father loses the phallus, symbolised here by the power to urinate, and a few lines later the Mother has figuratively acquired it. Similarly, in *Histoire de l'œil*, the feminine is seen to be dominant over the masculine and, ultimately, to torture and destroy it.

## Conclusion

Let us now return to the question of subjectivity, both within and outside the text and, more specifically, to the experience of the female reader. I have argued that *Histoire de l'œil* is a masochistic narrative which symbolically stages the expulsion of the father and the enthronement of the mother in the symbolic realm. Does this mean that this novel and narratives like it constitute a form of pornographic writing which is more accessible to the female reader?

One could object that there is evidence in *Histoire de l'œil* of an attack on the feminine-maternal in some of the urination scenes. Simone urinates on her own mother as well as on Marcelle's dead body. Yet, it seems to me that the real significance of these acts is less misogynistic than transgressive, especially since the agent, in both cases, is herself female.

It might also be objected that erotic urination in Bataille's text concentrates visually on the stream of urine, as phallic object which penetrates and ejaculates. Simone and the narrator urinate *into* each other's body, as when Simone asks the latter to 'piss into her cunt' or when he pisses into her mouth. In addition to her phallic urination, we have seen how Simone symbolically also acquires male testes by inserting the bull's testicles and other testicular shapes (eggs, priest's eye) into her vagina. Such representations appear to enthrone the phallus as sole sexual signifier and, in this perspective, the masochist's female dominatrix is also reborn as phallic woman. It might be argued, therefore, that the Father survives *in* the Mother, the masculine *in* the feminine, that such images keep us locked in a phallicist economy, which leaves little imaginary space for the female reader to play.

In Bataille's text female urination may reflect a masculine point of view in another sense. To eroticise urination as phallic is also to fetishise expenditure, which is exactly what Bataille does in his theoretical work, condemning the 'universal meanness' of capitalism.[49] Directly linking our social and erotic lives, he urges us to 'spend joyously'. Such an economy of pure expenditure without return is, arguably, a stereotypically masculine one, suggesting both phallic ejaculation and the 'generous' promiscuity of male sexuality. The narrative viewpoint, one might add, is, after all, itself masculine. The sexual subject of the narrative is arguably, therefore, male, masochistic and fetishistic.[50]

Fortunately, however, there are other ways of looking at the evidence which make Bataille's text just as accessible to the female as to the male reader. For example, not all descriptions of urination in the text serve a male-centred eroticism. Instead of a *visual* concentration on the stream of urine, the following passage, for example, represents urination as a shared activity between the narrator and Simone, foregrounding *tactile* sensations of mutual pleasure:

> [...] je sentis un liquide chaud et charmant couler le long de mes jambes et quand elle eut fini, je me levai et lui arrosai à mon tour le corps qu'elle tourna complaisamment devant le jet impudique et légèrement bruissant sur la peau. (p. 25)

> I felt a hot, enchanting liquid run down my legs, and when she was done, I got up and in turn watered her body, which she complaisantly turned to the unchaste and faintly murmuring spurt on her skin. (p. 21)

Simone's need to urinate, when ill, also provides opportunities for affection rather than prurience, on the part of the narrator:

> De temps en temps, je prenais Simone chaude de fièvre dans mes bras pour aller lui faire faire pipi dans la salle de bain, ensuite je la lavais avec précaution sur le bidet. Elle était extrêmement affaiblie et, bien entendu, je ne la touchais pas sérieusement [...] (p. 36)

From time to time, I would carry a feverish Simone to the bathroom to help her pee, and then I would carefully wash her on the bidet. She was extremely weak and naturally I never stroked her seriously; (pp. 32–3)

In any case, the phallicism of other descriptions is not necessarily problematic for some feminists. Linda Williams reminds us that, in a psychoanalytic perspective, it is not possible to imagine desire *without* the phallus. Moreover, Williams suggests that it is not the phallus as such which presents problems for psychoanalytically based feminists, but the system of difference it represents.[51] Deleuze's view of the maternal phallus of masochism as a neutral energy rather than a sexual organ suggests a phallus whose significance is not rooted in difference:

Le phallus maternel n'est pas un organe sexuel, mais au contraire l'organe idéal d'une énergie neutre, lui-même producteur idéal, c'est-à-dire, du moi de la seconde naissance ou du 'nouvel homme sans amour sexuel'.[52]

The maternal phallus is not a sexual organ, but on the contrary, the ideal organ of a neutral energy, itself, that is, the ideal generator of the second-born self or of 'the new man without sexual love'.

As to the problem, for a woman, of identification with the male masochist narrator and his point of view, she may adopt a number of different positions, identifying sometimes, for instance, with Simone's sadism and at other times with Marcelle's or even the narrator's masochism, shifting from active to passive as much as from male to female positions.[53] Laura Kipnis restates the argument succinctly: 'Identification is mobile, unpredictable, and not bound by either one's actual gender or by practical reality [...] as a male you can identify with a female character and vice versa.'[54] Sadistic or masochistic fantasy might even be thought liberating for women in that, as Williams argues, 'It may represent for women a new consciousness about the unavoidable role of power in sex, gender, and sexual representations and of the importance of not viewing this power as fixed.'[55]

There has been little serious critical discussion of sexual perversion and its representation in fiction, whether from a feminist or any other perspective, and it is high time that all of Bataille's novels were re-examined, following the lead first taken by Suleiman and then by the study of *Histoire de l'œil* undertaken here. It seems to me that Bataille's main contribution as a writer of fiction has been precisely to pose questions concerning both male and female sexuality which needed to be posed – questions relating to fetishism and to the links between sexuality and gender – and to suggest that these links are less clear-cut than might otherwise have been supposed. As Julia Kristeva has said in her brief analysis of Bataille's *Ma mère*, such writers go further, in content and in form, than the rest of us dare. They should be given every opportunity and every encouragement to continue to do so.

Ces aventuriers du psychisme qu'on appelle des écrivains vont au bout de la nuit où nos amours n'osent pas se risquer. Nous restons simplement troublés, inconscient oblige, par l'intensité du style ... Un style – témoin de la perte de sens, vigile de la mort.[56]

Those adventurers of the psyche whom we call writers go to the ends of the night where we lesser lovers dare not go. We simply remain perturbed, at an unconscious level, by their intensity of style ... A style which bears witness to the loss of meaning, a sentinel at death's door.

# 5

# 'O, Really!': Pauline Réage's *Histoire d'O*

In a piece in *The New Yorker* in August 1994, the writer and literary journalist, John de St. Jorre gave a detailed account of an interview with Dominique Aury, writer, translator and critic, in which Aury revealed that she and Pauline Réage are one and the same. In other words, Dominique Aury is the pseudonymous author of *Histoire d'O*, the first published novel of modern times to be both explicitly erotic and written by a woman. One of the greatest literary enigmas of the postwar years had finally been resolved.[1]

The novel takes the form of a third-person narrative, recounting how a young woman identified as O, a Parisian fashion photographer, is taken by her lover, René, to a château in Roissy, where she consents to the gradual erosion of her personal identity and autonomy. This process of enslavement involves being chained up in Gothic-style dungeons, frequent whippings and sexual penetration by a number of men, and the insertion into her anus of ever larger ebonite shafts in order to facilitate anal intercourse. It seems at first that O's submissiveness is motivated by her love for René, though during the course of her stay at the château, he 'gives' her to an English aristocrat named Sir Stephen, whose fatherly attentions are not without their attractions for her. O is also physically attracted to two females, Jacqueline, a young model and Natalie, Jacqueline's younger sister, both of whom she persuades to visit the château. Sir Stephen has O branded on her buttocks, and rings bearing his and her names are attached to her labia. By the final scene of the novel, O has apparently lost all humanity: wearing an owl-mask and led around by a chain attached to one of the rings in her labia, she is offered freely to guests at a party, though few show any real interest in her. In grotesque parody of the party wallflower, the now completely objectified O has no more significance than a piece of furniture.

Despite the explicit nature of the activities depicted in the novel, the style is contained, devoid of either emotion or vulgarity; the author explains the need for such stylistic restraint:

Il est passionnant d'être maître de soi dans ce qui est le contraire de la maîtrise de soi, sinon cela n'a pas le même prix.[2]

It is thrilling to be in control in what is the opposite of self-control, otherwise it doesn't have the same value.

Aury tells in the *The New Yorker* interview how, the long-term mistress of Jean Paulhan, she conceived the book as a love letter to the celebrated author, critic and academician. Though in his sixties by this time, Paulhan was known to have a high sex drive and a fondness for younger women. Fearful that he might be tiring of a woman approaching middle age and knowing his fondness for the writings of the *divin marquis*, Aury determined to compose a spicy narrative which might appeal to Paulhan's sexual predilections. Sheherazade-like, she was writing in order to keep their love alive. It did the trick. Paulhan was entranced by the first 60 pages which Aury dashed off almost automatically, basing the writing on fantasies of submission which she had had since childhood. He urged her to write more. Within weeks, the novel was finished. Paulhan begged Aury to let him find a publisher. She agreed, on condition that the novel be published anonymously. The pen-name Pauline Réage, it seems, had no conscious significance – Pauline was inspired by two famous women, Pauline Borghese of Renaissance Italy and Pauline Roland, a nineteenth-century defender of women's rights, whilst Réage was chosen at random from a property register.

Publication of the novel was not without its problems. Gallimard, after two years' deliberation, refused the book. René Defez, whose publishing house, Les Deux Rives, had already drawn attention to itself by publishing a critical account of France's involvement in Indochina, first accepted it, paying Aury an advance; but after being prosecuted for the book on Indochina, Defez finally sent the manuscript back in order to avoid another costly court case. Paulhan then showed it to Jean-Jacques Pauvert, who had already taken the risk of publishing the complete works of Sade. Pauvert accepted it enthusiastically and published it at once, with a preface written by Paulhan. The same year, 1954, saw the publication of the novel in English by the Paris-based Olympia Press.

The impact of the book was at first limited to a small circle of Parisian *lettrés*, the initial print run of two thousand remaining unsold ten months after publication. Nevertheless, Georges Bataille in *La Nouvelle Revue Française* and André Pieyre de Mandiargues in *Critique* praised it fulsomely and, in February 1955, less than a year later, it won the *Prix Deux Magots*, a small literary prize, usually awarded to new and unconventional writing.

Despite the book's favourable reception among the Parisian intelligentsia, moves to ban the novel began almost immediately. Both Pauvert and Girodias, the head of Olympia Press, suffered threats and harassment by the French government. The 'Commission du Livre' or 'Book Commission' were keen to prosecute, 'considérant que ce livre violemment et consciemment immoral, où les scènes de débauches à deux ou plusieurs personnages alternent avec des scènes de cruautés sexuelles, contient un ferment détestable et condamnable, et que par là même, il outrage les bonnes moeurs. (La Commission) émet l'avis qu'il y a lieu à poursuites' ('considering that this violently and consciously immoral book, in which scenes of debauchery involving two or more persons alternate with scenes of sexual cruelty, contains a detestable and condemnable ferment, and that this in itself is an affront to public decency. (The Commission) is of the opinion that there are grounds for prosecution').[3] The 'Brigade Mondaine', the French government's equivalent of the vice squad, made repeated attempts to discover the identity of the author, but although the police visited Aury and questioned her, nothing could be proved. Many magistrates wanted to prosecute Pauvert and Paulhan in the author's absence. This never actually happened, but the book was banned, the ban not being lifted until the early 1970s. Nevertheless, booksellers sold copies in secret. Indeed, in spite of (or perhaps because of) attempts to suppress it, the book has never been out of print, it has been translated into dozens of languages, has sold millions of copies and has been adapted (rather poorly) for the screen. Indeed, during the four decades that followed publication, it was to become for a time the bestselling and most widely read French novel outside France.[4] *Histoire d'O* has always proved a huge commercial success, to which the questions surrounding its authorship have doubtless contributed in no small measure.

For Roland Barthes and his fellow Structuralists, authorial identity was of only anecdotal interest. The text was enshrined as sole source of meaning, the author existing only as a textual construct or implication. More recently, however, feminists in particular have frequently dragged the author from the grave dug by Barthes, in the firm conviction that the identity and gender of a writer matter – especially in the case of 'pornography', which, because it depicts the exploitation of female characters, is not confined to the realm of books but is a political issue in the 'real' world. For many feminists, *Histoire d'O*, in which the eponymous heroine is subjected to all conceivable brands of male violence, was a voyeuristically pornographic account of female objectification that could not possibly have been the work of a woman. Some believed that the novel was the result of a group effort, like the erotica produced on demand by Anaïs Nin, Henry Miller and others in the 1930s and 1940s. Others were persuaded that Alain Robbe-Grillet's wife, Catherine, had written the book, a theory bolstered by the appearance in 1956 of the novel *L'Image* by the pseudonymous Jean de Berg, which had similar sado-masochistic themes, was dedicated to Pauline Réage and contained a foreword signed with the initials, 'P. R.'. (It had also been suggested that these initials were, in fact, those of Alain (Paul) Robbe-Grillet.) Most, however, felt that *Histoire d'O* was the work of a man – probably Jean Paulhan himself – and that the use of a female pseudonym by a male writer was nothing more than a convention of the erotic genre, designed to titillate the male reader even more, by suggesting that the novel was the confession by a real woman of events that had actually taken place – another convention of the genre. Andrea Dworkin, for example, speaking of the genre as a whole, argued that 'The female name on the cover of the book is part of the package, an element of the fiction. It confirms men in their fantasy that the eroticism of the female exists within the bounds of male sexual imperatives.'[5]

Forty years later, with both Paulhan and his wife long dead, the personal issues framing the writing of this novel seem trivial. However, Dominique Aury's disclosures should serve to remind us all of the dangers of drawing either artistic or moral conclusions from a writer's presumed identity: are we not, each one of us, a complicated mix of personae, social, psychological and sexual?

The question of authorial identity has haunted the novel from the outset, keeping the debate surrounding it at a relatively banal level. Perhaps now that the 'culprit' has come clean, critics of all persuasions can stop treating it like a 'True Crimes' confession, a real life 'Whodunnit' with every woman as victim, and consider whether, though born of an individual woman's sexual fantasy, *Histoire d'O* has a literary form that enables it to transcend the boundaries, either of gender or of individual experience.

The novel, we now know, was a 'lettre d'amour', but was the work based on real events or was it a product of pure imagination? What fascinated and excited Paulhan, Aury told St. Jorre, was the relationship of the story to her own life,[6] an issue going beyond mere authorial identity to the complex set of relationships between the text and the subject's desire. The author has already given an unambiguous answer to this question: she would never have tolerated violence, all the events of the novel are imaginary and not real.[7] Indeed, this is perhaps one of the main lessons to be drawn from *Histoire d'O*: sexual fantasies are not to be confused with reality, a woman being capable of deriving enjoyment from an imagined sexual violence unacceptable in real life. Both the story of O and Pauline Réage are constructs with no identity in the real beyond the text:

> *Histoire d'O* est une féerie pour un autre monde [...] qui n'existe plus maintenant qu'entre des pages de papier imprimé. C'est le livre d'une inconnue, dont je suis stupéfaite, à la limite, qu'elle ait été moi.[8]

> *Story of O* is a fairy tale for another world [...] which now only exists between pages of print. It was a book by an unknown woman, and I am amazed beyond belief that I was she.

Inside the text, too, the absence, or rather, the *obliteration* of identity becomes the main focus of interest – an ironic counterpoint to the enthusiasm shown outside the text for the *construction* of an authorial identity. This obliteration of identity begins in the novel's title. For Michel Butor, a title is not only, to use Gérard Genette's term, the *threshold* of a novel, but also a text in its own right:

Toute œuvre littéraire peut être considérée comme formée de deux textes associés: le corps (essai, roman, drame, sonnet) et son titre, pôles entre lesquels circule une électricité de sens, l'un bref, l'autre long [...] de même l'œuvre picturale se présente toujours pour nous comme l'association d'une image, sur toile, planche, mur ou papier, et d'un nom, celui-ci fût-il vide, en attente, pure énigme, réduit à un simple point d'interrogation.[9]

Any literary work may be thought of as consisting of two associated texts: the body (essay, novel, drama, sonnet) and its title, poles between which circulates an electricity of meaning, one short, the other long [...] in the same way the pictorial work always presents itself to us as the association of an image, on canvas, plate, wall or paper, and a name, even if this name is empty, waiting to appear, a pure enigma, reduced to a simple question mark.

The title of *Histoire d'O* illustrates this symbiosis so well that Butor could have cited it as an example. This title functions as a microtext which has the same enigmatic character as the macrotext that follows. It seems to reduce itself to a question mark, hanging over the zero that names (or unnames) the novel's main protagonist. This is a title that poses questions, stimulating the curiosity of the reader, a peephole into a text itself full of peepholes.

The first two words, taken together, carry an ambiguity which is lost in the English translation. Unlike 'Story of', 'Histoire de' in the spoken register can mean 'a question of', expressing aim or intention. 'A question of O', though less transparent than 'Story of O', sounds even more enigmatic, immediately foregrounding the thematic of identity.

There is also a more obvious ambiguity in the use of the preposition 'de': is the story in question *about* the eponymous heroine or is it simply narrated *by* her? This ambiguity in the title focuses our attention from the outset on the identity, not only of the character but of the narrator too, on the act of narration itself and therefore on the identity of the narratee implied in the title-text.

With the hindsight of our knowledge of the circumstances surounding the writing of the novel, the issue of a 'lecteur virtuel' or 'reader in the text' might seem clear-cut: if the work was a letter to Jean Paulhan and not a work intended for publication, then the woman depicted in the text is intended to be accessible not to *anyone* but to *someone*, a narratee who is both singular and known – a characteristic of confessional literature, in particular. Does this make *Histoire d'O* the most perfect example of reader-centred fiction or rather is the text closed off to the general and especially the female reader by the existence of a specific male narratee? Statements by the author would appear to support the latter hypothesis:

> [...] il faut un complice pour ce genre d'écriture [...] Une femme ne pourrait pas jouer ce jeu sans un complice masculin, et un complice masculin qui l'aime parce que rien de cet ordre ne peut être confié à un homme autre qu'un homme que l'on aime.[10]

> [...] you need an accomplice for this kind of writing [...] A woman could not play this game without a male accomplice, and a male accomplice who loves her, because nothing of this nature can be confided in a man, unless one loves him.

Once again, however, it is necessary to distinguish between the world outside the text, in which the intentions of the author are situated, and the text itself. In that this particular narratee's identity or presence is nowhere explicitly evident *in the text*, it seems to me that any reader, even a woman, who shares this narratee's tastes or who is able to identify with O's desires, is capable of taking his place. *Histoire d'O* is thus an *open* text in the sense of being accessible to all. Upon her arrival at Roissy, O is given lengthy instructions as to how she should behave, but the 'vous' seems after a time addressed as much to the reader as to the female protagonist:

Voici le discours que l'on tint ensuite à O. «Vous êtes ici au service de vos maîtres. [...] devant nous vous ne fermerez jamais tout à fait les lèvres, ni ne croiserez les jambes, ni ne serrerez les genoux (comme vous avez vu qu'on a interdit de faire aussitôt votre arrivée), ce qui marquera à vos yeux et aux nôtres que votre bouche, votre ventre, et vos reins nous sont ouverts. [...]» et seq. (pp. 48–51)

This is the speech they then made to O:
   'You are here to serve your masters. [...] in our presence you will at all times avoid altogether closing your labia, nor will you ever cross your legs, nor press your knees together (as, you recall, was forbidden to you directly you set out for this place), which will signify, in your view and in ours, that your mouth, your belly and your behind are constantly at our entire disposal. [...]' et seq. (pp. 25–6)

The ending of the story is certainly left open for the individual reader to determine, the final page of text presenting the following alternatives:

Dans un dernier chapitre, qui a été supprimé, O retournait à Roissy, où Sir Stephen l'abandonnait.[11]
   Il existe une seconde fin à l'histoire d'O. C'est que, se voyant sur le point d'être quittée par Sir Stephen, elle préféra mourir. Il y consentit. (p. 313)

There existed another ending to the story of O. Seeing herself about to be left by Sir Stephen, she preferred to die. To which he gave his consent. (p. 263)

'I didn't know how to end it,' Aury told St. Jorre, 'so I left it open. Why not?'[12] The author's unpretentiousness is not simply refreshing, it gives a green light to the reader's imagination. Such open-endedness is also appropriate in the context of the novel's role as aphrodisiac in a continuing love affair; but more importantly from the point of view of reception, it helps to make the story of O a gift from the narrator to any reader.

As for the identity of the narrative voice, the story is not in fact narrated by O but in the third person by a narrator who is both extradiegetic (remaining outside the diegesis) and heterodiegetic (absent from the plot).[13] And yet, everything is seen from the heroine's point of view: *Story of O, her* story. It is *her* voice that is heard in the free indirect style of the narrative and never that of the men; it is therefore the story of the woman, not René's or Sir Stephen's, the story not of their sexuality but of hers:

> Ce ne sont pas toujours des tortures joyeuses – je veux dire joyeusement infligées. [says Jean Paulhan in his *Préface*] René s'y refuse; et Sir Stephen, s'il y consent, c'est à la manière d'un devoir. De toute évidence, ils ne s'amusent pas. Ils n'ont rien du sadique. Tout se passe enfin comme si c'était O seule, dès le début, qui exigeait d'être châtiée, forcée dans ses retraites. (p. xvi)

> They are not always joyful tortures – I mean to say joyfully inflicted. René refuses to inflict them; and if Sir Stephen consents, it is as though he were performing a duty. From all evidence, the torturers do not find their work amusing. They have nothing of the sadistic in them. Everything happens as if from the outset it were O alone who demanded to be hurt, flushed from her retreat by punishment. (p. 277)

Having been invited into the text, as we saw earlier, to identify with O from the very beginning of the narrative, the reader is encouraged to continue this identification throughout the novel. Even passages which appear to privilege the viewpoint of one of her male lovers in fact present the woman's own stream of consciousness, as here during her first meeting with Sir Stephen:

> Tout étourdie qu'elle fût et haletante de bonheur, elle n'eut cependant pas de peine à y voir qu'il l'admirait, et qu'il la désirait. Qui aurait résisté à sa bouche humide et entrouverte, à ses lèvres gonflées, à son cou blanc renversé sur le col noir de son pourpoint de page, à ses yeux plus grands et plus

clairs, et qui ne fuyaient pas? Mais le seul geste que se permit Sir Stephen fut de caresser doucement du doigt ses sourcils, puis ses lèvres. (pp. 129–30)

Bewildered as she still was, and dizzy from joy, she was nevertheless very able to see that he was looking at her admiringly, and that he desired her. Who could have resisted her moist, half-opened mouth, her swollen lips, her white neck flung back against the black collar of her page-boy jacket, her wide open and bright eyes, her steady, unfugitive eyes? But Sir Stephen's single gesture was to caress her eyebrows and then her lips, softly, with the tip of his finger. (p. 97)

The last sentence makes it clear that this praise of O's beauty comes, not from Sir Stephen, but either from the narrator or – and this is the more likely and more psychologically interesting alternative – from O herself, as an expression of her own desire.

O is the central figure of the narrative in more than one sense. We are immediately struck by the use of a single letter to denote her identity. This usage has a long tradition in European literature and functions almost always playfully to arouse curiosity or else to conceal the identity of real people, but also on a symbolic level, to suggest the character and function of the actant in question.[14] This is the case in Alain Robbe-Grillet's *La Jalousie*, in which A ..., the most open vowel of the French language, points obliquely to the eroticism and sexual ambiguity of the role of the woman it denotes. In Réage's text, O, vowel neither fully open nor fully closed, suggests the pout of a Bard*ot*, of an O constantly accessible to the other's desire, but given neither wholly nor immediately to anyone.

This vowel above all reflects the holes of the female body, that open so many times in a narrative in which the permanent availability of this body is constantly demanded. Like the holes of her body – of her mouth, her vagina, penetrated by all, her anus, torn by Sir Stephen, reserved for him alone – the cupola and its columns against which O is whipped, the very ropes and chains that bind her, the iron rings attached to her loins, the iron bracelets that keep her fast as she is beaten, all of these circles seem to reproduce recursively the single letter of her identity, the void waiting to be filled.

On a physical level, O is also the cry of pleasure mingled with pain, the 'Oh!' that the branding iron forces from her lips, or the 'Oh!' of *jouissance*, or again, the 'Oh!' of submission, or even the 'Oh!' of disapproval that might escape from the lips of the more puritanical reader.

A material shape that reproduces itself incessantly in this perforated text, O is at the same time and above all the abstract metaphor, the non-material symbol of the structures of the narrative. This shape is to be found in the closed circle of initiates who visit Roissy to serve or to be serviced; in the circle of pleasure[15] or voyeurism formed by the relations between the characters. A scopic network links all the characters to O, eye that looks and is looked at.[16] This voyeuristic network reflects itself ironically in certain details of the narrative: Anne-Marie, voyeur *par excellence*, lives near the Observatory; and there is the statue that O 'avait vue enfant au Luxembourg [...] penchée en avant pour se mirer dans une source' (p. 234) ('[had] seen as a child in the Luxembourg Gardens [...] bending forward, gazing at her reflection in a spring' (p. 191)).

O is the question mark that persists in the mind of any reader whom the work of Sacher-Masoch fails to move: why suffer, why consent to pain? A question mark that repeats itself recursively in the suspension marks of an ending that may not be the real ending.[17] This question mark hangs above almost every aspect of the narrative, especially the identity of the female protagonist on a psychological and sexual level.

Andrea Dworkin sees the O of her name, which is emblematic of each of the orifices of her body, as no more than a zero symbolising her non-existence in a masculine world.[18] Not only from a literary but also from a psychological point of view, this analysis is a highly reductive and simplistic reading of a complex thematic and structural figure. As in her deadpan analysis of Bataille's *Story of the Eye*,[19] Dworkin flattens the narrative by completely ignoring the intricate workings of metaphor. On a literary level, the multiple semes engendered by this single letter form the basis of the entire metaphorical structure of the novel: whether in regard to the relations between the characters, the principal themes or figures of style, O is the linchpin that holds everything together, just as, in Robbe-Grillet's *Le Voyeur*, the figure eight is both the main stylistic figure and structural determinant of the narrative. Dworkin misreads the text also on a purely psychological level, since the character is not non-existent in the sense that she uses the word. Susan Sontag is far more sensitive to the complexity of this figure:

> 'O' suggests a cartoon of her sex, not her individual sex but simply woman; it also stands for the void, a vacuity, a nothing. But what *Story of O* unfolds is a spiritual paradox, that of the full void and of the vacuity that is also a plenum. The power of the book lies exactly in the anguish stirred up by the continuing presence of this paradox. 'Pauline Réage' raises, in a far more organic and sophisticated manner than Sade does with his clumsy expositions and discourses, the question of the status of human personality itself. But whereas Sade is interested in the obliteration of personality from the viewpoint of power and liberty, the author of *Story of O* is interested in the obliteration of personality from the viewpoint of happiness.[20]

Sontag identifies here O's essential motivation: hers is the story, not of the suppression of a woman's personality by others, but of the search by the woman herself for non-identity, or the non-entity known in familiar French as 'nul' (zero). The reasons for this quest are complex, stemming from a concept of happiness that to Sontag seems less phallocentric than Buddhist: 'The "perfect submissiveness" that her original lover, and then Sir Stephen, demand of her seems to echo the extinction of the self explicitly required of a Jesuit novice or Zen pupil.'[21]

Luce Irigaray seems to echo this idea, when she talks about the mystical discourse that for her is a privileged discourse of women. This discourse, says Irigaray in *Spéculum de l'autre femme*,[22] stresses the loss of identity of the subject. As for O, the complete surrender of the mystical woman becomes the moment of her liberation. Elsewhere, and in another context, Irigaray envisions the woman's 'sexed body' in the paradoxical terms of a zero that functions positively.[23]

Admittedly, the letter O also suggests the sex object that the character consents to become: the possession of Sir Stephen, whose mark is branded on her body. Yet, her aspiration to self-effacement seems to have a quasi-religious motivation which comes from within rather than from outside herself. The desire to erase her conventional identity, to achieve the neutrality of a being without a specific polarity, a being existing in every sense 'entre la vie et la mort' ('between life and death'), dictates her behaviour towards herself as well as towards others. 'In manus tuas, Domine,' O silently says to her lover, expressing a kind of spiritual death wish. For the writer, this is a widespread fantasy, resembling religious devotion:

> Elles veulent être possédées, possédées jusqu'au bout, jusqu'à la mort. Ce qu'on cherche, c'est à être tué. Que cherche le croyant, sinon à se perdre en Dieu. Se faire tuer par quelqu'un qu'on aime me paraît le comble du ravissement. Je ne peux pas arriver à penser autrement.[24]

> [Women] want to be possessed, possessed completely, until death. What one seeks is to be killed. What else does the believer seek but to lose herself in God. It seems to me to be the height of ecstasy to have oneself killed by someone one loves. I cannot think otherwise.

Religious imagery, indeed, abounds in the text. René is the 'god' to whom O must submit:

> [...] il lui semblait sacrilège que son amant fût à ses genoux, alors qu'elle devait être aux siens (p. 70)

> [...] it seemed to her sacrilegious that her lover be on his knees when she ought to be on hers (p. 44)

> Il la posséderait ainsi comme un dieu possède ses créatures (p. 73)

> Thus would he possess her as a god possessed his creatures (p. 47)

O était heureuse que René la fît fouetter et la prostituât [...]
parce que la douleur et la honte du fouet, et l'outrage que
lui infligeaient ceux qui la contraignaient au plaisir quand
ils la possédaient et tout aussi bien se complaisaient au leur
sans tenir compte du sien, lui sembaient le rachat même de
sa faute. [...] plus sa bassesse est grande, plus René était
miséricordieux de consentir à faire d'O l'instrument de son
plaisir. (pp. 164–5)

O was happy René had had her whipped and prostituted [...]
because the pain and the shame of the lash, and the outrage
inflicted upon her by those who forced her to pleasure
when they took her and at the same time delighted in their
own pleasure without concerning themselves for hers,
seemed to her to be the very absolution of her sin. [...] the
baser, the viler she was, the more merciful was René to
consent to make O the instrument of his pleasure.
(pp. 129–30)

As Michelson points out, O's will to self-effacement expresses
and illustrates a deeply rooted human desire 'to be free from
oneself, to have the gratifications one associates with the self
without the obligation of making the choices by which moral
character and personality are defined'.[25] Yet, O's self-denial
goes further than a simple yearning for the existential and
moral vacuum; it also recalls the act of pure devotion of the
Christian martyr. The very notion that love and pain are an
inseparable pair, notion reinforced time and time again in the
novel, is indeed a profoundly Christian one. The author has
spoken of the influence of her Catholic upbringing and how
this helped form her self-sacrificial tendencies.[26] Significantly,
the only word that Paulhan didn't like in Aury's text and
which he insisted she change was the word 'sacrificiel'.[27]

With regard to her own sexuality, she appears to waver
between at least two identities. On the one hand, she is a sexual
object, a feminine stereotype, madly in love with René to the
point of abasement, a passive woman who desperately wants
to be loved by a man, to be his sex toy. On the other hand,
not only is she reluctant to accept all of the rules imposed upon
her – she is never able to accept the rule that forbids her to look
at the men directly – but her sexual desire certainly does not

correspond to the male stereotype of female passivity; indeed, the lesbian in her is as dominant and as objectifying as the men who surround her.[28] Jacqueline, for example, attracts her so strongly that she fantasises about pinning her against the wall 'comme on fait d'un papillon avec une épingle' (p. 175) ('like a butterfly pinned to the table' (p. 139)) – the simile is aggressively phallic. Nor does she, in her relations with women, exhibit a stereotypically female fidelity rooted in emotion:

> [...] O n'était pas tellement amoureuse de Jacqueline, ni d'ailleurs de Natalie, ni d'aucune fille en particulier, mais seulement des filles en tant que telles, et comme on peut être amoureuse de sa propre image – trouvant toujours plus émouvantes et plus belles les autres qu'elle ne se trouvait elle-même. (p. 299)

> [...] O was not so very much in love with Jacqueline, nor for that matter with Nathalie, nor with any girl in particular, but simply with girls because they were girls, the way one can be in love with one's own image – always finding the others more arousing and lovelier than one finds one's own self. (p. 251)

Michelson argues that O's 'need for love forces her into a masculine cosmos, where morality is defined by masculine power and desire';[29] in other words, that she comes to embody a phallic power which is characteristic of porn, since, as Stephen Marcus puts it, 'The penis becomes the man: it does the thrusting and not the man; it is its own agent.'[30] While, on the surface, O is seen in her dealings with other young women to adopt a masculine role, this seems to me less because she is conforming to a male definition of the sexual than because she is quite simply drawn to act upon her desires in ways which we, in our culture, regard as male. In other words, it is not O herself but readers like Michelson who are guilty of stereotyping.

The portrayal of O goes beyond mere phallicism to explore the complex psychological responses of a woman, caught between her love of René and her love of Sir Stephen, between her attraction to men and her attraction to women, between her sexual desires and her emotional needs. In every sense, O exists *in between*, as reflected in her bodily postures. Her complete *disponibilité*, symbolised by the parted knees, the absence of underclothes, the permanently open entrances of her body, is a vessel neither full nor empty, a form of anticipation. O, like the mouth that names her, is both rounded and extended, an O of anticipation, denoting a woman without fixed identity, whose freedom frightens her,[31] whose sexuality is neutral or 'white' like the writing envisaged by Barthes – a *degree zero* of sexuality.[32]

Thus, in the end, O belongs neither to herself nor to anyone else: her body, shared by two men and two women, is in effect a *no man's land*, a neutral zone occupied by two allies, but without any specific ownership or identity; the zero point of impersonal pleasure, of Anne-Marie's, for example, 'dont O n'était que l'instrument' (p. 258) ('whereof O was the mere instrument' (p. 212)).

From a Lacanian perspective, O is the expression in language of the condition of lack which all language represents, the expression of a desire that is never fulfilled. On an emotional level, O seems to find in Sir Stephen what she had not known with René: 'Et O se disait que finalement elle n'avait aimé René que pour apprendre l'amour et mieux savoir se donner, esclave et comblée, à Sir Stephen' (p. 287) '[...] O told herself that she had only loved René as a means for learning of love and for finding out how to give herself better, as a slave, as an ecstatic slave, to Sir Stephen' (p. 240). Yet, one cannot help thinking that her quest for love will be as unending as 'l'anneau de fer qui [lui] troue la chair et pèse pour toujours, la marque qui ne s'effacera jamais' (p. 287) ('this iron ring which pierces [her] flesh and weighs eternally, this mark that will remain forever' (p. 240)), since her pleasure depends, not on knowing other, but on forgetting self, and total self-oblivion is only possible in death. O tries to destroy herself 'pour aller jusqu'au bout d'elle-même, pour atteindre cet absolu que la vie lui refuse [...] On ne peut trouver l'absolu que dans la mort'[33] ('to get to the very bottom of herself, to reach the absolute which life refuses to give her [...] One can only find the absolute in death.'). In the final tableau of the novel, O, it is true, does get close to death: dressed like an owl,[34] dragged on a lead by the young

Natalie, she is mute and no one speaks to her – she has finally achieved the degree zero of communication.

O does not necessarily die, as we have seen, but her desire to reduce herself to zero is the most direct expression of the death drive which, for Bataille, accompanies all eroticism and which has strong links with the religious instinct. At the end of the novel, O exists by proxy, in the pleasure of others alone.[35] What has died in her is her individual autonomy. In numerology, zero paradoxically represents both non-being and unity, its opposite. At the same time, however, zero has other positive symbolic meanings. It is also the 'Orphic Egg' (that is, 'entrancing' or 'mysterious' like the question of her identity itself); and finally, because of its circular form, the zero signifies eternity.[36] In abolishing the Ego, in privileging Other over Self, O mirrors the point of infinity which the perfect circle of her name symbolically represents, signifier of a lack that accepts itself, and in so doing, becomes eternal. The pleasure that Sir Stephen finds in her knows no limit:

> Oserait-elle jamais lui dire qu'aucun plaisir, aucune joie, aucune imagination n'approchait le bonheur qu'elle ressentait à la liberté avec laquelle il usait d'elle, à l'idée qu'il savait qu'il n'avait avec elle aucun ménagement à garder, *aucune limite* à la façon dont, sur son corps, il pouvait chercher son plaisir. (p. 293, my emphasis.)

> Would she ever dare tell him that no pleasure, no joy, nothing she even imagined ever approached the happiness she felt before the freedom wherewith he made use of her, before the idea that he knew there were no precaution, *no limits* he had to observe in the manner whereby he sought his pleasure in her body. (p. 246)

O therefore also suggests the infinity of the imagination, not only of the character and writer of fiction, but of the occasionally perverse, rarely compliant reader. If this reader is a woman, for instance, she may resist identification with the masochistic side of O to focus instead upon her tacit acknowledgement that loveless sex, too, can be pleasurable. At a time when 'respectable' ladies didn't talk about such things, such an implication must in retrospect be seen as a positive contribution to the sexual liberation of women.

In pushing against the boundaries of female sexuality, in voicing the fantasies and anxieties of one woman for other women to recognise as their own, and, above all, in presenting these fantasies and anxieties in a form of some artistic complexity, *Histoire d'O* is one of the best modern examples of erotic writing. An ironic reflection of the scopic circle formed by *text-character-reader-critic-author*, a loop which takes us back to identity as dominant theme in this work, informing and animating its structural images, the letter O is not only the focal point of the novel, but also the egg from which its symbolic structures emerge. It is this artistic exploration of a feminine psychology that makes *Histoire d'O* literature as well as pornography.

# 6

# *Emmanuelle* and the Sexual Liberation of Women

Emmanuelle Arsan's first novel, *Emmanuelle*, was published secretly in 1959 by Eric Losfeld in Paris, at a time of renewed public interest in erotic writing. Recent court cases in France had led to the unbanning of works by Henry Miller, Boris Vian and the Marquis de Sade. At the same time, the 1950s had seen the illicit and usually anonymous publication of many new erotic novels. In particular, Pauline Réage's *Histoire d'O* (1954), Vladimir Nabokov's *Lolita* (1955) and Jean de Berg's *L'Image* (1956); all of these, in their different ways, had prepared the 'cultured' French reader for the more explicit representation of an active female libido in *Emmanuelle*. In the cinema of the late 1950s,[1] too, the general as well as the educated public had become accustomed to more open representations of female sexuality.

As Jean-Jacques Pauvert tells us in his postface to the first full edition, published by Laffont in 1988, the novel was immediately acknowledged in literary circles: André Breton praised it lavishly on the front page of *Arts* magazine; André S. Labarthe devoted an entire issue of the monthly *Constellation* to it, hailing it as a landmark in the emancipation of human beings; and in the influential and prestigious *Nouvelle Revue Française*, André Pieyre de Mandiargues proclaimed its originality in a rule-bound genre and welcomed its 'optimistic' and liberating influence. Predictably, however, the lawmakers of Gaullist France were reluctant to acknowledge the increasingly liberal and even revolutionary social climate,[2] and sales of the book were not legalised until the end of de Gaulle's régime in 1968. Jean-Jacques Brochier was able to write at the time in *Le Magazine Littéraire* that not only was *Emmanuelle* about the importance of sex for a happy existence, but that the novel itself had helped to change attitudes and mores for the better:

L'apparition à la vitrine des libraires de *Tombeau pour cinq cent mille soldats* ou d'*Emmanuelle* est inséparable de l'acceptation – tacite ou non – du divorce, des produits anticonceptionnels, de la légalisation des 'minorités érotiques' en Angleterre [...][3]

The appearance in the windows of bookshops of *Tombeau pour cinq cent mille soldats* (*Tomb for Five Hundred Thousand Soldiers*) or of *Emmanuelle* is inseparable from the acceptance – tacit or not – of divorce, of contraceptive products, of the legalisation of 'sexual minorities' in England [...]

*Emmanuelle* had been several years in the writing, its author obsessively correcting and revising, and the novel may never have been completed, had it not been for a potentially lethal attack of rheumatoid arthritis at the age of twenty which kept her confined to bed for a whole year. The shadow of a premature death lent a particular sense of urgency to the author's creative impulse. Indeed, it was perhaps the very proximity of death that more than anything else generated the novel's life-affirming qualities. Unlike Sade and Bataille, Emmanuelle Arsan writes about a human sexuality which owes more to Eros than Thanatos.

In the 1990s, mainly thanks to the half a dozen or so films that it has spawned, the 'Emmanuelle' phenomenon remains a modern icon of pre-Aids sexual permissiveness. The novel, on the other hand, has received relatively little attention. Partly because of censorship of erotic literature generally, partly because the films were essentially soft-porn products for mass popular consumption and so never enjoyed serious critical acclaim, the novel has been largely ignored by critics,[4] in spite of the clear orientation of the text, as we shall see, towards an educated reader. A proper evaluation of a work acknowledged to have an important place in the evolution of literary pornography is, therefore, long overdue.

## Point of view

*Emmanuelle* is the story of a quest. Superficially, this quest takes the geographical form of a journey undertaken by the young female heroine from Paris to Bangkok to join her husband, who has already taken up a new post in Thailand. The novel thus follows a long-standing tradition of the genre, whereby erotic events are associated with exotic locales.[5] More profoundly, however, the heroine is also embarked on a quest for knowledge of self and of others, a quest for truth: 'Il y a certainement un progrès que je dois faire, quelque chose à trouver, qui me manque encore pour être une vraie femme [...]', Emmanuelle tells her husband early on in the novel, 'Je croyais connaître tant de choses, mais que sont-elles à côté de ce que j'ignore?' (p. 69) ('I know there's some kind of progress I have to make, something I lack and have to find before I can be a real woman [...] I thought I knew so many things, but what are they compared to what I don't know?' (p. 51)). The quest motif is certainly not new in erotic fiction, which, since the sixteenth century, has frequently related the sexual instruction of young females.[6] The subjugation of women by men which this structure implies and which has informed most other models of erotic narrative is the main reason why this genre continues to constitute a problem for many feminist readers.[7] How, then, can *Emmanuelle* be said to renew the French erotic tradition? In particular, is the eponymous heroine merely the object of a male voyeuristic focus or an autonomous subject, actively propelling the narrative forward?

As with Sade's Juliette, Emmanuelle's sexuality is certainly morally transgressive by conventional standards, yet her adulterous behaviour with the much older Mario, who becomes her sexual mentor in Bangkok, and the lesbian affair with her American friend, Bee, are presented in the novel as wholly positive; in this respect, the novel might be seen as helping to counter repressive attitudes to women's sexuality in particular. However, such a presentation might equally well be aimed at the voyeuristic male reader, particularly since a male character, Mario, plays a dominant role as Emmanuelle's sexual instructor.[8] According to this reading, that this is a woman's story told in a woman's voice would simply be a conceit, not uncommon in the erotic genre,[9] whilst the female pseudonym, Emmanuelle Arsan, may actually conceal a male writer[10] – another convention of the genre. These issues, however, can be addressed only through a detailed evaluation of the novel's formal properties. I shall begin by looking at the question of point of view, which depends on use of metaphor as well as on perspective (focalisation and narrative voice).

Metaphor frequently betrays an unconscious point of view which may be at odds with the consciously controlled rhetoric of a text. In this case, the rhetoric of female liberation which underpins the novel's thematic contents is to some degree undermined by a metaphorical discourse running counter to that rhetoric.

Though agreeing with Georges Bataille's theory of the erotic impulse as deriving from excess, Mario's definition of eroticism clearly attacks Bataille's emphasis on the desire for transgression, the awareness of sacred taboos and the drive towards death – the very last of these components, in particular, is explicitly rejected:

> – [...] Ses lois se fondent sur la raison, non sur la crédulité. Sur la confiance, au lieu de la peur. Et sur le goût de la vie, plutôt que sur la mystique de la mort. [...] L'érotisme n'est pas un produit de décadence, mais un progrès. Parce qu'il aide à désacraliser les choses du sexe, c'est un instrument de salubrité mentale et sociale. (pp. 173–4)

> '[...] Its laws are based on reason, not on credulity ... on confidence, instead of fear ... and on a taste for life, rather than on the mystique of death. Eroticism is not a product of decadence, but a progress. Because it helps to desanctify sex, it's an instrument of mental and social health. [...]' (pp. 116–17)

Mario directs his venom against the main source of Western taboos, religion, and those bourgeois cultural institutions (the couple, the family) which derive their authority from it. He warns Emmanuelle against the pernicious and repressive influences of cultural and religious taboos, against an Old Testament that reduces women to the status of animals, against a New Testament 'ideology of sin':

> – [Le progrès de l'homme] consiste à croire de moins en moins et à voir de mieux en mieux. Les dieux ne naissent que derrière les paupières fermées. [...] (p. 188)

'(Man's progress) consists in believing less and less and seeing better and better. Gods are born only behind closed eyelids. [...]' (p. 126)

The author has herself expressed her distaste for Bataille's preoccupation with 'the sacred' and his insistence on the relation between eroticism and death:

> Je ne me résigne pas [...] à la fatalité du couple obligé qu'Eros et Thanatos sont censés former. Tout au contraire, à mes yeux, l'érotisme est un défi à la mort, un déni de la mort. L'amour de l'amour, l'amour sexuel cérébralisé, la passion sensuelle faite art peuvent, mieux que toute croyance et que toute magie, nous guérir de la peur.[11]

> I am not resigned [...] to the idea that Eros and Thanatos are fated to go together. Quite the contrary, in my eyes, eroticism is a challenge to death, a denial of death. The love of love, sexual love made cerebral, sensual passion turned into art are better able than any belief or magic to cure us of our fears.

Yet, the metaphorical unconscious of Arsan's text tends to weaken the demystification of the erotic to be read at the text's surface. Mario's opposition to religion and the sacred is itself undermined by certain textual metaphors which hover stubbornly around religious/mythological themes. The titles of Chapters 1 and 3 are inspired by mythology: Chapter 1 is entitled 'La Licorne envolée' ('The Flying Unicorn'), 'La Licorne' being the name of the aeroplane which takes Emmanuelle to Thailand – an appropriately phallic image, given her experiences during the flight – and Chapter 3 'Des Seins, des Déesses et des Roses' ('Of Breasts, Goddesses and Roses) – *wives* of the Gods, we note! and there are Old Testament resonances in Chapter 2's 'Vert paradis' ('Green Paradise') and in Chapter 5's 'La Loi' ('The Law'), which announces a law of eroticism that seems to be as sacred as the Law of Moses.

Moreover, despite the thematics of female sexuality, textual metaphors are consistently drawn from the myths of male culture. This imagery may function ironically to suggest the substitution for a supernatural of a *human* divine (sexual freedom), yet images of the sacred escape the author's conscious control. In particular, the anti-religious messages of the novel are weakened by Mario's representation of sexual pleasure to Emmanuelle as the *transgression of the prohibited*. 'Le temps du sacré est fini' proclaims Mario (p. 195) ('the time of the sacred is over' (p. 132)), yet those sacred idols he despises so much reemerge in the metaphors of the narrative in counterpoint to Mario's humanistic atheism:

> Elle se sentait en accusation, coupable d'elle ne savait trop quel inexpiable péché contre l'esprit. (p. 216)

> She felt that she was on trial, guilty of some inexpiable sin against the mind. (p. 146)

> La nuit offre un silence si total que l'étrangère se retient de respirer et, davantage encore, de parler, comme par crainte d'un sacrilège. (p. 234)

> The night was thick with such a total silence that she scarcely dared to breathe, much less to speak, as though for fear of committing a sacrilege. (p. 159)

> Le cœur d'Emmanuelle bat en désordre. Sans nul doute, ce sont les sortilèges qui commencent. Dans un instant, des Mongols grimaçants vont jaillir de leur repaire: Emmanuelle sera livrée aux rites d'une magie sanguinaire. (pp. 240–41)

> Emmanuelle's heart pounded in disorder. No doubt of it, the sorcery was beginning. In a moment, grimacing Mongols would burst out of their lair and make her the victim of bloodthirsty magic rites. (p. 160)

In spite of Mario's contempt for religion and for the taboos it has created, it seems that, as in Sade's fiction, an awareness of those taboos is essential to those who seek pleasure in their transgression:

> [...] la survivance actuelle de fausses règles morales – ou simplement de conventions sociales [...] – ajoute à nos

plaisirs, en nous donnant, à nous qui les refusons, le pouvoir
de choquer [...] (p. 196)

[...] the present survival of false moral rules – or simply of
social conventions – gives us, who refuse them, the power
to shock. (p. 133)

Sodomy and adultery, opium-smoking and troilism would
all greatly lessen in appeal if they were not forbidden activities
– hence, what excites Emmanuelle, as she imagines deceiving
her husband, is the abstract notion of betrayal:

[...] le désir de principe de *tromper* Jean, le tromper autant
qu'elle l'aimait, le tromper d'urgence, beaucoup, de tout son
corps, de toute sa nudité, de toute la suaveté de son ventre,
où coulerait la semence d'un étranger. (p. 230)

[...] she was eager to *deceive* Jean as a matter of principle, to
deceive him as much as she loved him, immediately, fully,
with her whole body, with all her nakedness, with all the
softness of her belly, into which a stranger's semen would
flow. (p. 155)

Forbidden love is thrilling, which is also why Mario, echoing
Sade again,[12] finds sodomy erotic: 'Faire l'amour avec un
garçon est pour moi érotique dans la mesure où c'est, comme
le proclament à juste titre les imbéciles, contre nature.' (p. 252)
('For me, making love with a boy is erotic insofar as it's against
nature, as imbeciles rightly proclaim.' (p. 170)). As Bataille has
shown, prohibition is a universal component of both religion
and the erotic: 'La connaissance de l'érotisme, ou de la religion,
demande une expérience personnelle, égale et contradictoire,
de l'interdit et de la transgression.' ('Knowledge of eroticism,
or of religion, requires personal experience of the forbidden
and of transgression in paradoxically equal measure.')[13]

On the one hand, Arsan's novel is ostensibly a plea for
freedom from taboos,[14] and on the other, through both certain
metaphors of the narrative and certain character attitudes, her
text talks about the pleasures of a transgression which depend
on their continued existence. In this case, such taboos possess
the character of a religious sacred, derived from the Judeo-

Christian tradition. Far from liberating women, this tradition has helped perpetuate a patriarchal system which keeps them firmly in their place. At the same time, this contradiction between a conscious discourse of liberation from prohibitions and an unconscious desire to experience the pleasure of trans-gression[15] serves to emphasise the difficulty, and perhaps even undesirability, of creating an erotic imaginary that is wholly untransgressive.[16]

There is also in *Emmanuelle* evidence of a textual 'consensus' which seems to centre upon the phallus both as referent and as dominant image of the novel. On a thematic level, the work dramatises the sexual liberation of the female, but the male organ seems to take centre stage. The opening scenes on the aeroplane, during which Emmanuelle has sex with two different male passengers, immediately draw the reader's attention to the importance of phallic size:

Comme s'il se nourrissait d'elle, [le phallus] augmentait de taille et ses mouvements, d'amplitude et d'allant. A travers la brume de sa félicité, elle réussit à s'émerveiller que la course de ce bélier pût être aussi longue dans son ventre. (p. 34)

As if feeding on her, [the phallus] increased in size and its movements quickened. Through the mist of her ecstasy, she marvelled that this ram could go so deep inside her.

Elle faillit laisser échapper un cri lorsqu'elle vit le reptile herculéen qui se dressait devant elle hors de sa broussaille dorée. Parce qu'elle était sensiblement plus petite que l'homme, le gland trigonocéphale atteignait jusqu'entre ses seins. (p. 37)

She nearly cried out when she saw the reptile that had risen before her from its patch of golden underbrush. Because she was much shorter than he was, the blunted triangle of his glans touched her between her breasts. (p. 26)

As well as representing the male organ in terms of Freudian clichés (ram, reptile), both passages are structured around a stereotypical economy of male expansion as against female contraction: the phallus grows as if feeding off the woman (which implies a consequent diminishment of her), the woman is overawed by the gigantic dimensions of the predator that dwarfs her, a huge poisonous serpent of a phallus, ready for the kill.

This phallicist economy of expansion and contraction is paralleled in many of the novel's sexual metaphors by a similarly phallicist economy of emptying and filling: a man's penis empties itself into a woman, as a farmer ploughs, waters and inseminates the land he owns, 'se vidant jusqu'à la dernière goutte en elle, ne la quittant qu'ensemencée – argile fouie, hersée, irriguée, appropriée' (p. 165) ('emptying itself to the last drop in her, not leaving her until she was seeded, until she was a field that had been dug, plowed, irrigated, appropriated' (p. 110)). The essential thing is for the woman to stay full, not to lose a single drop of that sacred gift, the essence of man:

> Jean se déverse en elle, s'émerveillant d'avoir tant à lui donner, de la percer si profondément, de tant jouir [...] Elle ne bouge pas, pour qu'aucune goutte ne sorte d'elle. (p. 73)

> Jean pours himself into her, marvelling that he has so much to give her, that he can pierce her so deeply, come so much [...] She doesn't move, so as not to lose a single drop.

Such an economy is basically capitalist and patriarchal, in that it implies the need of the female to be filled by the male, like a vessel, an object, a money box, as though she were not whole, not '*full*filled', without her essential complement, the phallus and its regular deposits.

Like men, the women of the novel are also allowed to 'spend', since female sexuality is itself portrayed in the novel in largely phallic terms. Bee's pudenda, for instance, has an aggressively forward-thrusting shape:

> [...] le gonflement lisse et fendu de son bas-ventre était si sensuel, se jetait en avant avec un tel mouvement d'invite qu'Emmanuelle sentait son propre sexe fouillé comme par une main. (p. 107)

[...] the smooth, split bulge at the bottom of her belly was so sensual, and thrust itself forward so invitingly, that Emmanuelle felt as if her own sex was being probed by a hand. (p. 80)

Her clitoris is a 'phallus minuscule' (p. 121) ('a miniature penis' (p. 86)), while Marie-Anne's breast seems to Emmanuelle sufficiently pointed and firm to penetrate Bee 'aussi profond qu'une langue' (p. 129) ('as deeply as a tongue'). As for Emmanuelle herself, she fantasises about making love to Marie-Anne and then to Bee in a distinctly male fashion. Once again, masculine images of emptying and filling structure the discourse – 'je te viderai de toi et t'emplirai de moi' (p. 131) ('I'll empty you of you and fill you up with me') – and once again, female sexuality is seen as following an implicitly superior male model:

> Je jouirai dans sa bouche en même temps qu'Marie-Anne jouira dans son sexe. Elle avalera mon sperme imaginaire en même temps que coulera dans son vagin le lait de vierge de Marie-Anne. (p. 131)

> I'll come in her mouth at the same time as Marie-Anne comes up inside her. She'll swallow my imaginary sperm at the same time as Marie-Anne's virgin's milk flows into her vagina.

Later, in another scene, Emmanuelle wants to *become* the man she observes making love to a woman:

> 'Entre vite en elle, comme je le ferais si j'étais un homme!' Elle prit également la résolution de faire, un jour, l'amour, *en homme*, à une femme [...] (p. 154)

> 'Go inside her quickly, as I would do if I were a man!' She resolved to make love one day, *as a man*, to a woman [...]

However, even though her sexual desires are represented in terms of the active male role, the metaphors of her thoughts still conform to the passive stereotype – the violent penetration of woman's mind/body can make her cry out (with pleasure/pain, the double-edged sword of rape fantasy):

> Emmanuelle se sentit trouée par une pensée aussi aiguë qu'une épée grecque, si soudaine et violente qu'elle faillit crier. (p. 157)

> Emmanuelle felt herself pierced by a thought as sharp as a Greek sword, so sudden and violent that she almost cried out.

Is it in any case a promotion of the sexual liberation of women to show them taking the active role or is it rather the simple transference of the male stereotype on to women, who are thus trapped in the old phallocentric bind? Even Mario's 'Ce qui est érotique, ce n'est pas l'éjaculation, c'est l'érection' (p. 207) ('What's erotic is not ejaculation, it's erection' (p. 139)), though ostensibly favouring duration over consummation – the woman's endless multiplication of pleasure over the singular goal of man's solitary *jouissance* – is a maxim couched in terms of the male, not the female, body.

The sight of a naked Siamese impresses Emmanuelle so much that she begins a long rêverie about the phallus, about all phalluses, their colour, shape, and above all, size. Fantasising about the organ she has seen, Emmanuelle makes it stand up in her mind and, in doing so, she does indeed metaphorically *become* the phallus,[17] phallic woman, penis and vulva combined, the hermaphroditic ideal:

> A force de s'appliquer à cette création, Emmanuelle se fait elle-même phallus [...] Emmanuelle phallus s'introduira dans Emmanuelle vulve. (p. 239)

> By thinking about it, Emmanuelle makes herself into a phallus [...] Emmanuelle phallus will penetrate Emmanuelle vulva.

When Mario takes Emmanuelle to visit a Hindu temple dedicated to Priapos (god of procreation) in which hundreds of phalluses hang from trees, the mental images are transformed into visible icons, objects to look at, to touch, to worship. Emmanuelle is now ready to take Mario's penis in her hands, 'Il convient maintenant que l'illusion cède à la réalité' (p. 261) ('It's now time for illusion to yield to reality' (p. 178)), and God the Phallus is made flesh ....

Drawing on both feminist and psychoanalytic theory, Gertrude Koch explains the primacy of the phallus in pornographic films in terms of castration fear, which we may assume similarly afflicts the male reader of erotica: 'Seeing lots of penises confirms their durability and intactness; castration anxiety is also reduced by inducing the feeling of phallic omnipotence. The restless search for something that can't be found – the woman's penis – is compensated by an appeasing display of erections and potency. [...] John Ellis has shown that in the voyeuristic realm of pornographic films the invisible female phallus must be transformed into a visible fetish, so that pleasure can overcome the fear of castration.'[18] In hard-core cinema pornography, this need for an invisible phallus is met by having the woman 'borrow' the man's, as she smears his come into her face and breasts the moment he has ejaculated. The woman's pleasure is thus signified in her appropriation of the signifiers of male pleasure. However, the aim is not to please or excite the female spectator (though, as Koch points out, 'The pleasure of looking [...] is certainly a pleasure common to both sexes'[19]) but to soothe the male spectator's fear of castration.[20]

The dominant role played by the phallus in film erotica can, of course, be defended on the basis that sexual excitement and orgasm are displayed externally by the male only. This is not the case in the novel, in which it is perfectly possible to describe the woman's pleasure. Even more so than in pornographic films, this foregrounding of the phallus as both image and referent suggests an orientation towards the male rather than the female consumer. The final tableau of the novel, in which a rickshaw driver enters Emmanuelle and is simultaneously entered by Mario, presents us with a powerful image of the penetrating, active man and the receptive, passive woman. Only the boy, we note, is allowed to be both active *and* passive, functioning as orifice and phallus, and so, effectively, as Mario's phallic extension – the older man uses the younger man's body to penetrate the woman:

– Maintenant, je suis en vous, dit Mario. Je vous perce d'un glaive deux fois plus aigu que ne l'est celui du commun des hommes. Le sentez-vous?
– Oui. Je suis heureuse, dit Emmanuelle. (p. 275)

'Now I'm in you,' he said. 'I'm piercing you with a sword twice as sharp as that of common men. Do you feel it?'
'Yes. I'm happy.' (p. 189)

Thus, here the phallus physically enacts its metaphorical and symbolic role of linchpin, hyphen, 'trait d'union', *sine qua non*, the sharply pointed blade that must pierce (and so do violence to) a woman in order to make her happy.

The use of metaphor in this text is clearly problematic from the point of view of a sexual politics.[21] On the other hand, the perspective of the narrative, as defined by Gérard Genette, cannot so easily be reduced to a singular, masculine point of view. For Genette, narrative perspective is 'ce second mode de régulation de l'information qui procède du choix (ou non) d'un «point de vue» restrictif' ('this second mode of regulation of information proceeding from the decision to opt (or not to opt) for a limited "point of view"').[22] Genette analyses perspective in terms of *mood* (that is, which character's point of view determines the narrative perspective? or, in other words, who 'sees'?) and *voice* (that is, who is the narrator? or who 'speaks'?).[23] In Genette's terms, the narrative *voice* of *Emmanuelle* is both heterodiegetic (absent from the plot) and extradiegetic (remaining outside the diegesis). In traditional terms, this voice is therefore that of an apparently omniscient, third-person narrator.[24] Despite the externality of the narrative voice, the narrative *mood*, which Genette also terms more specifically *focalisation* (or focus of narration)[25] could frequently be said to be internal, in the sense that it is 'personal', as defined by Roland Barthes and discussed by Genette:[26] that is, it obeys the criterion that it is possible to rewrite the narrative in the first person without this operation involving any change in the discourse other than grammatical pronouns. This works perfectly with Arsan's novel, in which the reader sees most things from Emmanuelle's point of view. The frequent use of *style indirect libre* (free indirect speech) helps to reinforce this effect. During descriptions of sex between

Emmanuelle and two men on the aeroplane bound for Thailand in Chapter 1, it is *her* voice, *her* desire which provides the main focus of the narrative:

– of the air-hostess:

> Oh! si seulement sa compagne voulait, elle aussi, se dévêtir! (p. 29)

> Oh, if only the stewardess would undress, too! (p. 20)

– of her responses to the caresses of her first lover:

> Elle se plaignait, à petites plaintes, sans qu'elle sût exactement pourquoi cette peine. Était-ce le doigt qui la fouillait, si loin au fond de ses reins? Ou la bouche qui se nourrissait d'elle, avalant chaque souffle, chaque sanglot? Était-ce le tourment du désir ou la honte de sa luxure? (p. 33)

> She whimpered softly without knowing the exact cause of her distress. Was it the finger that was probing so deeply inside her, or the mouth that was feeding on her, swallowing each breath, each gasp? Was she tormented by desire or ashamed of her lasciviousness? (p. 23)

Emmanuelle's lovers remain shadowy figures; we are privy neither to their thoughts nor to their desires. It is her pleasure and hers alone that preoccupies the narrative. The following passage is typical:

> [...] Emmanuelle gardait assez d'imagination pour jouir du tableau qu'elle se faisait du méat dégorgeant des coulées crémeuses – qu'aspirait, active et gourmande comme une bouche, l'ouverture oblongue de son utérus.
> Le voyageur acheva son orgasme et Emmanuelle se calma à son tour, envahie par un bien-être sans remords, à quoi la moindre chose contribuait: le glissement du mâle qui se retirait, le contact de la couverture qu'elle sentait qu'il étendait sur elle, le confort de la couchette et l'opacité montante et tiède du sommeil qui la recouvrit. (p. 35)

[...] she still had imagination enough to enjoy the mental image of his penis disgorging creamy torrents that were lapped up by the oval opening of her uterus, as greedy and active as a mouth.

He finished his orgasm and she too became calm, filled with a sense of well-being without remorse, increased by his sliding motion as he withdrew, the contact of the blanket that she felt him spreading over her, the comfort of the reclining seat, and the warm, increasing opacity of the sleep that was covering her. (p. 25)

From the very first scene of this novel, in which this passage occurs, we are in no doubt that, like the responses of her own body, 'as greedy and active as a mouth', the eponymous heroine is no mere passive sex object.

There are two scenes, however, in which the focus is not Emmanuelle's: the brief scene between her husband, Jean, and his friend, Christophe, in Chapter 4 (the only scene from which Emmanuelle is absent) and the long 'instruction scene' in Chapter 5, in which the point of view appears to be zero (that is, with the external narrator) but which is actually dominated by Mario's voice. Indeed, in Chapter 5, this character achieves the status of intradiegetic narrator (or second-level narrator within a first-level narrative) with all the privileges this status entails. When quoting from authors ancient and modern, his voice appears to slide almost unobtrusively out of dialogue and into narrative. This impression is strengthened in Chapter 6 by a tendency for such quotations to be delivered without narrative introduction or acknowledgement of source. Because he is portrayed as a man of great wisdom and superior powers of expression, Mario's voice inevitably carries authority. It is also the dominant voice of the last two chapters in a more obvious sense, occupying far more narrative space than Emmanuelle's. The 'Mario' scenes therefore reinforce another ancient male stereotype: men speak, have the authority of language, while women listen. In fact, Mario's authority is not simply linguistic: in 'giving' Emmanuelle to other men – a young Thai boy, whom he instructs her to fellate, and a rickshaw driver, whom he invites to penetrate her – Mario both reaffirms his 'ownership' of the woman and derives pleasure from the process of exchange, as in the kinship system described by Lévi-Strauss.[27]

Use of metaphor and the dominant role played by Mario in the final chapters do suggest the education of a woman (and the woman reader) in the acceptance of male fantasies. On the other hand, outside the 'Mario' scenes,[28] narrative perspective broadly invites identification with the female character.

We must conclude then that, overall, the narrative perspective in *Emmanuelle* is a sexually ambivalent one. The identity of the implied reader in this text only serves to muddy the water further.

There are frequent attempts to bring the reader into the text so that the latter might feel voyeuristically present (another long-standing convention of the erotic genre.[29]) Initially, the use of epigraphs serves to define the reader's identity, inviting him or her to adopt a shared literary and cultural perspective, especially those highly literary quotations from Mallarmé, Artaud, Ovid on the novel's paratextual threshold. These gobbets from the classics, ancient and modern, act as a kind of entrance test, effectively filtering out the uneducated, deterring them from turning the page or buying the book. Once embarked upon reading the novel, the reader who makes it that far is allocated a decidedly voyeuristic role: Emmanuelle's blouse is sufficiently unbuttoned 'pour qu'un spectateur attentif puisse découvrir un profil de sein par la chance d'un geste ou la complicité d'un courant d'air' (p. 15) ('for an alert spectator to make out the shape of a breast, thanks to a chance gesture or the complicity of a draught of air'). This implied gaze soon becomes an explicitly masculine one; as Emmanuelle settles down in the seat of her aeroplane, she becomes aware of a man watching her: 'Elle a conscience que ses genoux sont levés vers ce regard pour qu'il prenne son plaisir' (pp. 19–20) ('She is aware that her knees are prominent enough for him to enjoy looking at them').

As the novel progresses, however, the nature of this gaze becomes more complex. The very process of *looking* is elevated by Mario to the level of art, thereby emphasising the reader's active, creative role: 'Il n'y a pas d'art heureux là où manque le spectateur' (p. 200) ('There can be no happy art without a spectator' (p. 134)), whilst the view of the gaze as both inherently masculine and as experienced negatively by the women it objectifies[30] is perhaps implicitly challenged in *Emmanuelle* in that the viewing subject is most often not a man. The site of this voyeuristic gaze moves from one character to another, as they function as proxies for the reader: English schoolchildren watch with wide-eyed fascination as Emmanuelle has sex on the plane;[31] Emmanuelle and her young friend, Marie-Anne, watch each other masturbating; the Sapphic French countess, Ariane de Saynes, enjoys the sight of Emmanuelle's bare breasts at the swimming pool before making love to her during a game of squash; most significantly, Emmanuelle herself becomes the *subject* of a female gaze in Chapter 6, as she views a succession of phalluses.

It is difficult, therefore, to draw unequivocal conclusions about the implied reader's sexual identity and the point of view presented by the novel's discourse. Many argue that the gaze can never be anything but male and objectifying, that even where the subject of the gaze is a woman she has simply taken on a 'masculine' role, and that even when women try to write erotically they cannot escape male discourse. Others claim that the gaze need be neither male nor objectifying.[32] Recent feminist film critics, for instance, have begun to suggest that, as Linda Williams puts it,

> [...] the male-active-voyeuristic-objectifying side of cinematic spectatorship has been stressed, at the expense of the female-passive-identifying-fetishized (instead of fetishizing) side. Even more problematic is the fact that activity and passivity have been too rigorously assigned to separate gendered spectator positions with little examination of either the active elements of the feminine position or the mutability of male and female spectators' adoption of one or the other subject position and participation in the (perverse) pleasures of both.[33]

The dissension, even among feminist critics, with regard to the nature and consequences of the gaze serves to underline the complexity of this issue and it seems to me that Arsan's novel exemplifies this complexity well. As we have seen, there are certainly passages containing a politically problematic use of metaphor. On the other hand, most of the physical portraits in the novel are redeemed by being drawn through Emmanuelle's eyes and by being psychological and poetic as well as erotic in tone. There is nothing objectifying in the portrait of the young Marie-Anne, for example, in which Emmanuelle admires her skin, breasts, hair and, finally, her eyes:

> [...] Obliques, allongés, se relevant vers les tempes d'un mouvement si rare qu'on les croirait fourvoyés sur ces joues claires d'Européenne – mais si verts, il est vrai! si lumineux! Emmanuelle y voit passer, comme surgit et vire le faisceau d'un phare, tour à tour des lueurs d'ironie, de sérieux, de raison, d'extraordinaire autorité, puis, soudain, de sollicitude, voire de compassion, et, encore, de malice rieuse, de fantaisie, d'ingénuité, de complicité: des feux d'ensorcelle-ment.
> «Les yeux de Lilith!», songe Emmanuelle. (pp. 47–8)

> [...] Slanting, oblong, rising toward her temples with such a rare line that they seemed to have been placed in that light Caucasian face by mistake. But so green, it was true! So luminous! Emmanuelle saw flashes pass through them like the revolving beam of a lighthouse, flashes of irony, seriousness, reason, extraordinary authority, then sudden solicitude and even compassion, followed by laughing mis-chievousness, whimsy, or candor – spellbinding flashes.
> 'Lilith's eyes!' thought Emmanuelle. (pp. 34–5)[34]

Marie-Anne's eyes, depicted here as the authoritative, com-passionate, captivating eyes of Lilith, of the first woman, may thus be seen as metaphorically representing a positive, active female gaze, which the reader may also share.

In addition to narrative perspective, the form of the novel has other important characteristics which may influence the reader's overall judgement.

## Intertextuality

*Emmanuelle* has an almost classically balanced structure. Five of its six chapters recall the five acts of a classical play: Chapter 1 describes the arrival of the heroine on the Oriental stage, the events of Chapters 2 and 3 resemble the plot development which we are accustomed to expect in the second and third acts of classical theatre, with a turning point reached in Chapter 4, as Emmanuelle struggles with her unrequited love for Bee and Bee is eventually replaced by Mario as focus of Emmanuelle's interest; Chapter 5 seems to function as a long philosophical interlude, all dialogue and no action, a kind of *entr'acte* during which everyone pauses to talk and think, to draw breath before plunging into the climactic activities of the *dénouement* in Chapter 6. It is as if the author had wanted to balance the chaotic promiscuity of the content with a rule-based structural symmetry.

In other ways, too, the structure of *Emmanuelle* is more classical than modern. The instruction of a young ingénue by both men and other women is a model of classical erotica. Marie-Anne and Ariane offer Emmanuelle lessons in masturbation and lesbianism respectively, whilst in Chapters 5 and 6, especially, Emmanuelle becomes the pupil of the cultured libertine, Mario, who takes her through the theory and, inevitably, the practice of promiscuous lovemaking.

The novel also contains many of the principal features of the *Bildungsroman*.[35] As in many *Bildungsromane* of the eighteenth century, names are often transparently symbolic. The paronyms, Marie-Anne and Ariane, seem to act as ironic reversals of each other and of the characters' parallel functions as Emmanuelle's guides to auto-eroticism and lesbianism respectively: the simplicity of the first suggests a deceptive 'little girl' innocence, while the sophistication of the second seems well suited to the pompous and predatory countess. Bee in French suggests the open mouth (*bouche bée*) of her shaven sex, which Emmanuelle longs to fill.

The narrative structure, too, corresponds closely to that of the *Bildungsroman*: the heroine undergoes a learning process, travelling to an exotic place where she passes from naïveté to knowledge; this voyage thus becomes a quest for truth, for self-awareness, for liberation; en route, the heroine has a number of edifying adventures; the reader is invited to identify with the heroine, to share her point of view; the narrative has discernible satirical/polemical purposes, linked to didactic authorial intentions; the structure and style have symbolic functions associated with these purposes and intentions. There is, of course, one essential difference: this *Bildungsroman* portrays the adventures of a woman, not a man (like Sade's Justine or Juliette,[36] but unlike the male heroes, typical of the genre). As Nancy K. Miller points out in her essay on *Juliette*, this type of narrative is a

> 'male affair,' 'a male form because women have tended to be viewed traditionally as static, rather than dynamic, as instances of femaleness considered essential rather than existential.' The typical subject of the genre is a sensitive young man, who, upon moving from a sheltered environment to the challenges of the world, loses an original innocence as he achieves a measure of social integration and *savoir-vivre*.[37]

Like Juliette, Emmanuelle conforms to this formula in every respect but one: she is a *female* apprentice, and her education, like that of Sade's resourceful heroine,

> is achieved by a reversal of the valorization assigned to the cultural and literary conventions encoding femaleness, the positively marked status of daughter, wife, mother. The novel thus builds upon the stages of emancipation from the familial, on the denegation of bourgeois femininity.[38]

Emmanuelle is not portrayed in terms of her status as daughter (her parents are not mentioned), she has no children and appears to have absolutely no maternal desires, and she is quickly disabused of the importance of her marriage vows. Again, like Juliette's, her enfranchisement from the family is 'all the more striking because undertaken by a woman'.[39]

In fact, Arsan's novel does appear to invert some of the dominant stereotypes of male-centred romantic fiction. Emmanuelle discovers that sex is not best in a loving relationship with one partner – on the contrary, such a relationship is seen to inhibit the experience of the erotic. Because the 'couple' is closely associated with the nuclear family, an essentially bourgeois patriarchal structure, this anti-couple rhetoric favours the sexual and social emancipation of women in particular.

The classical, *Bildungsroman* and romantic genres are, however, not the only intertextual contexts in which Arsan's novel may be read. There is also an extensive use of literary quotations as epigraphs, which help to promote the text as literature and situate it within a recognisable, multiple, intertextual framework. In addition to the use of epigraphs at the beginning of chapters, much of the writing itself appears epigrammatic in nature. Mario's discourse, especially, privileges the maxim, another self-consciously literary device, though many of his pronouncements are both pompous and banal. Here are just a few of numerous examples: 'La place naturelle de l'amant est au milieu du couple' (p. 204) ('The lover's natural place is in the middle of the couple' (p. 137)) '[...] tout changement est un progrès, toute permanence une tombe' (p. 255) '[...] every change is an advance, every permanence a grave' (p. 173)). His epigrammatic style is reinforced by direct quotation: he quotes, among others, from Goethe, Unamuno, Don Juan, the Bible, Montherlant, Rémy Belleau. He also refers obliquely to Sade and to the work of social anthropologists (the customs of the Muria tribe, which are the subject of the novel's only footnote). Above all, in the final chapter, he prefaces short sections of monologue with unattributed quotations, italicised in the text, thus underlining their importance for the reader.

It is difficult to find Mario's pomposity and condescension to Emmanuelle sympathetic and therefore to take his pronouncements seriously, as we are surely meant to do, and this is probably the novel's most serious artistic weakness. This impression is, however, to some degree mitigated by a lurking sense of irony, which at times escapes from the narrative, perhaps in spite of itself. Emmanuelle, for instance, joins in the 'maxim' game and tries to outperform her mentor:

> – [...] Serez-vous satisfait par ceci: 'Tout temps passé à autre chose qu'à l'art de jouir, entre des bras toujours plus nombreux, est un temps perdu.'
> – Très bien! approuva Mario. Vous avez le sens des formules, un don de synthèse. Il faudra que vous l'exerciez. Un de ces jours, je vous commanderai un ouvrage de maximes. (p. 201)

'[...] Would you be satisfied with this: 'All time spent on anything but the art of pleasure, in increasingly numerous arms, is wasted'?'

'Very good!' approved Mario. 'You have a sense of formulation, a talent for synthesis. You must practise it. One of these days, I'll buy you a book of maxims.' (p. 135)[40]

There is a self-referential irony in the exchange that frames Emmanuelle's maxim: we are invited to laugh with the heroine at Mario's pomposity: 'Mario n'avait pas l'air de plaisanter, mais Emmanuelle rit de bon coeur'. (p. 201) 'Mario did not appear to be joking, but Emmanuelle laughed heartily'.

On both stylistic and structural levels, the novel has decidedly literary sources, but this is not a case of simple plagiarism. These numerous allusions frequently seem to function ludically as fairground mirrors, offering reflections of both themselves and of their literary/erotic antecedents.

Chapter 1 begins with the following epigraph:

*Vénus a mille manières de prendre ses ébats, mais la plus simple, la moins fatigante, c'est de rester à demi penchée sur le côté droit.*
OVIDE («L'art d'aimer») (p. 13)

*Love has a thousand postures; the simplest and the least tiring is to lie halfway over on your right side.*
Ovid (*The Art of Love*) (p. 11)

These lines, which preface descriptions of fully penetrative sex in aeroplane seats, seem in retrospect to ironise both the discomfort of air travel and acrobatic sexual activity in public places.

In the last chapter, Mario cites Baudelaire to help persuade Emmanuelle of the importance of being open to all experiences:

Corps innombrables à notre ressemblance, hommes ou femmes, «enfer ou ciel, qu'importe ... au fond de l'inconnu pour trouver du nouveau»! (p. 254)

Innumerable bodies in our likeness, men or women, 'heaven
or hell, it matters not ... to the depths of the unknown to
find the new!' (p. 172)

The words in quotation marks are taken from the final stanza
of Baudelaire's long poem, *Le Voyage*, the theme of which is
the impossibility of escaping our spleen in the here and now,
and the need to travel beyond the human into the infinite to
find ultimate relief. Emmanuelle's 'journey', on the other
hand, is a journey among human beings – 'Innumerable
bodies in our likeness' – a journey in search of new experiences
certainly, but a journey into a heaven or hell very much of this
world. This oblique reference to *Baudelairien* spleen is,
therefore, a tongue-in-cheek reminder of 'the ideology of sin',
the guilt-laden view of the sexual generated by Christianity,
which Mario condemned earlier.

Alongside other writers, the very process of writing finds
echo in the text. The narrator, as we saw earlier, is strictly
speaking absent from her narrative, but we are directly
reminded of the novel's storytelling function:

– Que devrais-je encore apprendre? protesta-t-elle.
– Le plaisir de raconter: plus subtil, plus raffiné encore que
celui du secret. (p. 228)

'What else do I have to learn?'
'The pleasure of telling; it's even more subtle, more refined,
than the pleasure of secrecy.' (p. 154)

Mario's long instruction of Emmanuelle in itself becomes a
kind of intradiegetic narrative (a story within a story).

On a stylistic level, too, there are self-reflexive references in
relation to an intertextual context. In addition to Mario's
many allusions to and quotations from specific writers, the
discourse seems indirectly to echo the language and themes
of other French novelists and poets who have written about
love. For instance, a reference early in the text to the 'chienne
blasée' called O (p. 42) ('blasé little female dog that she called
"O"' (p. 30)), belonging to one of the indolent young wives
of the French expatriate community, does seem to function in
retrospect as an ironic counterpoint to the self-effacingly

submissive attitudes expressed by Emmanuelle a little later in the novel, as she makes love to her husband, Jean:

> Elle voudrait pouvoir se livrer plus encore, avoir plus complètement conscience d'être prise, au gré de celui qui la prend, être à sa disposition, ne pas être consultée, être faible, être facile, ne rien faire d'autre qu'obéir activement et s'ouvrir ... Existe-t-il, s'exalte-t-elle en secret, plus grand bonheur que de consentir? Cette pensée suffit à achever de la faire basculer dans l'orgasme. (p. 72)

> She wished she could surrender still more, be more obedient, more obliging, more open. 'Is there any greater happiness than consenting?' she elatedly asked herself. This thought was enough to drive her across the thin line that separated her from orgasm. (p. 53)

Such attitudes, which Emmanuelle will later be seen to modify considerably under Mario's influence, could not fail to remind the first readers of the novel of Pauline Réage's story of complete feminine subservience in *Histoire d'O*, which had appeared only five years earlier in 1954. Arsan's transparent homage to Réage's erotic classic is immediately undercut by the obviously sarcastic tones adopted by the narrative voice in the lines that follow:

> Puis, lorsqu'elle se retrouve bête abattue, échine brisée, jambes mortes, destin consommé, trophée heureux dans l'ombre aventurée du conquéreur:
> – Tu crois, dit-elle, que je suis la femme que tu veux? (p. 72)

> Then, when she was again a felled animal, a happy trophy in the shadow of the hunter, she said, 'Do you think I'm the woman you want?' (p. 53)[41]

## Conclusion

Use of irony, a ludic intertextuality and, indeed, the sheer poetry of much of the language, all make *Emmanuelle* more than just a trite example of popular fiction and worthy of a place on the 'Erotic Literature' shelf of the library or bookstore.

Yet, what makes the novel especially interesting for the contemporary reader is, perhaps, the contribution that it has undoubtedly made to the debate about female sexual freedom. It is true that, whilst Arsan aims to represent female desire, the rhetoric of her text sometimes betrays a 'masculinist' perspective – hardly surprising, perhaps, in a decade (the 1950s), in which there was little awareness of the dangers of phallocentrism.[42] Nevertheless, in privileging the spoken and unspoken thoughts and feelings of its female protagonist and thus foregrounding issues of female as against male pleasure, *Emmanuelle* focused renewed attention on Freud's rhetorical question 'What do women want?' and sincerely, if somewhat naïvely, attempted to provide some answers.

By the late 1960s, attitudes to sexuality had become so much more liberal that Losfeld was finally able to publish legally a manuscript he had held on to for ten years and which he describes in his memoirs as having 'une valeur de manifeste' ('the value of a manifesto').[43] It is to be regretted that censorship laws had kept out of public hands for a whole decade a novel with the potential to help change people's thinking about the sexual role of women. By the time *Emmanuelle* was openly available in 1968, its message of female sexual liberation may have begun to seem rather dated and the manifesto somewhat lacking in originality. On the other hand, judged according to the standards of the moment of writing rather than official publication, Arsan's first novel does represent a rare attempt to promote acceptance of an active female libido in a culture which still condemned the kind of behaviour indulged in by its heroine as that of the nymphomaniac or the whore.

# 7

# Progressive Slidings of Identity: Alain Robbe-Grillet's *Projet pour une révolution à New York*

The *nouveau roman* or New Novel is a term coined in the 1950s by Alain Robbe-Grillet himself to denote his own work and that of a number of other writers, principally Nathalie Sarraute, Claude Simon, Michel Butor, Robert Pinget, Samuel Beckett and, initially at least, Marguerite Duras, all of whom were published by Les Éditions de Minuit, and who shared a rejection of the traditional novel's approach to plot, characterisation and form, and so were considered experimental and avant-garde. As John de St. Jorre says of William Burroughs's *Naked Lunch*, however, most New Novels remain difficult and at times inaccessible books, belonging to 'that growing pile of great, unread classics, widely bought, knowledgeably talked about and little read',[1] and Alain Robbe-Grillet's books are, in general, no exception. On the other hand, Robbe-Grillet's fiction does contain strong elements of an explicit eroticism which just cannot be found in the works of other writers of the movement.[2] It is ironic then that, both as *chef de file* of the *nouveaux romanciers* and as the only writer of the group whose work has been called pornographic, Robbe-Grillet has enjoyed the least financial success and certainly less public acclaim than Claude Simon or Marguerite Duras. There is a double irony here in that while the accusation of pornographer has been levelled at him by feminist critics in particular, cinema-goers have on occasions reacted with incomprehension and even anger when their expectations of conventional pornographic images and scenarios were disappointed.[3] In the public imagination at least, Alain Robbe-Grillet's reputation has constantly slid between that of guru of the French avant-garde and purveyor of high-class sado-eroticism.

Robbe-Grillet's career as writer and film-maker, which spans nearly 50 years since the composition of his first novel, *Un*

*Régicide*, in 1949, has been marked too by 'slippages' of other
kinds: textual, intertextual, biographical, movements between
genres and forms, between the parodic and the postmodern.
'Glissements' (or 'slidings') is the first word of the title of one
of his most controversial films[4] and, indeed, in the context of
the erotic dimensions of his work, has clear sexual
connotations. The word 'glissements' could also be taken to
capture the essence of the relationship between author, work
and public – his obfuscations and disavowals, his playfulness
and, at times, downright mendacity.[5] Much has been written,
too, about the 'slidings' of his style of fiction, in relation to
*nouveau roman* theory as a whole: the blurring of character
identity, the repetitions and distortions of scenes, the
confusion between narrative voices.[6] It is not my intention to
reprise here what others have analysed in great detail.[7]
However, I would like to carry the use of 'glissements' further
as an overarching metaphor for an understanding of Robbe-
Grillet's writing.

As already intimated, Robbe-Grillet has constantly sought
to blur the boundaries between fact and fiction, between
reality and fantasy, most obviously, perhaps, in the three
autobiographical fictions which he has published since the
early 1980s.[8] The term of 'Romanesques' which he has applied
to these texts draws attention to their status as fictions rather
than as 'documentary' accounts, though within each text
there are sudden and imperceptible transitions from personal
history (for instance, accounts of various episodes 'lived' by the
author) to personal fantasy (most of which involves the
mythical authorial persona, Henri de Corinthe). In the novels
and films, too, as in 'real life', identity has come to play a
dominant role in the Robbe-Grillet universe. While Robbe-
Grillet the man has often expressed regret that the press have
labelled him the leader of the New Novel school, the narrative
voices, characters and settings of his fiction have always been
so mercurial as to render identification of a traditional linear
narrative or chronology, of rounded Balzacian characters and
'cause and effect' based plots virtually impossible by realist
standards. Nor can Robbe-Grillet's novels and films be properly
appreciated in isolation, without reference to the rest of his
*œuvre*. His work has to be viewed as a unitary whole in which

motifs slide from text to text, generating a seamless and open-ended intertext.

Against the background of these manifold slippages of identity between author and narrator, text and genre, invented character and historical figure, I shall extend the 'glissements' metaphor to erotic dimensions of Robbe-Grillet's work, focusing on *Projet pour une révolution à New York*, published in 1970. This work itself marks a noticeable slide in his writing towards the expression of a more explicit eroticism[9] on the one hand and of a more explicit humour on the other.

## Sado-eroticism – art or ethics?

Shortly after the novel's appearance, Structuralist critics such as Jean Ricardou and Bruce Morrissette focused their attention almost exclusively on its form, as indeed they had with all Robbe-Grillet's previous work.[10] For them, the world created in it bears little or no resemblance to the real world and the text is to be regarded as non-mimetic and non-referential, as art not life. John Fletcher, on the other hand, appears determined to impose a realist reading on the novel, which he describes as 'silly' and 'disappointing' and as projecting a 'naïve image of the United States'.[11] Fletcher curiously fails to understand that, like all *nouveaux romans*, *Projet* does not offer us real locations to be identified from our personal experience, Robbe-Grillet's New York being an essentially imaginary creation, a mix of comic book stereotype and personal fantasy. Similarly, any attempt to construct a comprehensible linear plot is doomed to failure. Morrissette might well be describing a huge, pop art mural when he says that *Projet pour une révolution à New York* combines 'an ensemble of New York scenes and locales [...] together with various quite contemporary "themes" (revolutionary cells, suspect activities in Greenwich Village townhouses, crimes and deliberately set fires in large, anonymous apartment houses, rape in the subway, and the like)'.[12]

Whether or not they are to be read as metaphorical rather than mimetic, there are, nevertheless, scenes in the novel depicting a sadistic sexual torture of beautiful young women and girls which are relatively new to readers of Robbe-Grillet (though perhaps less so to spectators of his films). This sudden increase in Robbe-Grilletian sado-eroticism was noted by Daniel Deneau in 1979, for whom *Projet* 'appears to be a degree or two more problematic than any of the five novels which Alain Robbe-Grillet published during the fifties and sixties'.[13] Deneau poses what he sees as an ethical problem in blunt fashion: 'Did he become by 1970 a "pornographer", a man engrossed with recording somebody-or-other's "dirty" sado-erotic fantasies?'[14]

Susan Suleiman, in a seminal essay on the novel two years earlier, had already opened up the novel's eroticism to feminist analysis.[15] Suleiman shares Deneau's and Fletcher's unwillingness to ignore the novel's contents, and there is no doubt that both Suleiman and Deneau have made significant contributions to an understanding of its erotic dimensions, though Suleiman's reading does more justice to the metaphoricity of the text. In the current climate of concern about abusive images of both women and children, it has undoubtedly become less easy to insist, as the author continues to do,[16] that the content of a work of art is simply its form. Recognising that the sexual contents of Robbe-Grillet's text do have a pornographic potential and directly confronting the issue raised by Suleiman in particular of the text's sexism and misogyny, I shall argue that any erotic response on the part of the reader is inevitably modified by the operation of a number of textual mechanisms, the most important of which is humour.

We may begin by looking at Suleiman's and Deneau's arguments in some detail. Suleiman calls attention to the response of the reader, especially the female reader. For her, a 'certain uneasiness' is engendered in this reader who has to confront scenes of the rape, sexual torture and murder of very young girls. She does acknowledge the distancing effect of parody, 'glissement' and 'coupure' in the text, such that the reader 'is caught up in two contradictory movements: one pulling him into a fiction that provokes erotic excitement, the other keeping him at a safe distance'.[17] However, for Suleiman, these 'de-realising devices' are also a means of sustaining the male erection, of deferring 'jouissance', and she is unimpressed by the author's well-known defence of the sexual content of his work as cathartic; a defence which is embedded in the narrative in an account of African religious rituals, 'une mythologie aussi meurtrière que cathartique' (p. 39) ('a mythology as murderous as it is cathartic'). Suleiman comments unsympathetically that 'catharsis is a *purgation* of passions: it must be preceded by their arousal'.[18] For Suleiman, this sexual arousal is exclusively masculine since the reader is directly inscribed into the narrative in the form of a number of narratees and is, therefore, strongly involved in the eroticism, and since 'all of the active (aggressive) roles are assumed by male figures and [...] only the male spectator can become an actor, the male narratee become a narrator – and presumably, the male reader become a scriptor'.[19] *Projet*, she concludes, is 'definitely a man's book', containing 'specifically masculine' fantasies; conflating both women with mothers and Robbe-Grillet with Sade, she attributes the degradation of young women in the novel to a 'tenacious hatred of the mother', which paradoxically goes hand in hand with incestuous fantasies attached to her.[20]

Suleiman's analysis, however, leaves an important question unanswered – if Robbe-Grillet's eroticism is indeed born of a hatred of the maternal, what precisely are the causes of such a hatred? What is the profound meaning of these sado-erotic fantasies? Like Suleiman, Deneau emphasises that critics did not know how to respond to the sado-eroticism of *Projet*, but he is far more sympathetic than Suleiman to the notion of catharsis, of literature as personal therapy and, unlike her, he identifies 'a large and important vein of humor' in the novel which, together with the more explicit eroticism, also 'distinguishes [it] from its predecessors'.[21] Suleiman's blind spot with regard to the humour is somewhat ironic, given that she accuses other critics of ignoring the *erotic* contents. The increase in *both* sexual explicitness and humour mark a significant departure (or 'glissement'!) from the author's earlier writing – even the text which immediately preceded it, *La Maison de rendez-vous*, which contains many erotic motifs and a great deal of irony, could in no sense be described either as explicitly erotic or as explicitly comic. Deneau, for his part, does not seem to think that the humour always attenuates the eroticism, since there is, he argues, one area of the novel in which 'little, if any comedy is allowed',[22] and this is the part dealing with the 16-year-old Laura, a girl held captive by the male narrator in his New York apartment and repeatedly raped by him.

It does seem to me, however, that the humour is not restricted to certain 'less erotic' or 'less violent' passages. Humour in this text is largely self-referential and intertextual, extending not only throughout the text of *Projet* itself (including the 'Laura' passages), but also beyond the text to Robbe-Grillet's writing as a whole. It also refers to pornographic and erotic material in general, and to recent feminist responses to such material. Humour therefore functions in a complex manner in this text and its effects are manifold, but its main consequence for a feminist reading, I would argue, is to flatten out the erotic potential, to transform Suleiman's 'male book' into metapornography, into an ironic, parodic and satirical commentary on the male-dominated pornographic genre. Since the humour is predominantly verbal, the reader's attention is, as we shall see, repeatedly drawn away from the signified to the signifier.

Suleiman does, as I have said, identify other distancing devices in Robbe-Grillet's text, but her conclusion that these devices merely serve to delay a male 'jouissance' which does finally occur, seems to me unconvincing, because of its conflation of textual with *extra*-textual responses.[23] *Projet*, she claims, is 'non-subversive', because it faithfully repeats 'male fantasies of omnipotence and total control over passive female bodies'.[24] The male reader, she implies, is obliged to become Robbe-Grillet's accomplice in this process. As just such a reader, it seems to me that, despite any conscious or unconscious search for *jouissance*, I never experience the eroticism of the text in an immediate (masturbatory) present, but rather that this *jouissance* is *indefinitely* deferred, because the erotic scenes (and this includes the scenes of intradiegetic orgasm) are either neutralised by a self-conscious humour which deconstructs both text and Sadean/Robbe-Grilletian intertext, or they are 'narrativised' (that is, recounted with the ironic distance of indirect speech) or generalised ('this is what normally occurs') or presented as past or future. I shall illustrate these processes, while attempting to locate the profound sources of Robbe-Grillet's eroticism and the reasons why it constantly slips from the male reader's grasp to become a metapornography, intelligent, self-aware and ultimately self-destroying, and so accessible to male and female reader alike.

There are, broadly speaking, three ways in which *Projet* might be described as pornographic, as we have defined the word: in its voyeuristic description of young women, in its depiction of rape and violent treatment of such women and in its implication of the male reader. Historically, all three are dominant features of the genre.[25] I shall examine these claims in turn.

## Voyeurism

Robbe-Grillet's writing has represented voyeurism either as a prelude to male sexual violence (*Le Voyeur*), as a signifier of jealousy (*La Jalousie*), or simply of male lust (*Glissements progressifs du plaisir*). *Projet*, however, goes further than previous novels in its inclusion of a voyeurism of an explicitly sexual nature. The following three passages are characteristic:

a)
Tout paraît se passer très bien – puisque la pointe menue du téton déjà se dresse (ou bien se raidit, s'allonge, grossit, se tend, se durcit, se gonfle de sève, entre en érection, en turgescence, etc., on a compris) [...] (p. 109)

Everything seems to be going well – since the slender tip of the nipple is already rising (or else stiffening, extending, swelling, hardening, bulging, becoming erect, turgescent, etc., the point is made) [...] (p. 89)

b)
Elle a l'air extrêmement jeune: seize ou dix-sept ans, peut-être. Sa chevelure est d'un blond éclatant; les boucles souples en désordre encadrent son joli visage terrorisé de multiples reflets d'or, fixés en plein vol dans la vive lumière venant de la fenêtre, qui l'éclaire à contre-jour. Ses longues jambes sont découvertes jusqu'en haut des cuisses, la jupe déjà courte s'étant encore retroussée dans la culbute, ce qui met à nu et bien en valeur leurs lignes plaisantes que l'on suit ainsi presque jusqu'au sexe, dont on pourrait même, à la rigueur, distinguer la présence dans le creux d'ombre, sous l'ourlet relevé de l'étoffe. (pp. 27–8)

She looks extremely young: perhaps sixteen or seventeen. Her hair is startlingly blond; the loose curls frame her pretty, terrified face with many golden highlights caught in the bright illumination from the window, against which she is silhouetted. Her long legs are revealed as far as the upper part of the thighs, the already short skirt being raised still farther in her fall, which exposes and emphasises their lovely shape almost up to the pubic region, which can in fact be discerned in the shadows under the raised hem of the material. (p. 18)

c)
[...] au milieu des cheveux blonds répandus en désordre, le visage de poupée aux yeux bleus entrouverts et aux lèvres disjointes a gardé sa couleur de porcelaine rose [...] La bête, qui semble attirée surtout par les blessures des sept poignards enfoncés dans les chairs tendres, en haut des cuisses et au bas du ventre, tout autour de la toison poisseuse, la bête velue est si grosse que, tout en conservant appui sur le sol, elle parvient ainsi à explorer la fragile peau déchirée, depuis l'aine jusqu'aux environs du nombril où la chair nue apparaît à nouveau, encore intacte à cet endroit, dans un large accroc effiloché du léger tissu de lin. C'est là que le rat se décide à mordre et commence à dévorer le ventre. (pp. 142–3)

[...] in the middle of her outspread blond curls, the doll's face with its wide-open blue eyes and parted lips has kept its pink china coloring [...] The animal, which seems particularly attracted by the wounds of the seven daggers thrust into the tender flesh at the top of the thighs and the lower part of the belly, all around the sticky pubic hair, the hairy animal is so large that, while still keeping its hind legs on the floor, it nonetheless manages to explore the fragile lacerated skin from the anus to the area around the navel where the bare flesh reappears, still intact here, in a broad, fraying rip of the thin linen material. It is here that the rat decides to sink its teeth, and begins devouring the belly. (pp. 118–19)

In the sense that they offer sexual descriptions of young women, penned by a male author, if not narrator (the narrators constantly change identity and gender), these passages certainly appear to constitute male voyeurism; and it is, in any event, impossible to police the subjective responses of the reader, whether male or female. However, there is, in each case, a framing of the description which has a distancing effect. This framing is partly intertextual in that we are confronted here with Robbe-Grillet stereotypes (blonde hair, half-open mouths, blue eyes, pretty young girls). If we are familiar with the Robbe-Grillet corpus, we can almost begin to write these very predictable descriptions with the narrator as we read.

Passage (a), which forms part of the description of a sexual encounter between two young criminals in the New York subway, appears at first sight to constitute a voyeuristic objectification of the female body, typical of a certain kind of pornographic realism. The use of language, however, produces a quite different effect from that associated with such material. In Robbe-Grillet's text, the focus veers away from the signified of female arousal to delight in a linguistic play along a metonymic chain of signifiers which simultaneously parodies the graphic language of commercial pornography. The impatient 'on a compris' ('the point is made') reveals a narrator, if not an author, ridiculing both his own fantasies and his verbal diarrhoea.

Over and above their stereotypical character, passages (b) and (c) are given theatrical settings which draw attention to their status as *mise en scène* and which make narrator and reader spectators of a self-conscious fiction:

b) cont.
En dehors de la posture des deux personnages [...], la scène comporte une trace objective de lutte [...] (p. 28)

Aside from the attitude of the two figures [...] the scene includes an objective trace of struggle [...] (p. 18)

We read on to discover that what we are watching is a series of poster stills from a play:

L'affiche bariolée se reproduit à plusieurs dizaines d'exemplaires, collés côte à côte tout au long du couloir de correspondance. Le titre de la pièce est: «Le sang des rêves»

[...] C'est la première fois que je vois cette publicité [...] (pp. 28–9)

The bright-colored poster is reproduced several dozen times, pasted side by side all along the subway passageway. The play's title is *The Blood of Dreams* [...] It is the first time I have seen this advertisement [...] (p. 19)

The use of language marks the scene in (b) as hypothetical rather than real, from the tentative opening – 'peut-être' ('perhaps') – to the conditional tense – 'pourrait' ('might') – of the penultimate line (which the English version renders inaccurately as 'can'), both of which suggest the passage's status as self-conscious fantasy.

Like passage (b), we soon discover that passage (c) is a scene from a play, watched on this occasion by a fascinated Laura:

c) cont.
Pour tenter de se soustraire à ce cauchemar, Laura fouille à tâtons dans l'étroite poche de sa robe, sans pouvoir quitter des yeux le spectacle. (p. 143)

In order to try and escape this nightmare, Laura gropes in the narrow pocket of her dress, without being able to tear her eyes away from the spectacle. (p. 119)

As Laura swallows the pill she was searching for, the scene begins to undergo the first of several modifications, announced by the narrator in explicitly cinematic terms: 'Reprise' ('Retake'). There is, additionally, a similar emphasis on semblance or supposition (as opposed to fact), rendering less direct our experience of the scene. The lines quoted are immediately preceded by the following:

La fin du sacrifice, en effet, ne *doit* dater que de quelques minutes: le corps *semble* encore chaud sous la lumière crue des projecteurs restés allumés (p. 142, my emphasis)

The end of the sacrifice, as a matter of fact, *can* only have occurred a few minutes ago: the body *seems* still warm under the harsh light of the spotlights which are still on. (p. 118)

The self-reflexive nature of the voyeurism in *Projet* is perhaps most graphically demonstrated in a series of abysmal reflections in each of which voyeurism is represented *as representation*. Laura tells the narrator a story in which she discovers a locksmith (alias a character named Ben-Saïd) trying to look at her through the keyhole of the door. Rather than poking his eye out with a knitting needle – an option which she briefly considers – she places the cover of a detective novel she happens to be reading in front of the keyhole. The image is that of a sinister man in a white coat, preparing to inject a female victim with petrol. This scene which is taken from a novel read by Laura and the narrator is repeated several times in the novel we are reading. Thus, fiction is depicted within fiction within fiction, and fictitious imagery is deployed in a story told by a character in a fictitious scene to displace the voyeurism from Robbe-Grillet's novel to Laura's narrative to printed image. In other words, the voyeuristic act is at two removes from our reading experience of it and at three removes from real life. Thus estranged from its narrative origins, it is effectively orphaned in a forest of narratives.

## Rape and Sexual Violence

In *Projet* there are undeniably many passages of a sexual violence committed exclusively against young women and any such passage quoted out of context could easily give a false impression of the functioning of such imagery. However, as with the predominantly voyeuristic (as opposed to violent) passages, what we are being presented with here is *mise en scène* rather than pornographic realism. Moreover, although there is indisputably a brutalisation of the women in *Projet*, sexual activity, whether violent or non-violent, is always implied rather than directly stated and there is none of the vulgarity associated with popular commercial porn:

> Je pénètre dans sa chambre, où je la trouve à demi nue, dressée de terreur sur son lit, bouleversée. Je la calme par les méthodes habituelles. (p. 55)

I walk into her room, where I find her half-naked, crouching in terror on her rumpled bed. I calm her by the usual methods. (p. 42)

Non, s'il vous plaît, ne faites pas ça. (p. 106)

No, oh please, don't do that. (p. 87)

When it is alluded to directly, rape occupies a future rather than a present and therefore immediate space: '"Je vais commencer par vous violer," dit-il' (p. 98) ('"I shall begin by raping you," he says' (p. 79).[26] The promised rape in fact never takes place, at least not in the diegetic space of the narrative.

Elsewhere, the male reader in search of pornographic realism would again almost certainly be dismayed to discover that apparent sado-erotic treatment of young women existed only in his own fantasies, prompted by taped moans and groans.[27] The virtual reader of pornography is, therefore, frequently duped into taking representation for reality. For instance, the detailed description of what appears to be a rape victim, a young girl bound and gagged, her skirt pushed up, her blouse torn, watched over by a white-coated, grey-haired man, who is in the process of preparing a sinister-looking hypodermic needle, turns out to be the illustration on the cover of a book that Laura is reading. The description, which is not, we note, of a rape in progress (of an act of rape), but of its consequences, itself contains strong clues as to the representational nature of the scene: the narrator is at pains, here as in most of the other passages of this kind in the novel, to emphasise that what he is conveying is supposition not fact – 'La fille a dû se débattre' (p. 88) ('The girl must have attempted to evade capture' (p. 71)), 'Elle essaie, dirait-on, de se soulever' (p. 89) ('She is apparently trying to prop herself up' (p. 71)), the man 'a l'air stéréotypé' (p. 89) ('has a stereotyped look' (p. 72)), and so on.

This passage is mirrored by similar *mises en scène* of rape and violence throughout the novel, culminating in the horrific torture of a naked young woman, suspended astride a sharp-toothed saw, which cuts more and more into her breasts, anus and vagina, all of which are 'smeared with sperm'. She is, naturally, surrounded by pools of her own blood. This is doubtless the most revolting scene of sexual violence in the entire novel, but once again, it is represented self-consciously as pornography, viewed through a keyhole by a locksmith/Ben-Saïd. The victim is described as 'la suppliciée de ce soir' ('tonight's torture victim'), as if she were a guest on some perverted TV game show.

In yet another 'rape' scene, the victim is a little girl, whom the narrator slaps repeatedly until she is compliant with his implied wishes:

> J'ai promené longuement le bout des cinq doigts de ma main libre sur sa peau, aux endroits où celle-ci est la plus délicate [...] je l'ai forcée à ouvrir les cuisses, en les écartant d'un de mes genoux, tout en écrasant avec mon poignet le tissu léger ramené en bouchon sur sa gorge, de manière à l'étouffer un peu à chaque pression comme moyen de persuasion supplémentaire. Mais, à partir de ce moment, elle a abandonné toute velléité de résistance et elle a obéi à mes ordres, bien sagement. (p. 171)

> For a long time I stroked her skin with the finger tips on my free hand, in all the places where the flesh is most delicate [...] I forced her to open her thighs, parting them with one of my knees, my wrist stuffing the delicate material down her throat as a gag to choke her a little with each application of pressure, as a means of additional persuasion. But from that moment, she abandoned any impulse of resistance and obeyed my orders without question. (pp. 144–5)

This passage is almost immediately followed by the account of a dream. As always in this text, the transition from apparent reality to apparent dream state is almost imperceptible and the implied distinction is certainly not reliable. *Projet* is a novel about representation, whether in fiction, in the media or advertising – representation of self, of other and specifically of woman as sex object, and it is in this dream section that we encounter one of the text's most striking metaphors of representation in a line of street posters. The narrator feels the need to decipher these posters and to 'attribute meaning to them', but fails to do so because of the darkness. Suddenly, however, the entire display is illuminated by street lamps and he discovers that there is nothing unusual about the poster ads which are the kind found more or less anywhere. Nevertheless, his attention is drawn to one particular ad, representing a young woman, blindfolded and her mouth half open:

> [...] seul détail remarquable (mais non pas exceptionnel) de cet exemplaire-ci: un graffiti géant [...] qui figure un sexe masculin de trois mètres de haut, dressé verticalement jusqu'aux lèvres disjointes. (p. 173)

> [...] the only remarkable (but not exceptional) detail of this particular one: a giant graffito [...] representing a male organ about ten feet high, raised vertically to the parted lips. (p. 146)

The graffiti artist had added to the 'demain...' ('tomorrow...') of the ad's caption the five words 'la hache et le bûcher!' ('the axe and the stake!'). We are not told what product the poster aims to sell, although the narrator tells us what other posters in the display are advertising – an electric iron, an apéritif, a clothing shop. Now this image clearly constitutes a *mise en abyme* of the reader's interaction with the text as well as of the dominant imagery of Robbe-Grillet's texts as a whole. The narrator tries to make sense of what he sees/reads, but experiences difficulty in putting the details together into a coherent whole – 'les replacer dans un ensemble' (p. 172). When the street lamps come on, he is then able to see the display properly, but only by stepping back from it, just as the reader or spectator of any Robbe-Grillet text must do to experience it as a unified construct. The image of the young woman is a Robbe-Grillet stereotype of female submission and already carries sexual connotations, even without the inclusion of the male penis thrusting itself into her mouth, forcing an act of fellatio. The image is thus heavily overdetermined by layer upon layer of representation: the graffiti artist's attempt to eroticise seems merely to make explicit what was already implicit in the poster image – just as Robbe-Grillet's text makes explicit the insidious eroticism of all media representations of women. The Robbe-Grillet stereotype (young woman, open mouth, blindfold) of the captive feminine refers ironically to itself and all other such images in his fiction. The graffiti is painted 'with a single stroke of an airbrush', referring us to the very act of writing this 'male book' with a transparently phallic implement. The added caption places us directly in the context of witch-burning – the sado-erotic destruction of the feminine by fire is a recurrent and dominant thematic in the novel. Like its Lacanian counterpart, the graffiti phallus is thus signifier of a signifier, to be read as a representation of a representation, an ironic image of that which is already imaged – a signified, the eroticism of which is so mediated by its signifiers as to be completely lost.

In spite of the author's teasing remarks about the cathartic exorcism of the 'monsters' lurking in his erotic imagination,[28] this representational character shared by all the scenes of rape and violence against women does, in my view, serve parodic purposes and, as already indicated, the targets of this parody include modern popular porn as well as the Sadean tradition and Robbe-Grillet himself.

The Sadean echoes are manifold, as Susan Suleiman has pointed out.[29] Suleiman, however, does not see these elements as parodic or deconstructive:

> Viewed in the light of the Sadean intertext, *Projet* takes on a curiously non-subversive aspect. Far from deconstructing male fantasies of omnipotence and total control over passive female bodies, *Projet* repeats them with astonishing fidelity.[30]

Yet, Suleiman provides little textual evidence for this claim. On the contrary, it seems to me, the Sadean allusions are transparently tongue-in-cheek. Dr Morgan, the hypodermic-wielding medic of the book illustration, defends crime as revolutionary, recalling the equally excessive and perhaps equally ironic declarations of the Sadean text on these matters:[31]

> 'Le crime est indispensable à la révolution,' récite le docteur. 'Le viol, l'assassinat, l'incendie sont les trois actes métaphoriques qui libéreront les nègres, les prolétaires en loques et les travailleurs intellectuels de leur esclavage, en même temps que la bourgeoisie de ses complexes sexuels.' (p. 153)

'Crime is indispensable to the revolution,' the doctor recites. 'Rape, murder, arson are the three metaphoric acts which will free the blacks, the impoverished proletariat, and the intellectual workers from their slavery, and at the same time the bourgeoisie from its sexual complexes.' (p. 128)

The juxtaposition here of a sexual and a political liberation is surely a sarcastic reference to both Wilhelm Reich and Herbert Marcuse. Elsewhere, there are the fantasised 'viols collectifs offerts à tous les passants sur des tréteaux dressés aux carrefours' (p. 202) ('collective rapes available to all passers-by on trestles set up at intersections' (p. 172)) – an ironic echo of Sade's call for universal prostitution ('maisons du peuple') – the outrageously cartoon-like dangling of a woman on the end of a rope thrown on to the track behind an underground train (p. 133), the fantastic account of the crimes of murder and rape committed by the 'Vampire du Métropolitain' ('Vampire of the Underground') against twelve young girls – a mocking reference, perhaps, either to the mystical belief in the power of certain numbers (the figure eight in *Le Voyeur* is another example of this) or to the circular completeness of the number twelve.[32] So little of their bodies remain that the authorities are unable to assess the extent of the injuries. Fortunately, the criminal himself writes the official report! This self-consciously exaggerated Sadean cameo also contains satirical references to the rapacious world of modern international finance, to the corruption of local politics, even the often unpredictable and occasionally perverse world of academe to which the author himself belongs!

The Sadean libertine's preoccupation with food as well as sex finds an echo in two humorous details. The rapist/torturer of the book that the narrator is reading requires his victim to serve ham and eggs during his break, and Laura's interrogator similarly talks of sending her to fetch him 'un sandwich au bœuf cru et une limonade à la cocaine' (p. 155) 'a rare roast-beef sandwich and a cocaine cocktail' (p. 130)!

These intertextual parodies do not exclude Robbe-Grillet's own intertext: we recognise names familiar from the Robbe-Grillet *œuvre* (Frank, Müller, Boris, Edouard Manneret, etc., including a homonymic play on the name of the author himself in the description of the dress that JR, the young métro prostitute, scorches with an iron as a 'robe grillée' (p. 82) or 'grilled dress'), detective-novel stereotypes like the doctor-criminal of *Les Gommes*, the figure of eight motif of *Le Voyeur* (p. 144), the labyrinthine corridors of *Dans le labyrinthe*, La Villa Bleue in the Hong Kong of *La Maison de rendez-vous* (p. 33) and all the familiar Robbe-Grillet motifs of broken glass, women's high-heeled shoes, blind man's buff, etc. (pp. 177–8). And in the mock interrogation of JR, the question 'A quoi rêvent les jeunes filles?' ('What do young girls dream about?') elicits the only logical answer in a Robbe-Grillet context, 'Au couteau ... au sang!' (p. 71) ('Knives ... and blood!' (p. 56)).

## Implication of the Male Reader

We have seen that, for Suleiman, *Projet* is a male book and by that she presumably means written by a heterosexual male with sado-erotic fantasies for an exclusively male target reader. Now, I have argued above that, although the text's obsessions with the bodies of young women may provide *prima facie* evidence that this is so, a closer look suggests that these elements are open to a more complex reading.

Looking in a general way at the narrators and narratees of the text, Suleiman forces the conclusion that, despite the presence of a number of female narrators (JR, Laura), 'the female narrative voice soon "slides" into that of the chief narrator (the one who begins and ends the book), and he does not relinquish control from then on'.[33] For Suleiman, of course, the dominance of male narrators means collusion with male readers in the enjoyment of 'specifically masculine' fantasies.[34] The fantasies may well be masculine in nature, but there is, as I have tried to show, a strong ludic dimension in *Projet* which undermines their eroticisation and which, as Emma Kafalenos argues in her insightful essay on the novel,

offers a consecrated space in which [the reader] can enjoy a freedom that can be experienced nowhere else. [...] the ludic text, with the nearly infinite possibilities it offers, requires more than passive *perception* from its reader. And the active *conception* of the work that it demands, offers the reader the chance to experience the only real freedom any of us can know.[35]

Such a freedom must be open to readers of any gender or sexual orientation. Furthermore, there is a sustained attempt in the text itself to explode the notion of a male-orientated fiction as the narrator is closely questioned by a critical and sceptical female narratee towards the end of the novel (pp. 188–9). This dialogue between narrator and narratee has, of course, been going on intermittently since the beginning of the narrative, undermining any attempt by narrator, narratee or reader to view its contents in terms of an *effet de réel* ('reality effect').

*Projet* is indisputably a book written by a man, but it is about the personal investment of any author in what (s)he writes and the processes of writing and reading themselves as much as it is about fantasies, which are, in any case, hardly representative of heterosexual male desire. As such, the novel is accessible to anyone, male or female, with an interest in the intimate and problematic relationship between author and work.

## Conclusion

We have seen that the identity not only of characters, narrators and scenes in *Projet* but also of the text itself and of its relationship with the implied reader slides ambiguously between a number of different positions: from a potentially pornographic account of authorial fantasy to a subversive parody of pornographic stereotype to a ludic self-irony which invites the reader to assist the author in deconstructing his own writing project.

It is, I have argued, the slippages of the text which help to make it accessible to the feminist as well as to the female reader. These slippages of meaning, many of which depend on the distancing devices which I have shown above to operate against an erotic response, may also be seen, in a psychoanalytic perspective, as displacement activity. The slippages of textual meaning, in other words, themselves act as signifiers, standing in for (or more accurately, deflecting attention away from) slippages of *sexual* identity. Thus, form and content in fact become inseparable. The ludic character of Robbe-Grillet's fantasies of sexual violence hide sexual anxieties located at an unconscious level. Humour in particular distances the reader, but also the writing subject from an anxiety which the feminine always generates, an anxiety associated with an inability to grasp and keep hold of the object of desire. In addition to their *textual* and *intertextual* dimensions, the 'glissements' of Robbe-Grillet's writing also function on an *intersubjective* level. This intersubjectivity, which manifests itself superficially in the slippages of identity between characters and narrators, has its deeper roots in an unconscious authorial presence in the text which slides between positions of gender and sexuality.

The author has claimed to identify more with his female than with his male characters. In *Glissements progressifs du plaisir*, which is based on Michelet's *La Sorcière* (*The Witch*), this is not hard to believe, as the young and vulnerable Alice is seen to defeat the three representatives of male power in our society (priest, policeman and judge), and here the narrative perspective is mostly hers. This claim seems less easy to accept in the case of *Projet*, in which the narrative voice (and therefore, perspective) is predominantly male, as Suleiman has shown. At least, this is so if identification is seen as a wholly conscious process. At unconscious levels, however, there is, perhaps, evidence in the Robbe-Grillet text of a bisexual focus in the obsessive repetition of fetishistic motifs – a broken bottle or wine glass, the nape of a young woman's neck, a woman's shoe, the doll-like characteristics of his female victims – fetishes representing, for Freud, an attempt to restore the castrated penis to the woman.

This authorial identification with the feminine, taken together with the need to control it by force,[36] which manifests itself both in the rigorously planned textual structures and in the sadism of the imagery (the image of the *captive* woman dominates much of Robbe-Grillet's work) appear as symptoms of an ambivalence towards the feminine, which, Suleiman suggests, is simultaneously an ambivalence towards the maternal.

Now, the avoidance of conventional identity labels, which is another characteristic of this author's work, may be associated, at an unconscious level, with a rejection of the fixity of the Lacanian Symbolic and with a desire to return to the pre-oedipal and undifferentiated relationship with the mother. We recall that, for Jacques Lacan, the very nature of desire is a constant slippery quest along an endless chain of signifiers for an object never to be recovered – the lost object of the mother's body. In a Lacanian optic, therefore, the 'glissements' of Robbe-Grillet's writing as a whole, the slippages of identity that they portray and, above all, the ambivalence towards the feminine-maternal which, I would agree with Suleiman, underlies the sado-eroticism, might be associated at deeper levels with this slippage of desire along the linguistic chain and so with the expression of an anxiety in relation to an unattainable object. This object, represented in his texts by impossible images of female perfection, has nevertheless to be controlled and ultimately destroyed, along with the fears of separation and loss which it embodies. A love/hate relationship with the feminine, expressed as it is in the extreme form of a sado-eroticism which is rendered similarly ambivalent by its ludic presentation, may, in part at least, be the pathological manifestation of an anguish generated by loss of the maternal object – anguish which both men and women may recognise. In this sense, one might say that Alain Robbe-Grillet's erotic fantasies speak unconsciously to us all.

# 8

# Homotextuality:
# Tony Duvert's *Récidive*

Born in 1945, Tony Duvert is the author of a dozen works of fiction, all of them homoerotic, and of two polemical essays. Although Duvert has never achieved the public acclaim of a Duras or the notoriety of an Arsan, the undoubted literary merit of much of his writing has not gone entirely unrecognised: his fifth novel, *Paysage de fantaisie*, won the Prix Médicis, a literary prize that rewards innovation, in 1973. Duvert now lives in seclusion in a small, provincial French town and has had no direct contact with his publisher, Éditions de Minuit, for many years. His last published work, *Abécédaire malveillant*, dates from 1989. Most of his writing, however, covers a ten-year period from the late 1960s to the late 1970s.

Duvert follows in a long tradition of homosexual writing in France, the twentieth century being particularly rich in this kind of literature. From Marcel Proust to André Gide, from Jean Cocteau to Jean Genet, homosexual themes run through the work of some of the century's major French authors. In the context of such an 'embarras du choix', it is therefore necessary to justify devoting the only chapter of this book that specifically deals with homosexuality to Tony Duvert. There are four main reasons for choosing Duvert against the others (given the need, within the restricted scope of the book, to make a choice at all).

Firstly, Duvert was one of a new wave of aggressively homosexual writers that emerged during the 1960s, aiming to depict homosexuality free of guilt for the first time. Duvert's positive portrayal of homosexual themes was in part a reaction to the largely negative portrayal of the homosexual in previous literature, for example, as 'an agent for the dissolution of society in Proust, an agent of death in Cocteau, a symbol of all that is conventionally evil in Genet',[1] and also a reaction to anti-gay legislation of the day: while it is certainly true that the 1960s saw a gradual relaxation of sexual mores in France, this was also a period in which legal sanctions were introduced against homosexuality for the first time.[2] Moreover, there was still a good deal of intolerance in the populus at large, especially outside sophisticated intellectual Parisian society, in the provinces, which provide the setting for much of his fiction.[3] Homosexuality had remained a clandestine activity throughout the 1950s and 1960s. Even among the Parisian intelligentsia, attitudes were slow to change: neither Roland Barthes nor Michel Foucault ever 'came out'.[4]

Secondly, Duvert stands at a crossroads in the literary representation of homosexuality, for, in spite of his aggressively positive approach to homosexual issues, the effect of Duvert's portrayal of homosexuality as furtive and sordid behaviour is unavoidably negative. Furthermore, there are pederastic/paedophilic elements in Duvert which demand attention from the point of view of a sexual politics, as does the sexual violence that runs throughout his work. His writing is artistically interesting precisely because its representation of homosexual desire is conflictual and, on a political level, its pederastic themes seem especially relevant to current concerns about paedophilia.

Thirdly, in past literature, homosexuality had largely been depicted in stereotypical terms, with homosexuals portrayed as drag queens or at the very least as effete or effeminate.[5] Undoubtedly the most positive aspect of Duvert's writing, from a political viewpoint, is his dismantling of such stereotypes and his representation of homosexuality as a fluid rather than a fixed position. In *Récidive*, Duvert's first novel, which I shall be focusing upon in this chapter, it is the *process of construction* of homosexual identity that is foregrounded, undermining attempts to view homosexuality as a fixed essence, which is why *Récidive* might be termed a 'homotextuality', since this is the term that has been used to stress the mobile nature of a homosexual identity which is constantly being constructed and deconstructed in changing social contexts.[6]

The representation of homosexuality in Duvert as fluid and resisting fixed categorisation is in itself a sufficient reason to reread him in the 1990s, given the recent emphasis of Queer

Theory on the destabilisation of identity and sexual and gender hierarchies.[7]

Fourthly, though much of Duvert's writing is now over 20, and *Récidive*, over 30 years old, its privileging of circularity, repetition and fragmentation puts it very much in tune with both modern gay theory in particular and what Jean-François Lyotard called 'the postmodern condition' in general.[8]

My presentation of Duvert will not be wholly uncritical: *Récidive* has considerable literary merit, but it does not entirely project the positive image of homosexuality that both Christopher Robinson and the author himself claim for his work.

## *Récidive*: Publication and Reception

The original version of *Récidive* appeared in 1967 and it was then rewritten in a much shorter version in 1976.[9] Before moving to a close reading of the text, I should briefly like to consider the novel's initial reception in the light of its highly controversial, explicitly pederastic themes.

Initial sales of the novel were modest, the first edition selling no more than 2000 copies. The second edition fared a little better, though at no time has the novel achieved anything like bestseller status.[10] Given the lack of public interest in the novel, it is hardly surprising that there has been very little critical interest.[11] Duvert's reclusiveness doubtless contributed to *Récidive*'s lack of impact;[12] his first novel, in fact, passed relatively unnoticed. Jérôme Lindon, Duvert's editor, recalls only one review by Madeleine Chapsal in *L'Express*. Even Jean-Jacques Pauvert curiously omits *Récidive* from his recent anthology of erotic writing in this century.[13]

This lack of critical and public attention perhaps helps to explain why *Récidive* was not the object of any direct attempt to censor. In spite of the radically changing attitudes to sex in general and to erotic fiction in particular which characterised the period,[14] the novel might well have attracted the attentions of the *Brigade des mœurs*, if there had been more critical interest.[15] Whilst the heterosexual excesses of *Emmanuelle*, published in the same year as *Récidive*, sold copies in their thousands and even attracted critical plaudits, the French establishment was no more ready for the open expression of homosexuality and paedophilia in the fictions of Duvert than in those of Sade, Pierre Guyotat or Bernard Noël.[16] Though the social and political upheavals of 1968 were just around the corner, the France in which *Récidive* was first published was still Gaullist, a France choked by political and literary censorship and repression.

Admittedly, this absence of public and critical response to the novel has to be placed in the wider context of the critical marginalisation of homosexual writing in France in general.[17] Yet, this explanation is not wholly satisfactory. After all, other novels by Duvert have not been so conspicuously neglected by the critics. One is bound to wonder, for example, why Robinson, though according Duvert an important place in his study of male and female homosexuality in twentieth-century French literature, does not even mention *Récidive*, which has the distinction of being both the author's first published work and the only work which he considered important enough to rewrite. Could it be that, in its unapologetic promotion of pederasty and of a sexual violence which is at times non-consensual on the one hand and its clear allegiance to a style of writing (the *nouveau roman*) which completely evacuates the social referent on the other, this is a text that sits uneasily between polemic and fiction, between sexuality and textuality, between the committed socio-political agenda of an author of the 1960s and the equally earnest sense of duty of a critic of the 1990s anxious to project positive images of homosexuality?

Recent critical approaches to gay fiction have tended to emphasise the 'mutual inextricability of textuality and sexuality'.[18] Robinson, for instance, ends his book by insisting that gay body and gay text are one, that gay readers look for life and not merely signs within the pages of gay literature: 'They happily collude with the texts they read in the "experience" of gay desire, deciphering the literary systems as a translation of lived or liveable experience.' At the same time, he continues, this experience is an *aesthetic* one, 'A set of responses to a particular literary discourse.'[19]

In thus making out a special case for homosexual fiction, in re-establishing a circle of identification and influence between text and reader, Robinson and others recreate a tension between the mimetic and the purely aesthetic functions of the text, which has serious political implications in the case of all representations of sexual abuse and violence. I have argued in other chapters of this book that such representations are textual and not real and, as such, are contained within an erotic imagination which not only has every right to exist but probably needs to do so for the sake of the physical and mental health of us all. Like many other gay writers of the contemporary period, who do write scenes of sexual violence, Tony Duvert is problematic, therefore, in wanting to bring the textual and the real closer together. In what follows I should like to focus on both the political and the artistic dimensions of *Récidive* or on what we might term in shorthand the 'sexuality' and the 'textuality'. Notwithstanding their 'inextricability', I shall attempt to deal with them separately, but first we need to consider the novel's overall shape and structure.

## Themes and Forms

*Récidive* embarks us on a journey which takes on the character of a quest for sexual experience or, more profoundly, for sexual identity, in a dimly remembered past, or perhaps in the virtual realm of fantasy, as a shadowy male narrator struggles to reconstruct his adolescent sexual experiences. Instead of a conventional, linear plot, the novel consists of a series of scenes. From scene to scene, but also sometimes within scenes, the narrative voice migrates from first person to third person, from a 15-year-old boy who appears to have run away from home in search of sexual adventure, to what may or may not be an older writing persona and, on occasions, to some of a number of passing lovers or objects of desire, who include a forester in a jeep, a young sailor whom he first meets in a station waiting room and eventually follows to a hotel bedroom, a lonely old man, living in a manor house, a handsome 17-year-old, a cute young blond boy, a 15-year-old builder's apprentice with tight jeans and a bulging crotch, a group of young lads out playing by a river. The perspective therefore circulates with the narrative voice between homosexual adolescent and adult pederast, between boy and man.

Circularity, in fact, underpins all the novel's thematic and structural levels. The word 'Récidive' comes from the medieval

Latin, 'recidivus', meaning 'that which returns'. The modern French word has three basic meanings: 1. 'Recurrence of an illness (especially an infectious illness) following a recovery, due to a new infection by the same germs'; 2. 'The act of committing a new offence after conviction for a previous offence; condition of a person who has committed a new crime or a new misdemeanour'; 3. 'The act of relapsing into the same fault, the same error'.[20] Duvert's title, therefore, broadly covers two semantic fields: repetition and circularity on the one hand and criminality on the other. Both of these *isotopies* can be seen to underpin the representation of (homo)sexuality in the novel. The circularity, dislocation and fracture of the novel's narrative form directly mirror its presentation of homosexual identity as constantly self-questioning, constructed from fragments of memory and fantasy, and both criminalised by and alienated from the surrounding society. Duvert's text thus harmoniously combines the disharmonies of form and content.[21] Not only do the scenes of the narrative repeat themselves as the narrative voices return again and again to the same locales (railway station waiting room, woods, seedy hotel bedroom, etc.),[22] but thematically, too, there is repetition – in the obsessive preoccupation with homosexual stereotypes (sailor boy, blond, blue-eyed cherub), in the endless circularity of desire. Memories are filtered through the subject's (and the virtual reader's ) fantasies to produce a 'narrative on the loose' in which the time perspective constantly oscillates between past, present and future.

In addition to *isotopies* of circularity and repetition, the word 'Récidive' also generates an *isotopie* of criminality which forms another kind of circle, this time between the textual and the real. Like all of Duvert's fiction, the novel represents 'pédérastie', the literal meaning of which is sexual relations between adult males and pubescent or pre-pubescent boys. It is true that 'pédéraste' and 'homosexuel' have been used more or less interchangeably in the French language, although the former term carries more pejorative connotations.[23]

Tony Duvert's reputation derives principally from his defence of pederasty and, indeed, Duvert is a self-proclaimed 'pédhomophile' ('paedhomophile'), a term he invented for himself in *L'Enfant au masculin*, the second of his two polemical essays.[24] As far as Duvert's distinction between paedophiles and pederasts is concerned, those who favour pre-pubescent boys are the former, while those attracted by post-pubescent boys belong to the latter category. For him, all other distinctions are merely 'effects of the penal code'.[25]

All of the sexual behaviour depicted in *Récidive* would have been criminal in 1967, when the novel first appeared: the age of consent for homosexuals in France had been 21 since 1942 (compared with 15 for heterosexuals since 1945). Moreover, in 1960, an amendment to existing law had made homosexuality one of a list of 'plagues' from which children must be protected.[26] In 1974, two years before the second, revised edition of *Récidive* came out, the general age of majority was reduced to 18, still three years above the age of consent for heterosexuals. The 15-year-old boy whose sexual adventures dominate the narrative of the novel would have been permitted by the laws of 1967 or 1974 to have sex with girls or women, but his homosexual activities remained criminal acts, and his older partners pederasts, for readers of either version.[27]

Admittedly, there is a clear case here of discrimination against homosexuals, given the disparity between the homosexual and heterosexual ages of consent. One might also argue that in either case this age is culturally and temporally relative and not necessarily indicative of biological, or even emotional maturity. As Duvert insists himself, 'Le dépeçage juridique de l'homosexualité [...] ne correspond à aucun clivage des sexualités réelles' ('the legal categories of homosexuality [...] in no way correspond to real sexual divisions').[28] On both grounds, novelistic representations of sex between an adult male and a 15-year-old boy are neither pederastic nor paedophilic in the strict sense. All the same, illegality and, from a conventional point of view, immorality, hang disturbingly over the writing like ghosts at the feast.

Moreover, Duvert's representation of pederastic acts is far more direct and explicit than anything that had been written before and would have been novel in the 1960s, even for French readers.[29] A matter-of-fact, prosaic style goes some way to creating the impression that these activities are quite ordinary, even day-to-day, but overall, as the novel's title implies, we feel drawn again and again into a world of transgressive activity. In this respect, one could argue that Duvert's portrait of the homosexual and especially of the pederast, as isolated by his community and driven to seek sexual satisfaction in secret, is just as negative as that of many previous gay French writers (notably Jean Genet).

Is Duvert's fiction, then, guilty of promoting activity that is both criminal and ethically and morally reprehensible or is it a fiction bearing no direct relation to reality and so unbound by social or political responsibilities? In answer to this question, let us first consider those aspects of the novel which reinforce its status as a text of fiction or a 'homotextuality' and which therefore suggest the constructedness of homosexuality in the real, before turning to examine its problematic representations of promiscuous and violent sex involving adolescents and children.

## Discontinuity

*Récidive* assaults the expectations of the reader accustomed to more traditional narratives. A story told by voyeurs rather than by a single voyeur, it presents the plural, shifting and therefore limited viewpoint of the *nouveau roman* rather than the all-seeing perspective of an omniscient Balzacian narrator: there are uncertainties and contradictions throughout. Moreover, the novel is constructed in a largely episodic, even fragmentary manner: the narrative jumps arbitrarily from one scene to another and there are even unfinished paragraphs and sentences. The most glaring examples of the text's self-mutilation are probably the abrupt ending of sections and even chapters in mid-sentence.

There are some passages in which punctuation is self-consciously absent, others in which the syntax breaks down completely. The lack of punctuation frequently suggests the incoherent and breathless delivery of a child and, even though it is not always clear in these cases that the narrative voice *is* that of a child, the child's perspective manufactured in this way displaces narrative and thereby moral responsibility. The fragmentation of syntactic structures also suggests a child's language, serving to confuse fantasy and reality in a 'stream of consciousness' flow.

Time, in *Récidive*, is not represented in a chronological or linear manner either, but serves an internal, textual logic, dictated by the unreliability of memory, the unsatisfactory nature of fantasy and, above all, by the movement of desire. The central role played by desire in the novel is beautifully evoked by the recurrent images of the railway station waiting room, a furtive meeting place for those whose age and sexuality put them outside the law, and of the ever-moving train:

> Et, quand on va de train en train et de gare en gare à la rencontre de quelque chose, qui n'est plus là depuis longtemps, qui est peut-être ailleurs, plus tard, ou qui était ici, à la minute précédente, ou qui n'existe pas, on ne voit plus rien, on oublie ce qu'on voulait, sinon un train et un autre, on vit dans un couloir. (pp. 77–8)

> And when you go from train to train and from station to station in search of something which disappeared long ago, which is perhaps somewhere else, some time later, or which was here, just a minute ago, or which doesn't exist, you don't see anything any more, you forget what you were looking for, unless it's one train or another, you live your life in a corridor.

Elsewhere, the use of future and conditional tenses, alongside the more dominant past, suggests a need to escape linear time and emphasises the role of fantasy and desire in the construction of sexual scenarios.

Such changes in time and space construct a world which is virtual, not real, a world of desire rather than fulfilment, in which the subject's identity drifts between the insecurities and anxieties of adolescent desires and a predatory adult sexuality, between the perspective of a 15-year-old boy and those of his older lovers. It is a highly subjective perspective, hedged around by the admission of its own limitations, often doubtful, contradictory, playing on the reader's own needs to fantasise and underlining the discontinuous nature of homosexual identity.[30]

This privileging of the plural and the fragmented undermines the binary structures of heterosexuality and its exclusivity,[31] and it also serves in *Récidive* to blur the boundaries between adolescence and adulthood, aiding and abetting the evasion of responsibility.[32] Such discontinuity of form may not, in fact, strike the 1990s' reader as especially unusual. After all, as Michael Worton points out, 'It is now virtually axiomatic that the text is not only ambiguous, but actively polysemic and enticingly protean.'[33] In 1967, however, Roland Barthes had not yet published *S/Z*[34] and the fragmentation of subjectivity was still a relatively novel feature of fiction writing.[35]

## Self-referentiality

There are strong elements of a self-referentiality in *Récidive*, which extends to the interaction between the reader and the text. We are reminded on more than one occasion that we are reading fiction, implying that the fantasies which it contains can therefore not be thought criminal. Such passages often exhibit a dry humour that also offsets the novel's harsher elements. The sailor, declares the narrator with relief, robbed me but didn't take my watch: 'Les précisions horaires ont trop d'importance dans mon récit.' (p. 89) ('Precise details of time are too important in my narrative.') There are direct references to the architecture of the novel – 'Je me contenterai d'utiliser les rochers d'un chapitre antérieur' (p. 93) ('I shall make do with using the rocks of a previous chapter'), 'Oui. Voilà des faits plausibles, enchaînés correctement' (p. 116) ('Yes. These are plausible facts, appropriately linked') – and to the very process of writing – 'Je suis en train de raconter un suicide' (p. 116) ('I'm in the process of relating a suicide').

A particularly novel feature of this textual self-referentiality in *Récidive* is the ironic *mise en scène* of the reader's active role in the construction of the text. The narrator claims that he feels the need to justify the invention of a character who does not conform to the pederast's ideal object of desire, that is, a blond, blue-eyed 13- or 14-year-old, with pale skin, no glasses or spots, a cute little bottom and a big penis. The reader, explicitly positioned as pederastic, is invited to compensate for the omission by exercising his own imagination:

> Mais je sais, pédérastes qui me lisez, que vous avez aimé l'un d'eux. Cherchez donc dans vos souvenirs, vos photogra-

phies, vos personnages de roman, quelque joli gamin qui
vous ait fait bander, ou pleurer. Le voyez-vous? Retrouvez
votre blondinet: qui n'en a pas? [...] Voyez ses lèvres, que
votre bouche aurait su mordre [...] (pp. 74–5)

But I know that you pederasts who are reading this have
loved one of them. So search your memories, your
photographs, among your novel characters, for some pretty
boy who gave you a hard-on, or who made you cry. Can you
see him? Find your little blond boy: who hasn't got one? [...]
Look at his lips that your mouth could have bitten [...]

Having thus excited the reader's private fantasies, however, the
narrator mockingly dashes any hopes he might have nurtured
that the text was about to satisfy them:

Enfin n'y pensez plus. Car ces fadeurs troublent l'ordre
public, ces mièvreries sont criminelles, ces gentillesses vous
mèneraient en cour d'assises – et surtout cela m'ennuie de
leur consacrer ce chapitre. (p. 75)

Don't think about them any more. For these sick tastes
disturb public order, these delicate matters are criminal,
these attentions could land you in court – and anyway, I find
it boring to devote this chapter to them.

The text thus ironises the potential criminality of the desires
it may conjure up whilst projecting any responsibility for
them upon the irresponsible reader. At the same time, Duvert
acknowledges the tradition of reader seduction which has
helped define the erotic genre since the seventeenth century,
a tradition which includes the portrayal within the text itself
of a reader substitute, a voyeur whose job it is to teach the
reader how to respond.[36] Thus, Duvert creates a mock
complicity between reader and narrator. Later in the text, for
instance, the narrator humours the reader with a brief portrait
of his stereotyped pin-up, the 'little blond boy', in the most
clichéd of romantic settings. This time, the reader appears at
first to have achieved equal status with the narrator,
accompanying him into the narrative, taking an active part in
it as a homosexual with strong paedophilic tendencies:

Le gamin se sera promené avec moi, en forêt, un jour d'été, il y aura eu un ruisseau [...] Votre héros avait emporté un roman policier. Il ne parle guère, déçu d'être avec moi, avec vous qui l'importunez.

Couché à plat ventre, torse nu, il s'étire tout au long de la pierre et il lit. Vous et moi, nous regardons son profil sage [...] Sa main droite lance un doigt sur son avant-bras gauche et le caresse mécaniquement. Nous nous fascinons à cette caresse: notre blondinet s'aime devant nous.

Yeux fermés, nous nous étendons près de lui pour chauffer nos dos contre le rocher; [...] nous effleurons ses côtes soyeuses [...] (pp. 93–4)‧

The boy will have gone for a walk with me in the forest, on a summer's day, there'll have been a stream [...] Your hero had brought a detective novel with him. He hardly speaks, disappointed to be with me, with you pestering him.

Lying on his tummy, with his shirt off, he stretches himself out on the rock and reads. You and I observe his chaste appearance [...] He strokes his left forearm absent-mindedly with a finger of his right hand. We watch him do this with fascination: our little blond boy is making love to himself in front of us.

With our eyes closed, we lie down next to him to warm our backs against the rock; [...] we gently caress his silken body [...]

The boy, however, does not take kindly to being propositioned in this manner and leaves – cue for the now smug narrator to reassert his superiority over the reader: 'Ce n'était pas le moment de nous intéresser à lui, je vous avais prévenu' (p. 94) ('I warned you that it wasn't the right time to pay him attention'). The link back into the 'sailor' storyline, favoured by the narrator, is nothing short of brilliant, playing as it does on the boundary between the inside and the outside of the narrative. The disappointed reader is teased and coaxed back into a creative partnership with the narrator which has, nevertheless, proved far from equal : 'Non cette tête. Le marin, comment il s'appelle?' (p. 94) ('Oh, what a face you're pulling! What's the sailor's name?') The narrator immediately turns from the truculent reader to address the sailor directly –

'Comment tu t'appelles?' ('What's your name?') – and the *récit* continues with the former firmly in control.

Whether ironic or not in character, such self-referential interludes as these might be considered a form of *textual* narcissism, paralleling the *sexual* narcissism which, in a Freudian perspective, underlies homosexual desire[37] – a further sense in which sexuality and textuality can be said to mesh together in Duvert's well-crafted novel.

## Intertextuality

This meshing of the sexual and the textual can also be found in *Récidive*'s numerous intertextual echoes, which place it on the avant-garde side of the French novelistic tradition and give it a ludic character, generally associated with the 'New Novels' of Alain Robbe-Grillet, Raymond Queneau, Marguerite Duras, Robert Pinget and other writers of the genre. Unorthodox handling of syntax and punctuation recalls Marguerite Duras, whilst the playful orthography of 'causons zinpeu' (p. 57) ('let's chat a little'), 'pêchons lézam' (p. 57) ('let's fish for souls'), 'oussadon pourquidon' (p. 58) ('where then? who for, then?') and 'sitorévu' (p. 136) ('if only you'd seen'), whereby written language is distorted to humorous effect to give a phonetic transcription of slangy, spoken expressions – is clearly a homage to Raymond Queneau.

Above all, *Récidive* owes a large debt to Alain Robbe-Grillet, whose novels, in both its sexual and its textual transgressions, especially the sadomasochistic elements, it closely resembles. Some scenes may even be read as a parody of Robbe-Grillet's preoccupation with geometric description, of his 'chosiste' style or of his experimentation with structure and page layout.[38]

There are echoes, too, of more traditional literature. For example, *Le Grand Meaulnes*, the modern French novel of adolescent desire in the Romantic tradition, gets a tongue-in-cheek mention:

> alors il est parti, parce qu'il veut trouver ce qu'on trouve
> toujours en forêt quand on a quinze ans, lisez des romans
> > un château
> > avec un parc [...] (pp. 49–50)

> so he left, because he wants to find what you always find in
> a forest when you're fifteen, just read novels
>     a castle
>     with grounds [...]

Unlike Meaulnes, it is a beautiful young boy, not a girl, that
the narrator fantasises about meeting, and the language is far
more explicit than in Alain Fournier's novel: 'Ils seraient
soudain face à face, son sexe durcirait dans sa culotte déchirée'
(p. 50) ('Suddenly they would come face to face, and his penis
would harden inside his torn pants').

This ironic intertextuality injects humour into an otherwise
rather sombre narrative and, at the same time, could be
argued to function, precisely as it does in Robbe-Grillet, to
underline the novel's status *as text* in a universe of texts and
not as a reality, for which the author/narrator must be held
morally responsible.[39] For Michael Worton, intertextuality
in gay fiction generally decentres the text and the reader,
saturating the text 'with so many intertextual signals that no
single position can be adopted by "his" reader',[40] and so
serves a similar function to that of the plurality of narrative
voices in *Récidive*.

Duvert's first novel is, in so many respects, such a good
example of the New Novel's ludic formal experimentalism and
self-conscious literariness that at times it reads like a homage
to the genre's main proponents. However, unlike the fiction
of Alain Robbe-Grillet or Robert Pinget, Duvert's novel contains
passages of a startling psychological and social realism in
which sexual violence predominates.

In fact, Tony Duvert is a writer with a social and political
mission much more reminiscent of the *littérature engagée* of a
Sartre or a Camus than of the *nouveau roman*, to the extent that
his fiction might be seen as an extension of his polemical
essays, *Le Bon sexe illustré* (1974), a fierce attack on conventional
sex education material, and *L'Enfant au masculin* (1980), which
is more directly concerned with the defence of adolescent
homosexuality. Both works promote sexual freedom, regardless
of age or inclination, a freedom which, for Duvert, is closely
linked to social liberation. Parents and what Duvert calls
'heterocracy' impose heterosexuality on children.[41] There is no
essential difference, he argues, between pederasty and other

forms of homosexuality. Above all, he wants the sexuality of adolescents to be free from adult exploitation.

Duvert's vision of human sexual behaviour, which simply ignores certain harsh realities, is decidedly utopic. The view that an adolescent, whether pre- or post-pubescent, is emotionally and psychologically mature enough to sustain a sexual relationship with an adult on an equal footing must be highly questionable. Indeed, it seems nothing short of naïve to imagine that any sexual relationship in which power were not an issue could exist.

Other aspects of Duvert's representation of homosexuality demand attention from the point of view of a sexual politics: the tendency of his characters to objectify the other, their rampant promiscuity and especially the violence which never seems far from his characters' desires.

## Objects of Desire

The narrative vehicle of *Récidive*, a man recalling scenes from his adolescence, is necessarily a voyeuristic one. Indeed, very early on, the narrative specifically draws attention to this: 'Je vis toujours par les yeux, par eux seuls' (p. 20) ('I always live life through my eyes, through them alone'). Like the eye of a sex tourist's camera, the viewpoint moves from scene to scene, pausing to capture moments of interest, focusing on visual detail with the prurience of the pederast: 'Je regarde les autres garçons, bras crispés, grimaces, culottes étroites et sales qui précisent les reins quand ils s'accroupissent et s'étirent pour embarquer ce qui est lourd' (p. 17) ('I watch the other boys, with their clenched arms, their grinning faces, their tight, dirty shorts that reveal the shape of their bottoms when they crouch down and stretch to carry something heavy on board'); 'son pantalon lui dessina la bite' (p. 85) ('you could see the outline of his prick through his trousers'). In the description of a naked young sailor asleep, there is a sense of the mastery of the other's body as the narrator follows each contour, inspecting every crack and fold, mapping the territory of his desire:

Il ne se réveilla pas. J'étais libre enfin. L'obscurité, son corps assoupi, ma légère hébétude me faisaient vivre un rêve éveillé. Je pouvais m'accorder toutes les licences et, malgré mon âge, être, à l'insu du marin, le maître de ce grand corps. (p. 98)

He did not wake up. I was finally free. The darkness, his sleeping body, a slightly dazed feeling put me into a waking dream. I could do whatever I liked and, in spite of my age, without the sailor's knowing, I could be master of his big body.

This polymorphous narrator is in many important respects Alain Robbe-Grillet's voyeur, obsessively surveying the physical geometry of his subjects, his vision shaped by the subjectivity of passion.

The voyeurism of Duvert's text is dependent on a descriptive detail which is remarkably well observed and, I would suggest, justifed as a structural element of a narrative quest conveyed in images which are predominantly visual. Visual description, after all, is a mainstay of the novel as a genre (even the New Novel) and if what is being described is the male body it is because the quest is for a *homosexual* identity. Moreover, objectification of the other's body is an inescapable function of sexual desire and even of what we popularly term 'romantic love'.

As we have seen, the reader, too, is invited to take an active part in the quest, but often feels intentionally led astray by a non-linear narrative which seems to delight in its aleatory movements. The climate of confusion is increased by frequent changes of narrative voice from 'he' to 'I' and the mixing of character roles, which suggest a polymorphous perversity, overspilling the bounds of individual subjectivity. The narrator of *Récidive* is thus a chorus of subjectivities, each one determined to have its solo spot.

This promiscuity of narrative form is, of course, perfectly suited to the promiscuous sexual content of Duvert's novel, in which the narrative voices relish the memories (or the fantasies) of sex with a plurality of partners. Promiscuity is a stereotypical characteristic of homosexual behaviour in a Euro-American context, but the homosexuality depicted in Duvert's novel certainly confirms the stereotype: 'J'ai probablement aimé déjà l'un d'entre eux' ('I've probably already loved one of them'), says the narrator, thinking of an adolescent boy he encounters in a railway station waiting room, and of many others like him, and he adds ironically, 'Je l'ai connu, touché, nommé de son prénom' (p. 21) ('I've known him, touched him, called him by his first name'). Like so many homosexuals in the real world, 'Il aimait trop les garçons pour se contenter de n'en déculotter qu'un seul' (p. 123) ('He liked boys too much to be content with taking down only one boy's trousers').

Worton suggests that, like the narcissistic component of homosexual desire, promiscuity (or what he calls 'cruising') does not have to be viewed negatively: 'Rather than denying the narcissism and the episodicity of their erotic lives, gay men can, and should perhaps, strive to rewrite their self-images, for instance, seeing the multiple encounters of cruising not as a fragmentation and shattering of desire, but (potentially, at least) as serial plenitude.'[42] Foucault, Worton reminds us, openly advocated gay promiscuity when he declared that gays must invent different models of desire to 'make ourselves infinitely open to pleasures'.[43] In *Anti-Oedipus*,[44] Gilles Deleuze and Félix Guattari had redefined desire as fragmented, as somehow divorced from real subjects and objects, operating mechanically, with people as 'desiring machines'. For Deleuze, 'There is no subject of desire, any more than there is an object [...] Only the flows are the objectivity of desire itself. Desire is the system of meaningless signs with which flows of the unconscious are produced in a social field.'[45] Guy Hocquenghem picks up this argument and applies it to the homosexual's promiscuity, which he attempts to rehabilitate as what Worton calls a 'mechanical scattering' that corresponds to the 'mode of existence of desire itself'. Hocquenghem goes even further, praising homosexual promiscuity as 'anti-capitalist' and 'revolutionary' in potential.[46] Not only do these arguments seem childishly self-indulgent (and Hocquenghem's in particular quaintly dated after the demise of Eastern European communism – *Le Désir homosexuel* was originally published in 1972), but set against the background of a worldwide AIDS epidemic, they are loftily irresponsible.

Worton presents a similar pro-promiscuity argument, emphasising the *process* of cruising, attempting to draw attention away from the object of desire to the act itself:

'Cruising is essentially about desire [...] unfocused. In cruising, it is the act rather than the individual object of desire that is important. This act is necessarily and compulsively repeated, and what is sought is simply an encounter, a fleeting encounter where pleasure may be had (often anonymously), rather than an encounter *with* someone, a meeting with an individual who could have an identity and therefore become an Other.'[47] However, by depersonalising homosexual sex in this way, it seems to me that Worton stresses instead its negative character.

Both Robinson and Steven Smith seem uncritically to characterise Duvert's eroticisation of adolescents as wholly positive, but their arguments in favour of promiscuity appear much more acceptable from an ethical viewpoint than those of Hocquenghem and Worton. For Robinson, Duvert's adolescent is not an object but a subject of desire, an autonomous agent, positively assuming his own sexuality, and the pederasty he depicts is not a separate sexual condition or set of acts.[48] The pleasure principle is seen by Robinson to be an absolute moral defence: what matters is mutuality so that sex between adult and adolescent is acceptable, provided that the younger partner experiences equal pleasure, but his view that gay male writers 'have had to reclaim the role of object' seems at variance with his 'mutuality' argument and sounds far too absurd to take seriously as an attempt to justify abuse.[49]

In fact, not all of the acts of pederasty depicted by Duvert are consensual, and there are passages of a brutal violence. Even in cases of apparent consensuality, issues of power, abuse and exploitation in relation to the seduction of boys by adult males remain unresolved.

## Sexual Violence

Erotic violence is not only a current focus of fiction and media alike, but it is also 'a key theme of recent gay writing, notably in the work of [...] Tony Duvert'.[50] Heathcote, Hughes and Williams argue that violence in a gay context may have a 'subversive force': 'These writers [Duvert *et al*] key into contemporary debates about gay/lesbian erotica, pornography and sexual abuse.'[51] Heathcote sees sexual violence specifically as a way of highlighting what Judith Butler calls 'gender trouble'.[52] He even suggests that gay violence can play a positive role: 'Violence between single-sex male protagonists can be used to question not only stereotypical male violence but also stereotypical male homosexuality as an orientation and as an identification.'[53]

All of these recodings of violence as positive presuppose (one assumes) that it is consensual, which in Duvert's writing is not always the case. Duvert's novel is replete with sexual violence of both kinds, from descriptions of the pain of being sodomised to sadomasochistic torture, multiple rape, suicide and finally murder. All of these events are brought to life with realistic physical detail and psychological observation.

In a scene which combines both promiscuity and paedophilia, the narrator, now an adult, watches a group of young boys playing by a river. As elsewhere, there is a strong voyeuristic element, rendered more acceptable, perhaps, by a keen sense of observation and an impressive insight into the sexual psychology of young male adolescents: '[ils] glissent la main dans leur maillot de bain pour remonter leur pine et avoir le ventre arrogant. Il y en a un, le plus grand, qui ne retire pas sa main' (p. 107) ('[they] slip a hand into their trunks to pull up their prick and make it stand out proudly. One of them, the biggest, doesn't take his hand away'). But this narrator goes beyond the merely voyeuristic, actively manipulating what he sees, as his fantasies orchestrate the gang-rape of a nine-year-old boy by three older companions. Narrative distance and a deadpan, matter-of-fact style give an impression of harmless child's play, an impression reinforced at the end of the passage as the boys return to their more usual games, but the horror of child-rape persists, both in the slow transformation of the victim's screams into a sort of naïve acquiescence and in the ostensibly disinterested presence of a fifth, much younger child:

Le petit est tout nu, maintenant. [...]

On lui court après. Cris. Le gosse est attrapé, mis par terre. Palabres. Le mioche frétille pour se dégager. Ils rigolent. Ils le maintiennent bras et jambes écartés, à plat ventre. Le grand lui claque les fesses et se couche dessus. On n'entend plus rire, mais des aïe répétés, suraigus.

Le petit ne dit plus rien. L'autre l'encule à coups de reins très vifs. Pudique, en se remettant debout il cache sa bite et se rajuste.

Il prend un bras et une jambe du gosse à la place d'un second, qui court à genoux pour s'installer sur le petit.

Il a enfoncé sa queue, il remue. On dirait qu'il se bat avec un polochon, serpent de dortoir coincé sous lui, maîtrisé à grand-peine.

Puis le troisième l'imite. On ne tient même plus le gosse; le nez écrasé dans l'herbe, il répond aux plaisanteries.

À présent ils se baignent. Le cinquième, le tout petit, qui a observé la scène d'un oeil froid, grignote un croûton, le dos tourné à la rivière. Il y en a deux qui sont immobiles dans le courant, l'eau à mi-corps. On les asperge. (pp. 107–8)

The little boy is now naked [...]

They run after him. Shouts. The kid's caught and thrown to the ground. Palaver. The child tries to wriggle free. They laugh. They hold him face down, with his arms and legs apart. The big boy slaps his behind and lies on him. The kid stops laughing and starts screaming.

The kid falls silent. The big boy pushes into him, with short, quick thrusts. He stands up again, modestly covering his prick and puts his clothes straight.

He grabs hold of an arm and a leg from a second boy, who quickly kneels down to take his place on top of the youngster.

He's stuck his cock into him and is moving it about. It looks as if he's fighting a pillow, holding it underneath him with great difficulty.

Then, the third boy does the same. They're not even holding on to the kid any more; he's joking along with them, face down in the grass.

Now they're having a swim. The fifth boy, the really young one, who has watched the whole scene cooly, is nibbling a crust, with his back to the river. Two others are standing in the current, with water up to their waist. They're being splashed.[54]

The writing is so persuasive, the detail of the scene so well observed that we cannot help but be simultaneously gripped, and moved, and angered, and morally outraged. And yet, all of these emotions are immediately undercut in the passage that follows, in which the first-person narrator, this time the 15-year-old boy, rehearses different narrative possibilities, implying that all these activities are virtual, not real, fantasy, not documentary. Moreover, we tell ourselves, his perspective is certainly more respectable than that of an older male. Throughout the novel, the narrative point of view drifts in this way from man to boy, from sodomiser to sodomised, displacing moral responsibility and criminal agency. The representation of a homosexuality, which is not only promiscuous but abusive, is thus somehow made artistically respectable by an equally promiscuous and abusive textuality.

The novel concludes with a gruesome scene in which a young boy is tortured and then murdered by two others. Thus, the text ends on a grim note, not simply because the final scene involves murder, but because the possibilities of youth have given way to the certainties of adulthood. These closing pages seem to make an irrevocable, depressingly fatalistic statement about the fixed nature of adult homosexual identity. It is, in the *excipit*, the 15-year-old of the *incipit* that is murdered.[55] In the hotel bedroom, the sailor awakens next to the boy and pushes his hardening penis into the boy's anus, fantasising that the boy is dead and that he is sodomising the corpse. This final act of the narrative, however, is less sexual than symbolic, a gesture not born of excitement but of a need to bid an affectionate farewell to a memory of adolescent sexuality: 'Il restait immobile, pétrifié comme s'il craignait de défaire les chairs d'un cadavre. Sa bite, rigide, une artère qui joignait les deux corps.' (p. 143) ('He remained motionless, petrified as if he was afraid of damaging the flesh of a corpse. His cock, rigid, an artery joining the two bodies.') Both sailor and boy are immobile, fixed by the penis that turns them into a single dead body, the corpse of their virtuality. The death of the boy, therefore, signifies the death of a fantasy- and/or memory-based desire. The sailor finally withdraws from the boy and brings himself off by hand: 'Comme la première poignée de terre qu'on jette sur un cercueil' (p. 143) ('Like the first handful of earth thrown on to a coffin'). The narrative ends with an image combining death and *jouissance*, the 'petite mort' of the masturbator signifying the end of the narrative subject's 'recidivism', of his repeated forays into memory and fantasy, journeys which prevented his sexual identity from coagulating in the mire of adult homosexual stereotypes. Duvert's morbid ending emphasises the solitude of the adult male homosexual whose search for identity is complete:

> Il avait eu besoin d'imaginer cette mort pour oser enfouir dans les entrailles tièdes sa présence entière, si solitaire qu'un vivant l'eût rejetée. Ensuite, il pourrait partir. (p. 143)

> He had needed to imagine this death to dare to bury his entire presence, so solitary that a living person would have rejected him, in those warm bowels. Then he could leave.

A new life, in a new direction may be about to begin, but it is a life empty of sperm, devoid of fantasy and desire.

*Récidive* is ultimately a celebration of adolescent *disponibilité*, as opposed to adult fixity – the Gidean influence is obvious – and implicitly a plea for the sexual freedom of the young.

## Conclusion

There is no doubt that in addressing adolescent homosexual desire openly, unashamedly and directly, Tony Duvert's first novel is an important milestone in gay fiction, both inside and outside France. Rather than hanging on to the coat-tails of France's strong novelistic tradition, Duvert speaks with the voice of a new authority, that of a literary avant-garde for whom there is no discourse that is taboo, since art does not answer to any ideology or ethical code. Though in our more politically correct times, there are repeated calls for the artist to be morally and ethically responsible, we should perhaps remember that *Récidive* is a text of the 1960s, when the principal defence against the allegation of pornography was to persuade a court that a written text (or a film or a painting) had aesthetic value.

*Récidive* presents itself, therefore as a work of literature because, according to both the legal and cultural climate of the day, any other kind of text which explicitly appeared to promote sex with adolescents would have been deemed immoral, and dangerously so. From this perspective, *Récidive* is a 'homo*text*' because it has no other alternative.

As in the case of Robbe-Grillet's fiction, the *nouveau roman* format of the novel appears to provide a perfect vehicle for the presentation of a sexuality which refuses conventional descriptions and categories, and which questions its own status as real. The guilt associated with the text's homoerotic and, in particular its paedophilic elements, is displaced from reality to fantasy, from sexuality to textuality. The text thus finds ways of evading responsibility for its own contents by disguising them as formal experimentation.

However, as we have seen, there are enough reasons to judge the novel on realist terms and so to hold it responsible for the images it contains. Where Robbe-Grillet insists on the unreality of his text, or the gap between art and life, indeed, on the subordination of content to form, the reader of Tony Duvert's fiction is implicitly encouraged to view it in tandem with his polemical essays, since the former illustrates the views expounded in the latter, and thereby to focus upon the sexual content. In Robbe-Grillet's work, form merges with content to the point of becoming it, whereas there is no such fusion in Tony Duvert. The most problematic passages of *Récidive*, that is, the passages of sexual violence, for instance, do not exhibit *nouveau roman* characteristics and indeed are relatively conventional in form. It is therefore not convincing to suggest, as Robinson does, that 'insistence on details of the sexual act itself coupled with a fragmentation of the text'[56] prevents the reader from seeing the characters as individuals to focus instead on a pleasure that somehow exists independently of them, or that 'a reader might be excited by description of the acts, but the form of the text prevents him from voyeuristically possessing the actors',[57] since there is no sense in which the form can actually be said to prevent the reader from constructing individual characters (the adolescent runaway, the sailor, the pederastic forester, the young boys playing by the river) or from enjoying them voyeuristically. Nevertheless, such voyeuristic enjoyment is indeed a feature of all of the texts we are considering in this volume and, as I have suggested above, is not reprehensible in itself. The realistic and yet uncritical depiction of an aggressive promiscuity and, in particular, of a repugnant sexual violence is quite a different matter.

On a purely artistic level, *Récidive* has considerable merit as a narrative form that skilfully (and in some ways, ironically) mirrors its thematic content. The title entices the reader to join a quest that is both sexual and textual, so that he becomes a textual construct, alongside all the other narrative voices, and ultimately one of many homosexual virtualities. The novel's chief merit, on a political level, is its subversion of normative labelling and its promotion of a more liberated version of desire than that imposed on homosexuals (and indeed others) by an age-obsessed society. One cannot help feeling, however, that Duvert attempts too self-consciously to persuade the reader that this is experimental fiction inhabiting a space, like Robbe-Grillet's, beyond the troublesome area of political and ethical responsibility, and that the attempt founders on the rock of a frequently sordid and gruesomely realistic depiction of violent sexual abuse. In spite of his choice of the anti-realistic New Novel as his writing vehicle, Tony Duvert wants to engage seriously and directly with the realities of homosexual experience, an ambition difficult to reconcile with the virtual absence in his fictional writing of any ethical dimension. It is precisely this problematical relationship with social reality which makes Tony Duvert an important voice in the current debate on both paedophilia and the influence of texts on sex.

# 9

## 'Enfin, une érotique féminine?': Two Contemporary Novels by Women

### *Corps de jeune fille* by Élisabeth Barillé

In its thematic preoccupations with masturbatory fantasy and its essentially romantic treatment of sexual attraction, Élisabeth Barillé's *Corps de jeune fille*, which was published in France in 1986 and in England as *Body of a Girl* in 1989, is an excellent example of contemporary erotic writing by women. Barillé displays a remarkable maturity of style, her narrative voice fizzing with ironic wit and more than a touch of self-mockery. Her first fictional publication (the author is also a journalist) is not so much a novel as a series of vignettes about sex written from a young woman's point of view – well observed but loosely linked. In an ironic reversal of the *Bildungsroman* or picaresque novel, in which a male protagonist learns from a series of (usually) unfortunate experiences, often with women, this 22-year-old female protagonist pursues the illusory image of a male writer across Paris. On the way, she discovers the truth about herself and about him. The specular image on the cover of the original French edition, which shows a semi-naked young woman looking at her reflection in a mirror as she dresses, turns out to be a key metaphor for an understanding of this moral tale, in which she and we learn not to take appearance for reality.

Like the first-person narrator of the traditional *Bildungsroman*,[1] the heroine of Barillé's text, a young student and would-be novelist named Élise, writes her story, recording her experiences as they are lived on a day-to-day basis, as in a diary. Élise thus positions herself as her own implied reader, while appearing to confide her experiences to another young woman. This is a novelistic format which has most often

173

been associated with the limited point of view of an emotionally and sexually inexperienced *ingénue*.[2] And yet, this heroine is no female Candide reacting naïvely to events. Again, reversing the conventional character of the innocent male hero, she not only comments on her experiences with sardonic insight, displaying a self-awareness that *Bildungsroman* figures conventionally do not possess, but she also reveals a distinct lack of innocence as she muses about the past, in particular about her early sexual encounters. It quickly becomes clear that her erotic responses are rooted in fantasies rather than in real experiences.

I have already suggested that the novel's paratextual threshold[3] raises interesting questions concerning the heroine's identity and, above all, her self-image. The title implies both a reification ('corps/body') and an infantilisation ('fille/girl') of women, which a reading of the text itself shows to be heavily ironic. In the absence of such a reading, this reification appears to be reinforced by the image on the cover, which frames a voyeuristic gaze that feminist critics have generally defined as masculine. Inside the cover, a two-line epigraph[4] implies the veracity of a woman's autobiographical reminiscences, which is also characteristic of an erotic genre historically dominated by male writers, who frequently used female pseudonyms:

> Élisabeth Barillé est journaliste. *Corps de jeune fille* est son premier roman, écrit à vingt-trois ans – l'âge de sa narratrice.

> Élisabeth Barillé is a journalist. *Corps de jeune fille* is her first novel, written at the age of twenty-three – the same age as the female narrator.

However, on closer examination, the image on the book's cover constitutes an ironic staging of the voyeurism and appropriation of the ostensibly female erotic novel by male publishers. The effect of this *mise en scène* is, firstly, to undermine the male gaze because, despite the reification of the female body suggested by the title, the active subject of this gaze is a woman, not a man: as she faces away from the reader and towards a mirror, the reader is invited to share her gaze rather than to focus on her as object. Moreover, the gaze is, in a sense, inverted, because she (and we) are looking at an invisible mirror image. This inversion satirises a specularity that is characteristic of male voyeurism. Instead of viewing the woman as object, the potential reader is therefore forced to consider her as subject. Similarly, if (s)he reads the text that follows, this reader is forced by the narrative to share the female narrator's point of view. At the same time, as we shall see, Barillé's novel constructs a female eroticism which not only avoids but also mocks male stereotypes.

The text constantly refers to the writing process itself, thus displaying an ironic awareness of its own status as erotic fiction. The effect of this self-referentiality is to undercut the traditional male use and appropriation of the erotic. In a *mise en abyme* of the writing activity, Élise narrates the pursuit of a self-styled novelist who wants to use her as model for the heroine of his latest novel. Refusing this symbolic objectification as a male writer's female character, however, she instead becomes the heroine of her own novel: 'L'écrivain était libre de faire ce qu'il voulait. Il m'avait remplacée. Je n'étais plus son héroine' (p. 156) ('The writer was free to do what he wanted. He had replaced me. He had finally understood that I was no longer his heroine' (p. 116)). The narrator thus enacts the process, whereby the feminist woman takes control of her own identity, seeing herself, not through men's eyes, but through her own: 'L'héroine avait fait place à une romancière en herbe' (p. 157) ('The heroine had given way to a budding novelist' (p. 117)). At the same time, the narrative questions the validity of any conception of human identity based on physical appearance. Sifting through old albums, Élise comes across a photo of herself taken at the age of 13 and wonders how to reconcile the constructed nature of this image with memories of how she really was. As with the image on the cover, this photo seems to bear little resemblance to the 'real' her:

J'ai peine à reconnaître dans cette sainte-nitouche la précoce que je croyais être, celle qui se branlait dans sa chambre, se shootait à l'éther, léchait son sang noir.

Pourtant ce corps lourd est le mien, ce ventre rebondi, ce visage lunaire aux joues généreuses m'appartiennent. Qui dit vrai? Mon souvenir ou cette photo? (p.137)

I hardly recognise the precocious girl I thought I was, the one
who used to masturbate in her bedroom, shoot up with
ether, lap up her dark blood.

Yet this heavy body is my own, this podgy stomach, this
moonlike face with its generous cheeks belong to me. Which
is telling the truth? My memory or this photo? (p. 101)

For Roland Barthes, in a photograph, 'le référent adhère' ('the
referent is stuck on to it').[5] Barthes sees the photograph as a
'certificat de présence' ('proof of presence'), unlike the literary
text which, like memories, has fundamentally subjective
origins:

Dans l'image, l'objet se livre en bloc et la vue en est *certaine*
– au contraire du texte ou d'autres perceptions qui me
donnent l'objet d'une façon floue, discutable, et m'incitent
de la sorte à me méfier de ce que je crois.[6]

In the photographic image, the object is wholly accessible
and my view of it beyond doubt – unlike a text or other ways
of perceiving which give me a hazy, equivocal view of the
object, and in this way, encourage me to distrust my own
perceptions and beliefs.

The text, for Barthes, is imprecise, whereas the camera honestly
provides a 'whole' image.[7] Barillé's novel reverses this
opposition, seeing the photograph as bearing an image that
is less 'real' than memory. Now, it seems to me that Barthes's
distinction between a representation (photo) and a perception
(text) of the self is quite close to the Lacanian dichotomy
between the Symbolic (realm of the father) and the Imaginary
(pre-oedipal realm of the mother). Barthes doubtless borrowed
from Lacan the concept of *méconnaissance* or 'misrecognition', which is the basis of the ego's self-perception in the
Imaginary.[8]

In a symbolic gesture of rejection of a self defined in physical
terms, Élise burns all the photos of her childhood. Following
Barthes and Lacan, the feminine subject thus refuses an
identity as object of a masculine 'eye' (the lens of the camera)
in favour of her own 'imaginary' self-image. Even when, a little
later in the narrative, she describes her 'writer' physically,

there is a nice touch of irony in this blatant role reversal, as she runs a critical eye over the man's body: 'Je le contemple sans un mot. Il est torse nu, en lewis. Le jean, trop neuf, lui moule les fesses. Il les a charnues, comme une femme' (p. 158) ('I contemplate him without saying a word. He is barechested, in Levi's. His jeans, too unused, cling to his thighs. They are fleshy like a woman's' (p. 118)). The writer of her imagination was far more attractive!

In this novel, the feminine 'imaginary' (memories, impressions) is valorised, as against all symbolic representations (photos, the 'writer''s novel), which are seen to be nothing more than *trompe-l'œil*, as the 'girl' of the title takes possession of her own body, rescuing it from the implicitly male gaze both of the camera and of the 'writer'. This perhaps explains why the self-pleasuring to which the heroine's fantasies lead is far more satisfying than past encounters, which involved penetration by the gaze and the penis of a real man.

This inversion is repeated elsewhere in the novel, sometimes in the form of intertextual allusions to antecedents in the French erotic tradition. Élise compares herself, for example, to the heroine of *Senso*, but changes the latter's mental humiliation into a physical one. Like the eponymous heroine of *Histoire d'O*, she has 'atteint le stade où le dégoût de moi-même devenait excitant' (p. 66) ('reached the stage where self-loathing is becoming exciting' (p. 47)). In both cases, it is through masturbation, an activity long viewed as negative, but represented here objectively as a simple means of satisfying sexual hunger, that Élise experiences feelings of excitement and self-loathing. Like O, Élise reaches orgasm through self-abasement, but unlike O, she does so not to please any man but to please herself.

Barillé thus narrates female sexuality from a female point of view, avoiding the male stereotypes of women as passive sexual objects or nurturing maternal figures. Élise's sexuality is both active and aggressive, her fantasies driven by physical rather than affective impulses, founded less on the need for emotional security than on the pursuit of *jouissance*:

J'aime l'amour facile, étourdi, inconséquent; les brèves étreintes, les corps qui basculent. Je me passe de preuves; la sueur suffit. Odeur de la passion. Il sue donc il m'aime.

Quand les corps sont secs, on se quitte. Je hais les croissants du réveil, les promesses. (p. 166)

I like straightforward, heedless, inconsequential love; fleeting embraces, bodies which topple over. I can do without proof; sweat is enough. Odour of passion. He sweats therefore he loves me. When bodies are dry, people leave each other. I hate croissants when I wake up, and promises. (p. 123)

The text thus insists on women's right to seek pleasure on the same basis as men, to be as promiscuous as they are:

Il n'est qu'une seule chair: celle dont je jouis. [...] J'ai choisi d'oublier le sexe qui m'a ouverte; ceux qui m'ont fait jouir; ceux dont le sperme a giclé sur mon ventre; ceux qui m'ont blessée; ceux que j'ai sucés jusqu'à la nausée. Oubliés. (p. 114).

There is just one flesh: that which is giving me pleasure. [...] I have chosen to forget the cock which opened me up; those which made me come; those the sperm of which spurted over my stomach; those which hurt me; those I sucked until I was nauseous. Forgotten. (pp. 82–3)

Élise looks for sexual partners 'like a man', and her sexual desires, at times, appear rooted in a fetishism which Freud saw as exclusively masculine in nature. The body of one of her ex-lovers reminded her of the Christ figure on a primitive crucifix that she used to see every summer behind the altar of a Catalan church:

[C'était] un homme comme je n'en avais jamais vu. Chaque été, je m'attendais à ce qu'il descendît de la croix et qu'il m'écrasât contre son poitrail de chêne. (p. 165).

[He was] a man like no other I had seen before. Every summer I expected him to come down from the cross and crush me against his chest of oak. (p. 123)

Her attitude towards fellatio avoids all stereotypical views of the woman's role in this activity, from that of ever-willing nymphomaniac to that of 'victim' of male violence: 'Un seul acte me répugne: avaler le sperme. La fellation me rappelle des attitudes: la bouche tendue vers l'hostie, la langue prête à la saisir. Je crache. [...] Avalerait-il son sperme s'il était une femme?' (p. 167) ('A single act disgusts me: swallowing sperm. Fellation reminds me of poses: my mouth reaching out for the Host, my tongue ready to fasten on to it. I spit it out. [...] Would he swallow his own sperm if he were a woman?' (p. 124)). Her dislike of fellatio seems related less to puritanical sexual attitudes than to an aversion for the demeaning rituals of Catholicism. Her sardonic humour similarly deflates the sacred phallocentric traditions of erotic literature: sperm is nothing but 'une gelée incolore' ('a colourless jelly') or 'cette espèce de colle blanche' ('that sort of white glue'),

> Alors pourquoi ces rougeurs, ces allusions, ces sourires en coin; pourquoi ces périphrases ou ces mots: «semence, liqueur, germe, foutre, purée»? Toute cette littérature pour ça. (p. 168).

> So why those blushes, allusions, half-smiles; why that periphrasis or those words: 'seed, semen, sperm, spunk, juice'? (p. 125)

Thus, the humour of Barillé's text repeatedly debunks the male abuse of female fantasies. The voyeurism of both her 'writer' and of any male reader listening to the account of the heroine's sexual flowering is, for example, undermined by the repulsive images that punctuate it:

> [...] maman avait accueilli mes premières règles d'un unique commentaire: «Te voilà grande», puis elle m'avait ordonné d'aller me changer. J'avais ôté mon slip. Je l'avais reniflé à la dérobée avant de le porter, du bout des doigts, jusqu'au panier à linge. Il sentait les boyaux de lièvre, chapelets de chair tiède que mon père, fin chasseur, détachait soigneusement à l'aide d'un couteau de cuisine. Papa me disait de rester à ses côtés. Il me tendait les intestins sanguinolents en me demandant de les jeter à la poubelle. (pp. 125–6).

[...] Mummy had greeted my first period with one single remark: 'Now you're a big girl,' then she ordered me to go and change. I took off my panties. I sniffed them surreptitiously before carrying them in my fingertips to the laundry basket. They smelt of hare's entrails, strings of warm flesh which my father, an expert hunter, would carefully remove with the aid of a kitchen knife. Daddy would tell me to stay by his side. He held out the bleeding intestines, while asking me to throw them into the rubbish bin. (p. 92)

To assist him in a writing project which turns out to be nothing more than a means of seducing young impressionable women, the 'author' asks Élise to recount to him in detail what he calls her 'aventures galantes' ('amorous adventures'). Suddenly, the text explodes the potential eroticism of the account of her deflowering with a comic imagery that subverts the male exploitation of female fantasies:

Il m'a caressé les seins, les a léchés évasivement. Je me laissais faire. Je promenais mes mains sur son dos. À un moment, il les a saisies pour les poser sur ... ses couilles. J'avais l'impression de tenir des fruits. Je me disais que c'étaient des prunes'(p. 126)

He caressed my breasts, licked them cagily. I let him do what he wanted. I ran my hands over his back. At a certain moment, he seized them to place them on ... his balls. I had the impression that I was holding some fruit. I told myself that they were plums. (p. 92)

And as she relates an act of fellatio, performed on a different occasion, on a different man, this time to the reader alone, her rather serious tone is suddenly undercut by a verbal and visual comedy, which ridicules the male organ: 'Avec cette pine dans la bouche, gonflant mes joues, mon visage ressemble à un masque de la commedia dell'arte. Pantalon ....' (p. 172) ('With that cock in my mouth swelling my cheeks, my face looks like a *commedia dell'arte* mask. Pantaloon ...' (p. 128)).[9]

Not only does Barillé reject male-centred eroticism, but she goes even further to produce a writing which could be described as 'feminine'. We have already seen that there is in this novel a valorisation of the feminine imaginary at thematic levels. The heroine's rejection of fixed representations of her identity also seems to constitute a rejection of any essentialist definition of woman. At stylistic levels, too, the novel has several of the principal characteristics of what has been called 'écriture féminine'. There is a reluctance in this text to name, which Hélène Cixous has identified as a significant trait of feminine writing.[10] Moreover, there is a noticeable lack of linearity in the narrative, which rather possesses the Proustian character of an excavation of the past, thus creating a temporal circularity that Julia Kristeva recognises as predominantly feminine.[11] This circularity reflects itself in the comings and goings of the female protagonist, as she pursues her 'writer', constantly returning to the Paris bar in which they first met. Finally at the level of the senses, the narrative privileges what Hélène Cixous and Luce Irigaray consider to be the more feminine senses of smell and touch at the expense of the visual.

*Corps de jeune fille* is, above all, a text full of surprises, a text which disrupts and ultimately explodes the presuppositions of any reader conditioned to expect a more conventional male eroticism. There are surprises in store, too, for the reader who is seduced by the paratext into buying a novel which (s)he thinks belongs to the 'Mills and Boon'[12] genre. After the excessively sentimental self-portrait of the heroine as a Heidi figure, sketched in Chapter 1, the reader abruptly encounters quite a different tone at the beginning of Chapter 2, where this innocent young girl tells in deadpan style of her impatience to get home after meeting the 'writer' for the first time so that she can masturbate. The first chapter now reads, in retrospect, as a parody of the popular romance.[13] The discovery is refreshing, to say the least.

This explosive and subversive description of female masturbation, a time bomb primed by the author to go off well into the narrative, implicitly challenging the stereotype of masturbation as an exclusively male activity, is repeated in an ending which challenges another stereotypical view of female sexuality, concerning rape and its consequences. Immediately after she has been seriously sexually assaulted by her 'writer', Élise enters a men's toilet to masturbate (the 'Ladies' is out of order). Both the agent of this act and its location ironically invert the conventional scenario. But in this tongue-in-cheek *dénouement*, we learn with the narrator, who is wearing 'tarty' fancy dress, that nothing is as it seems: the so-called writer turns out to be an imposter, fantasy safely substitutes for a dangerous reality which was, in any event, a fraudulent one, and a liquid is spilt that is far more banal than male sperm:

> Je me suis mise nue. Debout, je me suis branlée, sanglotante, avec des bruits de gorge de bête qu'on achève. J'appelais l'orgasme. La délivrance. Mes tempes tintaient, tintaient. Mon coeur s'emportait. Mon sexe grondait. Mon cÏur ...
> Un filet bleu coula sous la porte. J'avais entraîné la bouteille de détartrant dans ma chute. (p. 183).

> I stripped. I masturbated standing upright, sobbing, with the sounds in my throat of an animal which is being finished off. I summoned the orgasm. The release. My temples were ringing, ringing. My heart was bursting. My fanny was rumbling. My heart ...
> A trickle of blue ran underneath the door. I had dragged down the bottle of bleach in my fall. (p. 137)

The text ends, then, with the image of an ejaculation that mockingly juxtaposes the sublime and the ridiculous, and underlines at the same time that, for women as well as for men, *jouissance* has its origins in the imaginary. It is in this imaginary, more exciting than any reality, that the constantly shifting identity of the feminine subject is formed and reformed, an identity determined largely by physical exigencies.[14] In perfect safety and in spite of the sexual violence which she has just suffered, Élise claims her right to enjoy her own fantasies, constructed in a virtual reality which she controls. This virtuality appears much less absurd than the banal day-to-day reality surrounding her.

## *Truismes* by Marie Darrieussecq

An erotic black comedy, which appeared in France in 1996 and in English translation the following year, *Truismes* is the story of a gorgeous young masseuse-cum-prostitute who gradually turns into a pig. This first novel by the young woman writer and academic, Marie Darrieussecq, explores contemporary political issues, both sexual and non-sexual, and satirises a society that increasingly views human beings as entries on the profit and loss sheet. At the same time, Darrieussecq pays homage to Kafka (*Metamorphosis*) and perhaps, given its erotic themes, to Philip Roth's Kafka-inspired tale of a man who wakes up to find himself transformed into his favourite part of the female body (*The Breast*).

The young pig/woman tells her own story, beginning with a warning to any potential publisher of the dangers of publication:

> Je sais à quel point cette histoire pourra semer de trouble et d'angoisse, à quel point elle perturbera de gens. Je me doute que l'éditeur qui acceptera de prendre en charge ce manuscrit s'exposera à d'infinis ennuis. La prison ne lui sera sans doute pas épargnée, et je tiens à lui demander tout de suite pardon pour le dérangement. (p. 9)

> I know how much this story might upset people, how much distress and confusion it could cause. I suspect that any publisher who agrees to take on this manuscript will be heading for trouble – heading for prison, probably – and I'd like to apologise right now for the inconvenience. (p. 1)

Echoes, then, on an intertextual level, not only of specific texts, but also of the conventions of the pornographic genre in France: a first-person female narrator, a playful title (see below), an awareness of the threat of censorship and of draconian punishments awaiting both author and editor of illicit materials as recently as the 1950s.

One might protest that such a caveat is superfluous, since, as we saw in Chapter 1, there *is* no longer any legal censorship in France. The Darrieussecq case, however, clearly demonstrates that a form of censorship does still exist, more subtle, more insidious, less easy to counter than the old repressive laws – a censorship not at the point of production, but at the point of promotion and distribution.

Literary journalists have a great deal of influence on the reading public, and some of the reviews of the book which appeared in the French press following its publication could certainly be described as censorious. *Le Figaro-Magazine* described the novel as 'un peu osé' ('a little daring') and 'à ne pas mettre entre toutes les mains' ('not for all readers'),[15] while for one critic writing in the right-wing *Valeurs Actuelles*, 'Marie Darrieussecq réussit le prodige [...] d'écrire un roman pornographique avec une écriture frigide' ('Marie Darrieussecq accomplishes the marvel [...] of writing a pornographic novel in a frigid style').[16] It is unclear whether the book is here being condemned for being too pornographic or not pornographic enough!

Despite (or even in some measure thanks to) the adverse publicity that the novel has attracted since its appearance in the autumn of 1996, its editor (Paul Otchakovski Laurens or P.O.L.) is not only unlikely to go to prison, but stands to make a fortune from a novel which has sold more than 2000 copies a day, has been nominated for the Prix Goncourt and made into a film by Jean-Luc Godard. As Nicholas Harrison argues, censorship often draws public interest to works which might otherwise pass unnoticed.[17]

In any event, the author is acutely aware of censorship issues, declaring herself an enemy of political correctness – 'Je déteste le "politiquement correct" et tout le discours de la pensée obligatoire et j'aime la résistance sous toutes ses formes'[18] ('I hate the "politically correct" and the whole discourse of obligatory thought and I love resistance in all its forms') – and even expressing some disappointment that the book did not create more of a scandal: 'Je pensais que cela allait choquer pas mal les esprits et je me retrouve face à un consensus. C'est un petit peu decevant [...]'('I thought it would really shock people and yet, I find a consensus view. It's a bit disappointing [...]').[19]

Literary censorship is, not surprisingly, therefore, thematically inscribed into the text itself. In addition to the caveat of the incipit, the narrator lives under a totalitarian régime described as 'Social-Franc-Progressiste' ('Social Free Progressionism') which holds *autos-da-fé* for the socially and physically undesirable and sets up a Minister of Public Morality and a Censorship Office which burns any book considered unsuitable.

So would the censorship office burn *Truismes*? In what sense, in other words, can Darrieussecq's own book be called 'censurable'? In fact, though there are many scenes of sexual activity, ranging from fellatio to sodomy, the narrative style avoids vulgarity, partly by being allusive rather than direct and partly because of the feigned naïvety of a female narrator, modelled, no doubt, partly on Candide and Justine, but lacking their sexual ignorance. The following exemplifies this 'degree zero' style of eroticism well. Short of funds to travel on the métro, the heroine has to exploit her feminine charms:

> [...] j'ai été obligée, pour franchir la barrière, de me coller contre un monsieur. Il y en a toujours beaucoup qui attendent les jeunes filles aux barrières du métro. J'ai bien senti que je faisais de l'effet au monsieur; pour tout dire, beaucoup plus d'effet que je n'en faisais d'habitude. Il a fallu [...] que je lave discrètement ma jupe. (pp. 12–13)

> [...] to get through the turnstile, I was forced to squeeze up against some man. There are always lots of them waiting around for girls at the Métro turnstiles. I definitely felt that I'd made an impression on the gentleman – bluntly put, much more of an impression than I usually made. I had to wash my skirt discreetly in one of the changing rooms at Aqualand. (p. 4)

More generally, *Truismes* has been characterised as 'anti-feminist' and politically incorrect. The author responds to such charges with a vigorous, if somewhat vague, promotion of the rights of the female body:

> Il me semblait pourtant qu'on n'avait pas encore parlé de ce qu'est un corps de femme. Qu'on avait parlé de l'avortement, de la sexualité, de la contraception, mais du corps non! Après tous les combats essentiels, graves et décisifs qu'ont menés les féministes de la génération de ma mère, il fallait avancer un peu, avoir une vision plus large, et essayer d'aimer les hommes.[20]

> It seemed to me, however, that women's bodies hadn't yet been properly discussed. That we'd talked about abortion, sexuality, contraception, but not about the body. After all those very important battles that the feminists of my

mother's generation had fought and decisively won, it was time to go a little further, to adopt a broader vision, and to try to like men.

Any close reading of the novel suggests that what she is promoting is the unqualified right to use this body in whatever manner she wishes, whether this be in prostitution, in 'glamour' modelling or simply in self-gratification. If there is a case for considering the book worthy of inclusion in the 'forbidden' category, it has to be because of its sexual politics rather than because it is too explicitly erotic or obscene. A view of the body, in other words, which might be considered collusive with phallocratic power structures, will hardly be compatible with conventional feminist thinking. I shall argue that the novel's radical sexual politics turn upon the notion of metamorphosis, which in fact structures the entire narrative, and that this notion invites a less judgemental approach to the body of either gender. Let us begin by focusing on the title.

The novel's French title is a wordplay, 'Truismes' meaning truisms, but also pointing to 'truie', the French word for 'sow'. Pigs have been much in the British media of late, from the recent children's movie, *Babe*, to the case of the 'Tamworth Two', a pair of piglets which made a bid for freedom from an English slaughterhouse in January 1998 and managed to evade recapture for two whole days. Media coverage of both phenomena reflects a current tendency to see pigs and some other animals (dolphins, gorillas) as intelligent neighbours rather than as objects for human sport or consumption. They also remind us of the complex relationships which have existed between the human and the porcine since ancient times on cultural and linguistic levels. Darrieussecq's story sets this positive view of the pig against its traditionally pejorative connotations – 'sale truie' in French has the same offensive force when applied to a woman as 'dirty cow' in English. In both cases, there is an implication of sexual misconduct. The irony is, of course, that the real 'pigs' are the men that sexually exploit Darrieussecq's porcine heroine.

The title encapsulates the idea of change or metamorphosis and, specifically, a process of movement from the personal to the political which the single portmanteau word of the title both symbolises and linguistically enacts, the diphthong acting to metamorphose the French word for sow, 'truie', into 'truismes', 'truisms', hackneyed or self-evident truths. To label something a 'truism' is therefore to make a political statement about truth as a given or absolute. The title moves therefore from pigs to politics, from the animal to the abstract. The author has confirmed in press interviews that she quickly realised that individual appearance always impacts on the surrounding community, that the personal *is* political. The heroine's transmutation thus becomes a prism through which to view all sorts of 'isms' – careerism, sexism, Lepenism, racism. Any ideological absolute, whether relating to beauty, fitness, racial purity, but also political correctness, is heavily satirised in this novel.

There is, of course, another way of reading the 'ismes' of the French title which is equally pertinent to the text's political contents: its sociopolitical message is nothing if not clichéd, purveying, as it does, a few platitudinous and self-evident truths about the material and spiritual corruption of contemporary French society. There is hardly anything new in drawing attention to the manipulative populism of a Le Pen, for example, to the exploitation of women in the sex industry or to the potentially fascistic character of the current cult of the body (the novel depicts an exaggerated obsession with health and physical appearance). 'Ma réflexion politique ne va pas très loin,' admits the author with disarming frankness, 'Tout ce qui est dit dans le livre sur le monde est de l'ordre de l'évidence – d'où le titre, d'ailleurs' ('My political thinking does not go very far. Everything that is said in the book about the world is self-evident – hence, the title, moreover').[21] What *is* worth focusing on, however, is Darrieussecq's positive representation of the objectification of the female body. As I draw my own discussion of the 'forbidden' genre to a close, it is worth asking how useful metamorphosis is as a metaphor to describe the evolution of this genre at the end of the millennium in France[22] at a time itself defined by change and upheaval, as the twenty-first century approaches.

As we have seen, Darrieussecq's novel situates itself playfully in the erotic/pornographic genre in its opening paragraph, which implicitly satirises the history of book censorship. On the other hand, I have suggested that, notwithstanding the scandalised reactions of a handful of reviewers in the right-wing French press, the book hardly conforms to accepted definitions of pornography. Descriptions of sex are allusive, never direct – the passage quoted earlier is typical in this regard. In other ways too, *Truismes* evades easy categorisation.

Too long to be a *conte* or short story, too short to be a novel in the traditional sense (one reviewer suggested resurrecting the medieval term 'sotie', meaning 'satirical farce' or 'allegory of contemporary society'), Darrieussecq's text seems to ignore the basic rules of conventional narrative form – there are no divisions into chapters, the story told in one breath, so to speak, by the autodiegetic heroine.[23] There is no dialogue and so no stylistic variation.

The satirising of political positions by means of sexual misbehaviour follows a long tradition in France, dating back to the eighteenth century,[24] but it does suggest a confused orientation for readers, especially those in the anglophone tradition with no experience of politically subversive pornography, who may wonder whether they are being invited to respond physically or intellectually. The essentially intertextual basis of a story about a woman changing into an animal and its uneasy self-positioning between fact and fable, fantasy and reality, contribute to the sense of reading a narrative which defies formal categorisation by straddling many different categories, just as, on a political level, it attacks the dictatorship of homogeneous thinking. Although this anti-dogmatism of form and content is certainly a feature of much postmodern writing, in the particular context of the erotic, it can only be welcomed as further evidence not only that French erotic writers are reforming a genre too often characterised in the past by male-centredness and stereotype, but that the genre itself is actually ceasing to exist as such. Eroticism, and even obscenity, are, in other words, becoming features of writing of a more heterogeneous nature, writing by women as well as by men, writing by and for both.

If books and other media are still to be called 'forbidden' at the end of the 1990s, it is not because they are censored by governments or other public authorities, as in the past, but because a kind of consensus emerges among the well-educated that they do not conform in some way to the politically correct stereotype. In the case of the erotic, this stereotype, as we saw in Chapter 1, is defined largely by crude notions concerning objectification of the (mainly female, though sometimes male) body.

Darrieussecq's text implicitly challenges the facile assumption that objectification of the female body is wrong by perversely taking such a body as her central focus. Indeed, the reader is encouraged to share in the heroine's own narcissistic pleasure in viewing it. The heroine notes how, in the early stages of her transformation, she became physically more appealing:

> À cette époque-là de ma vie, les hommes s'étaient tous mis à me trouver d'une élasticité merveilleuse. [...] ma chair était plus ferme, plus lisse, plus rebondie qu'avant. [...] mes cuisses étaient devenues roses et fermes, musclées et rondes en même temps. (pp. 11–12)

> At that point in my life, men in general had begun finding me marvellously elastic. [...] my flesh had become firmer, smoother, plumper than before. [...] my thighs had grown pink and firm, curvaceous, yet muscular. (pp. 2–3)

At Aqualand, the swimming pool and relaxation centre where young women can 'earn a good living', she admires herself in the mirror, a gesture which the reader is implicitly invited to share: '[...] je me suis trouvée, je suis désolée de le dire, incroyablement belle, comme dans les magazines mais en plus appétissante' (p. 13) '[...] I thought I looked – forgive me for saying so – incredibly gorgeous, like a fashion model, but more voluptuous' (p. 4)). 'Forgive me for saying so' is not so much an apology for the gesture, as an ironic expression of the awareness that it may well be deemed politically incorrect and at the same time an implicit challenge to the need to apologise.

What in fact shocks most in *Truismes* is the positive eroticisation of the female body. The heroine's gradual metamorphosis makes her more highly sexed, a 'cat on heat' or a 'real bitch', in her boss's words:

> Ce qui se passait d'extraordinaire, c'est que maintenant j'aimais ça, je veux dire, pas seulement les massages qu'on peut afficher en vitrine et la démonstration de produits, non,

tout le reste, du moins ce dont je prenais moi-même l'initiative. (p. 40)

What was astounding was that I liked it now, I mean, not only the massages you can advertise in the shop window and the product demonstrations, no – all the rest of it, at least what I undertook on my own. (p. 29)

The author emphasises in interviews her determination to separate morality and physical pleasure:

Je voulais montrer qu'une femme peut vraiment aimer les hommes, qu'elle peut coucher avec plein d'hommes, mener une vie dissolue et prendre son pied. J'avais envie de parler de la sexualité autrement que de façon gynécologique, féministe ou moralisatrice, dire que prendre son plaisir, cela n'a rien à voir avec la morale.[25]

I wanted to show that a woman can really like men, that she can go to bed with lots of men, lead a dissolute life and carve out her own niche. I wanted to speak about sexuality in a way different from the gynaecological, feminist or moralising standpoint, to say that taking one's pleasure has nothing to do with morality.

If, as her character knows too well, humans are frequently perverse and corrupt, the animal side of our nature can also be sensitive, tender and even poetic. *Truismes* is, in this respect, a hymn to the body, both sensuous and bestial and at the same time a scathing attack on the new puritanism of the hygenic society and its 'éthique de la pureté': 'Moi, je n'ai pas envie d'être propre. Il faut vivre, aimer, se salir'[26] ('I don't want to be clean. You've got to live, love and get dirty'). This 'ethic of purity' also includes political correctness. The view of prostitution that she presents is certainly not a feminist one:

[...] le féminisme de la génération précédente m'a donné une liberté totale vis-à-vis de mon corps. Et à partir du moment où j'ai cette liberté, je peux me permettre d'écrire des choses horribles sur l'image féminine. Une chose est certaine: si c'était un homme qui avait écrit le livre, il se serait fait assassiner![27]

[...] the feminism of the preceding generation gave me total freedom with regard to my body. And given this freedom, I can write horrible things about the image of the female. One thing is certain: if a man had written the book, he would have been lynched!

As she becomes more and more porcine, Darrieussecq's character begins to take a strong sensual pleasure in earthiness, as represented by the smells and tastes of roots and truffles. The woman-pig thus indulges her heightened senses, boundaries and inhibitions dissolve, so that her own body, the bodies of others and the body of the earth itself become confused in an orgy of purely physical delight:

Ma robe tenait raide autour de moi, elle sentait bon la sueur fraîche, la chair vivante, le sexe chaud. Je me suis roulée dans mon odeur pour me tenir compagnie. [...] Je rêvais de fougères et de terre humide. Mon corps me tenait chaud. J'étais bien. Quand le soleil s'est levé j'ai senti la lumière couler le long de mon dos et ça a fait du jaune vif dans ma tête. (p. 85)

My dress stuck out stiffly around me, smelling richly of fresh sweat, warm crotch, living flesh. I curled up in my smell to keep myself company. [...] I dreamed of ferns and damp earth. My body kept me warm. I was just fine. When the sun came up I felt the light run along my back and turn bright yellow in my head. (p. 69)

The metamorphosis of woman into pig is thus accompanied by other bodily metamorphoses. Her new boyfriend, the director of a cosmetics firm, called 'Loup-Y-Es-Tu' (literally, 'The Wolf In You', but rendered in the English version as 'Moonlight Madness'), sniffs her bottom rather than shaking her hand when she meets him and, in true corporate loyalty, turns into a wolf on their first date. Fear on her part quickly turns to love. The social body ('corps social'), on the other hand, proves anything but lovable, transforming more and more, as the novel progresses, into a totalitarian nightmare, in which corrupt politicians abuse and murder for pleasure, animals are privileged over humans and blacks 'disappear'. These metaphors of change in Darrieussecq's fantastic world engage us with the changes confronting us in the real, as our own bodies and those of our partners become aged and corrupt, as the societies in which we live become increasingly obsessed with purity of mind and body at the expense of its capacity for sensual pleasure and *jouissance*.

While the political changes undergone by the surrounding society are presented as wholly negative, the monstrous trans-formations of individuals in the novel are viewed, paradoxically, in a positive light. Darrieussecq's plump, porcine heroine is, in the end, happy as she is, as is her lycanthropic boyfriend, who clearly has his own 'body image' problems to cope with, not to mention a morally problematic though low-fat diet – when the pig orders pizza for home delivery, the wolf eats the pizzaman! Fat, in this novel, is not so much seen as an issue, feminist or otherwise,[28] but as a different condition, associated with a lifestyle deviating from the puritanical norms of a health- and size-obsessed society, and appealing to different people (as she puts on weight, some of the heroine's massage parlour clients are more excited by her, others less so).

These physical changes seem to mirror generic changes – of novel into novella,[29] of male into female narrative perspective – which must also be viewed as positive.

## Concluding Remarks

At the beginning of the twentieth century, erotic literature in France was still essentially male-centred, a genre written by and for men. As the end of the century approaches, France has seen the emergence of many women writers of the erotic, some of whom, like Alina Reyes, appear merely to offer a female version of the male gaze. There is, nonetheless, a significant number, among whom both Barillé and Darrieussecq, who write for both men and women about the bodies of both, inviting us to confront male desire without any of the damaging hostility that has characterised so much writing inspired by the political feminism of the 1970s and 1980s.

The effective deregulation of gendered desire which these writers are helping to bring about is the product, too, of an increasing fragmentation of values, beliefs and tastes, a pluralist society served by a World Wide Web, decentred, lacking consensus, control or limits. If pornography has gradually become more acceptable since Apollinaire wrote *Les Onze Mille Verges* at the beginning of the century, it is in large measure because of the almost total erosion of the religious and moral codes underpinning the laws which were used to censor it.

On the other hand, even if the laws governing the print media have been greatly liberalised in the latter half of the century, the urge to censor is still powerfully present in all Western countries – one only has to think of recent calls for controls of the Internet – and so, the anti-authoritarian themes of *Truismes* make the book a fitting subject for the final chapter of my own.

In some important respects, Darrieussecq's novel might be said to be remarkably similar to Apollinaire's: both are fables of a kind, both illustrate well the fantastic rather than realist character of the genre. Both, too, are heavily intertextual, using irony and parody to make us think about society, human nature, politics and the erotic genre itself (which in the French tradition has rarely been just pornographic: following Sade, Apollinaire, Louÿs, Robbe-Grillet and many others have used the obscene as a satirical weapon).

Described by some as a 'fin de siècle' novel,[30] *Truismes*, in fact, looks both backwards and forwards, warning of the dangers attendant upon the religious fundamentalist and puritanical forces which threaten to take Western society back to the Middle Ages, and at the same time demonstrating that the real possibilities of sexual liberation for all lie in the expansion of the erotic across the borders of gender and sexuality, not in its suppression by those who want to police those borders more vigorously.

# Notes

## Chapter 1

1. Lucienne Frappier-Mazur points out that, in France, the erotic novel as a genre began to appear in the sixteenth century and slowly followed the evolution of the novel in general: see Lucienne Frappier-Mazur, 'Marginal Canons: Rewriting the Erotic', *Yale French Studies*, vol. 75, 1988, pp. 112–28; this reference, p. 112, n. 2.
2. Pierre Guyotat's *Éden, Éden, Éden*, however, has a certain notoriety, which is, in a sense, unrelated to its literary qualities: when it appeared in 1970, the novel became a *cause célèbre* in the battle against legal censorship: see later.
3. See, for example, Alex Hughes and Kate Ince (eds), *French Erotic Fiction. Women's Desiring Writing, 1880–1990* (Oxford: Berg, 1996). This volume is an excellent recent example of such criticism, comprising essays by women on erotic writing by six twentieth-century French women writers, at least four of whom – Colette, Leduc, Wittig and Cixous – can be described as writing about lesbian experience.
4. André Pieyre de Mandiargues, *Le Désordre de la mémoire*: *Entretiens avec Francine Mallet* (Paris: Gallimard, 1975) pp. 174–5. Mandiargues called this list his modern 'Enfer', a reference to the collection of books of the same name, considered unsuitable for public consumption, mainly on the grounds of their obscenity, and set up by the Bibliothèque Nationale in 1874. The last addition to the collection was made in 1972. As Nicholas Harrison points out in *Circles of Censorship. Censorship and its Metaphors in French History, Literature, and Theory* (Oxford: Clarendon Press, 1995), p. 54, n. 12, the 'Enfer' preserved books which otherwise might have been burnt or simply forgotten, so inclusion in this particular 'hell' represented both condemnation and salvation.
5. 'La pornographie, c'est l'érotisme des autres'; cited by Jean-Jacques Pauvert, *Nouveaux Visages de la Censure* (Paris: Les Belles Lettres, 1994), p. 59.

6. *Jacobellis* v. *Ohio*, 1964; cited by Catherine Itzin, 'Harm in Porn' in *The Law* (June, July, August 1995), p. 22. Itzin is one of Britain's leading anti-pornography academics: as an example of her work, see Catherine Itzin (ed.), *Pornography. Women, Violence and Civil Liberties* (Oxford: Oxford University Press, 1992).

7. See Linda Williams, 'A Provoking Agent. The Pornography and Performance Art of Annie Sprinkle' in Gibson and Gibson (eds), *Dirty Looks. Women, Pornography, Power* (London: BFI Publishing, 1993), pp. 176–91; this reference, pp. 181–2.

8. Quoted by Stephen Heath, *The Sexual Fix* (London and Basingstoke: Macmillan, 1982), pp. 105–6.

9. See Linda Williams, 'Second Thoughts on Hard Core. American Obscenity Law and the Scapegoating of Deviance' in *Dirty Looks*, pp. 46–61; this reference, p. 47, n. 1.

10. Susan Sontag, 'The Pornographic Imagination' in Douglas A. Hughes (ed.), *Perspectives on Pornography* (New York: Macmillan, St. Martin's Press, 1970), pp. 131–69; this reference, pp. 153–4.

11. The Obscene Publications Act, 1959.

12. Williams, 'Second Thoughts', pp. 48–9.

13. Ibid., p. 54.

14. Angela Carter, *The Sadeian Woman. An Exercise in Cultural History* (London: Virago Press, 1979), p. 17.

15. Quoted by Andrew Ross, 'The popularity of pornography' in Simon During (ed.), *The Cultural Studies Reader* (London: Routledge, 1993), p. 232.

16. Ibid., pp. 232–3.

17. Jennifer Wallace, 'What does it take to be a woman?', *The Times Higher Education Supplement*, 8 May 1998, pp. 16–7; this reference, p. 17.

18. Laura Kipnis, 'She-Male Fantasies and the Aesthetics of Pornography' in *Dirty Looks*, pp. 124–43; this reference, p. 135.

19. See Frappier-Mazur, 'Marginal Canons', p. 119.

20. For a detailed account of this process, see Vernon A. Rosario, *The Erotic Imagination. French Histories of Perversity* (New York and Oxford: Oxford University Press, 1997).

21. See Jean-Jacques Pauvert, *Anthologie historique des lectures érotiques. De Guillaume Apollinaire à Philippe Pétain, 1905–1944* (Paris: Stock/Spengler, 1995), p. 8.

22. Ibid., p. 15.

23. Frappier-Mazur, 'Marginal Canons', p. 116, n. 13.

24. Ibid., p. 123. The final stage of this evolution is presumably the representation of female sexuality from the female standpoint and for the female reader: see below.

25. Pauvert, *Anthologie*, p. 10.

26. Ibid., p. 27.

27. Frappier-Mazur, 'Marginal Canons', p. 120.

28. For example, Françoise Rey, Raphaële Billetdoux and Catherine Cusset.

29. Frappier-Mazur, 'Marginal Canons', p. 121, n. 24.

30. *Corps de jeune fille*, p. 151.

31. See, for instance, *Troubles de femmes. Nouvelles érotiques* (Paris: Spengler, 1994). This collection of stories by Jeanne de Berg, Françoise Rey, Régine Deforges, Calixthe Beyala and others offers a characteristic selection of contemporary French erotic writing by women.

32. The work of Alina Reyes is a notable exception to this trend in French women's writing of the contemporary period. Her first, highly successful novel, *Le Boucher* (*The Butcher*) (1988), foregrounds the intense physicality and the ephemerality of erotic experience occurring outside emotionally-based relationships and celebrates the erotic body, whether male or female, as fragmented and objectified like pieces of butcher's meat.

33. For a detailed discussion of the evolution of specifically lesbian-oriented fiction, see Hughes and Ince, *French Erotic Fiction*, Introduction.

34. Ibid., p. 18.

35. 'Marginal Canons', p. 128.

36. Ibid.

37. John de St Jorre, *The Good Ship Venus. The Erotic Voyage of the Olympia Press* (London: Pimlico, 1994), Preface.

38. The best known of these were Henry Miller's *Tropic of Cancer* and *Tropic of Capricorn*; Samuel Beckett's trilogy, *Molloy*, *Malone Dies*, and *The Unnamable*; J. P. Donleavy's *The Ginger Man*; Vladimir Nabokov's *Lolita*; Pauline Réage's *Story of O* (published in English and French); and William Burroughs's *Naked Lunch*. For a full and fascinating account of the history of the Olympia Press, see de St Jorre, *The Good Ship Venus*.

39. Even publication in Paris by an American author was risky – Nabokov, for instance, initially wanted the Olympia Press publication of *Lolita* to appear under a pseudonym for fear of losing his teaching job at Cornell University: see ibid., p. 125.

40. See Robert Netz, *Histoire de la censure dans l'édition* (Paris: PUF, 1997), p. 13.

41. Between 1678 and 1701, for example, roughly half the books seized had religious contents, with very few concerning the internal politics of Louis XIV: see ibid., p. 37.
42. Ibid., p. 45.
43. The best account in English of the trade in forbidden books in eighteenth-century France is Robert Darnton, *The Forbidden Best-Sellers of Pre-Revolutionary France* (London: HarperCollins, 1996).
44. Ibid., p. 87.
45. See Darnton, ibid., pp. 169–246 for a detailed analysis of the political power of the printed word. Although, as Darnton himself concedes, the hypothesis of a causal link between the printed word and political radicalism is difficult to prove, there is some evidence that the French authorities believed in it: in 1823, *Les Liaisons dangereuses*, which had appeared in 1782, was condemned to be destroyed by a Paris court for having helped cause the Revolution of 1789 – see Harrison, *Circles of Censorship*, p. 28.
46. Netz, *Histoire de la censure*, p. 75.
47. Ibid., p. 85.
48. Cited by Netz, ibid., p. 91.
49. Harrison, *Circles of Censorship*, p. 53.
50. Netz, *Histoire de la censure*, pp. 90–1.
51. The *Index Librorum Prohibitorum* was not officially ended until 1965 – see Harrison, *Circles of Censorship*, p. 11.
52. Netz points out that, far from constituting a 'wave of pornography', only 21 books per annum on average ended up in the Bibliothèque Nationale's 'Enfer' between 1890 and 1912 (*Histoire de la censure*, p. 99).
53. Ibid., p. 98.
54. Ibid., pp. 111–13 for the detail of this legislation and its effects.
55. de St. Jorre, *The Good Ship Venus*, p. 67.
56. Netz, *Histoire de la censure*, p. 116.
57. *Magazine littéraire*, no. 37, February 1970.
58. For a detailed discussion of the 'Guyotat Affair', see Harrison, *Circles of Censorship*, pp. 174–80.
59. Netz, *Histoire de la censure*, pp. 117–18.
60. Pauvert, *Nouveaux Visages*, p. 188.
61. Ibid., p. 189.
62. Hugh Dauncey, summarising Girodias's views in 'Publishing, pornography and personal freedom: l'Affaire Dreyfus, l'Affaire Miller, l'Affaire Lolita and l'Affaire Kissinger', *French Cultural Studies*, iii (1992), pp. 203–9; this reference, p. 208.
63. Ibid., p. 2.

64. In the USA, anti-pornography feminists have recently secured new limitations on sexual speech, persuading courts to ban a wide range of sexually orientated expression from campuses and workplaces: see Nadine Strossen, *Defending Pornography. Free Speech, Sex and the Fight for Women's Rights* (London: Abacus, 1995), p. 82.

65. See Catherine MacKinnon, *Only Words* (London: HarperCollins, 1994), Andrea Dworkin, *Pornography: Men Possessing Women* (London: The Women's Press Ltd, 1981) (originally published 1979), and *Intercourse* (London: Secker & Warburg, 1987).

66. Among recent studies, opposing the censorship of pornography, see especially, Alison Assiter and Avedon Carol (eds), *Bad Girls & Dirty Pictures. The Challenge to Reclaim Feminism* (London and Boulder, Colorado: Pluto Press, 1993); Bill Thompson, *Soft Core. Moral Crusades against Pornography in Britain and America* (London: Cassell, 1994); Avedon Carol, *Nudes, Prudes and Attitudes* (Cheltenham: New Clarion Press, 1994); Nadine Strossen, *Defending Pornography* (London: Abacus, 1995); Laura Kipnis, *Bound and Gagged. Pornography and the Politics of Fantasy in America* (New York: Grove Press, 1996).

67. Thompson, *Soft Core*, Chapter 4: 'Pornography Effects Studies', pp. 116–51.

68. This is still true in the modern era, as the Guyotat affair or Tony Duvert's homoerotic fiction show.

69. de St. Jorre, *The Good Ship Venus*, p. 273.

70. Pauvert, *Nouveaux Visages*, 'Une Histoire Officielle', pp. 131–44.

71. This is the main thesis of Harrison's *Circles of Censorship*.

72. Michel Foucault, *Histoires de la sexualité 1: La volonté de savoir* (Paris: Gallimard, 1976).

73. Even in pre-Christian or pagan cultures, sexual knowledge was wrapped in taboo; indeed, the Greek word for sex manual authors, 'anaiskhuntographos', means 'writers of shameless things': see Roy Porter and Mikulas Teich (eds), *Sexual Knowledge, Sexual Science: The History of Attitudes to Sexuality* (Cambridge: Cambridge University Press, 1994).

# Chapter 2

1. Quoted by Jean-Jacques Pauvert in his *Anthologie historique des lectures érotiques. De Eisenhower à Emmanuelle, 1945–85* (Paris: Stock/Spengler, 1995), p. 928.

2. The first edition was in 1907, according to Louis Perceau's *Bibliographie du roman érotique, II* (Paris: Fourdrivier, 1930), pp. 56–7.

3. 'Les Maîtres de l'Amour', Bibliothèque des Curieux.

4. *L'Oeuvre du Marquis de Sade* (Paris: Bibliothèque des Curieux, 1909).

5. Guillaume Apollinaire, Fernand Fleuret et Louis Perceau, *L'Enfer de la Bibliothèque Nationale* (Paris: Mercure de France, 1913).

6. Pascal Pia, in his *Apollinaire*, 'Écrivains de toujours' (Paris: Seuil, 1965), practically ignores the poet's pornographic output, merely observing that the two erotic novels were written to make much needed money, while Julia Hartwig in *Apollinaire* (Paris: Mercure de France, 1972) suggests that these pseudonymously published works have little artistic merit and respect for their author will prevent them from ever seeing the light of day!

7. In Apollinaire's best-known collection of poetry, *Alcools*, for instance, there are many instances of erotic imagery, such as this potentially blasphemous, yet visually amusing and delightfully original image from *L'Ermite*:

> O Seigneur, flagellez les nuées du coucher
> Qui vous tendent au ciel de si jolis culs roses
> O Lord, flagellate the clouds of sunset
> That thrust such pretty pink arses at you in heaven

8. Robert Desnos, quoted by Jean-Jacques Pauvert, *Anthologie historique des lectures érotiques. De Guillaume Apollinaire à Philippe Pétain, 1905–1944* (Paris: Stock/Spengler, 1995), p. 76.

9. Preface to a clandestine edition of *Les Onze Mille Verges*, edited by René Bonnel in 1930, and quoted by Jean-Jacques Pauvert, 'Un pornographe ou les deux Guillaume', *Magazine Littéraire*, November 1996, pp. 48–53; this reference, p. 50.

10. Apollinaire was accused of stealing the Mona Lisa and imprisoned for six days in 1911. He was briefly famous for this and almost thrown out of the country.

11. Frans Amelinckx, 'Apollinaire's *Les Onze Mille Verges*: Humor and Pornography', *West Virginia Philological Papers*, vol. 29 (1983) pp. 8–15; this reference, p. 9.

12. Michael Perkins, *The Secret Record: Modern Erotic Literature* (New York: William Morrow, 1976), p. 44.

13. Peter Michelson, *Speaking the Unspeakable: A Poetics of Obscenity* (New York: State University of New York Press, 1993), p. 13.
14. The first two syllables of 'Culculine' replicate 'cul', the French for 'arse', whilst her surname is a homophone of 'enconner', meaning 'to fuck'.
15. Amelinckx, 'Apollinaire's *Les Onze Mille Verges*'.
16. Michelson, *Speaking the Unspeakable*, p. 14.
17. Umberto Eco attributes all metaphoric substitution to identifiable links between beads in a metonymic chain, identifiable, that is, in terms of contiguities established according to cultural associations by the reader himself (see Umberto Eco, 'The Semantics of Metaphor' in *The Role of the Reader* (London: Hutchinson, 1981), pp. 67–88).
18. Paul Ricœur, *La métaphore vive* (Paris: Éditions du Seuil, 1975), p. 236.
19. Pierre Guyotat, *Littérature interdite* (Paris: Gallimard, 1972), p. 12.
20. Marina Yaguello, *Les mots et les femmes* (Paris: Payot, 1978), p. 156.
21. Roland Barthes, *Sade, Fourier, Loyola* (Paris: Éditions du Seuil, 1971), pp. 128–9.
22. Ibid.
23. For a detailed discussion of the comic transparency of many of the characters' names, see Amelinckx, 'Apollinaire's *Les Onze Mille Verges*', p. 10.
24. See *Histoire de Juliette*.
25. In a psychoanalytic perspective, such representations of the vagina might suggest male fear of castration by a voracious feminine, as symbolised by the nightmare image of the *vagina dentata*, an image which Culculine brings starkly to mind when she tears off Chaloupe's penis with her teeth! Beware of bearded vaginal mouths – they may look alluring, but they can bite!
26. There are clear references in the text to the assassination of King Alexander of Serbia and the Russo-Japanese war.
27. The most accessible account of Bakhtin's theories is to be found in his essay, 'Discourse in the Novel' in Michael Holquist (ed.), M. M. Bakhtin, *The Dialogic Imagination* (Austin: University of Texas Press, 1981).
28. This narratological term, coined by Gérard Genette, means 'within the narrative'.
29. Holquist, *The Dialogic Imagination*, pp. 420–1.

30. Julia Kristeva, 'Word, Dialogue and Novel' in Toril Moi (ed.), *The Kristeva Reader* (Oxford: Basil Blackwell, 1986), pp. 34–61; this reference, p. 37.
31. Ibid., p. 36.
32. Jean Mainil, 'Érotisme carnavalesque dans un roman obscène de l'Ancien Régime', *La Chouette*, no. 26 (1995), pp. 26–35; this reference, p. 28.
33. Mikhaïl Bakhtine, *L'œuvre de François Rabelais* (Paris: Gallimard, 1970), p. 28; cited by Mainil, 'Érotisme carnavalesque', p. 28.

## Chapter 3

1. Since the eighteenth century in particular, the erotic genre in France has shown strong ludic tendencies: witness, for example, the parodic *mises en scène* of Nerciat's *Le Doctorat impromptu*, Diderot's *Les Bijoux indiscrets* or Crébillon fils's *Le Sopha*, not to mention the many linguistic and formal innovations to be found in Sade's fictions.
2. The word 'pornographic' is used descriptively, but not pejoratively, to denote any writing that transgresses sexual taboos with the sole aim of exciting the reader sexually.
3. The erotic was certainly not a peripheral activity for Louÿs: after his death his heirs discovered 400 kilos of erotic writings; a recently published anthology of his work in the genre covers more than a thousand pages: see Jean-Paul Goujon (ed.), *Pierre Louÿs: L'Oeuvre érotique* (Paris: Sortilèges, 1994), p. xvii. Louÿs's interest in the history of eroticism as evidenced by the many unpublished works he wrote on the subject led Goujon to describe him as a 'real encyclopedist of sex' (ibid., p. xxix).
4. Ibid., p. xxviii.
5. Stephen Heath, *The Sexual Fix* (London and Basingstoke: Macmillan, 1982), p. 107.
6. Raymond Queneau's tomboyish young heroine in his classic novel, *Zazie dans le métro*.
7. Goujon, *Pierre Louÿs*, p. xxx.
8. Ibid.
9. Ibid., p. xxiv, n. 26.
10. In his representation of women as sexually voracious, Louÿs also reflects a dominant characterisation of women by Decadent *fin de siècle* writers, that of the dangerously destructive *femme fatale*: see Jean Pierrot, *The Decadent Imagination* 1800–1900, translated by D. Coltman (Chicago and London: University of Chicago Press, 1981).

11. Andrea Dworkin, *Pornography: Men Possessing Women* (London: The Women's Press Ltd, 1981), p. 149.

12. Jean-Paul Goujon observes that *Trois Filles de leur mère* could be considered a self-parody, in that it appears to replicate in a a humorous and obscene way one of Louÿs's mainstream novels, *La Femme et le pantin*: see Goujon, *Pierre Louÿs*, p. xvi.

13. Louÿs's text addresses itself initially to a female addressee (see above).

14. See, for example, *Les 120 Journées de Sodom* (Paris: La Collection P.O.L., 1992), p. 70: 'Le nom de Dieu n'y sera prononcé qu'accompagné d'invectives ou d'imprécations et on le répétera le plus souvent possible.' ('God's name will only be pronounced if accompanied by curses and abuse and will be repeated as often as possible.').

15. As the narrator of *Les 120 Journées de Sodom* recognises, laughter and eroticism are incompatible: 'Le moindre rire, ou le moindre manque d'attention ou de respect ou de soumission dans les parties de débauche, sera une des fautes les plus graves et les plus cruellement punies.' (The slightest laughter, or the slightest lack of attention or respect or submission in the sessions of debauchery, will be one of the gravest and most cruelly punished faults) (*Les 120 Journées*, p. 69).

16. See my discussion, above, of the *Avis à la lectrice*, which introduces the narrative.

17. The reader will note that the English translator has raised the age of the child from ten to fourteen, effectively censoring the paedophilic implications of the French text.

18. Note the mistranslation of the word 'caca' which means 'shit', not 'cocoa'.

19. It was Jean-Jacques Rousseau who coined this expression in the eighteenth century to denote pornographic novels, read as masturbatory aids: see Jean-Marie Goulemot, *Forbidden Texts. Erotic Literature and its Readers in Eighteenth-Century France* (London: Polity Press, 1994), p. x; originally published as *Ces livres qu'on ne lit que d'une main* (Paris: Éditions Alinea, 1991).

20. These terms were developed by the French structuralist, Gérard Genette: 'extradiegetic' describes a narrator or narratee who is invisible in the story (remaining outside the diegesis), 'homodiegetic' describes a narrator who is present as a character in the plot which (s)he unfolds, and 'metadiegetic' denotes a second-level narrative or 'narrative within a narrative'. Genette also uses the term 'intradiegetic' to describe a second-level narrator (or narratee), who is a

character telling (or listening to) a tale which is embedded in a primary narrative. (Genette, *Figures III* (Paris: Éditions du Seuil, 1972), pp. 238–41).

21.  Ibid., pp. 265–6: Genette argues that the real reader cannot identify with intradiegetic narratees addressed by an intradiegetic narrator, as here, but only with an extradiegetic narratee adressed by an extradiegetic narrator. Louÿs breaks the conventional rules of narrative, however, by having an intradiegetic narrator address an extradiegetic narratee.

22.  *Les 120 Journées de Sodom*, p. 76.

23.  The interpretive participation of the reader is one of the characteristic strategies of the erotic narrative: see Goulemot, *Forbidden Texts*, Chapter 6.

24.  A *mise en abyme* is a mirror image within the text of the writing of the text itself.

25.  Louÿs succeeded for years in persuading classical scholars and literary critics that *Les Chansons de Bilitis* (*The Songs of Bilitis*), which he himself had composed, were the rediscovered work of an ancient Greek poet. These erotic prose poems about a Greek courtesan were published in 1895 by the Librairie de l'Art Indépendant, with the subtitle, 'Traduites du grec pour la première fois par P. L.' ('Translated from the Greek for the first time by P. L.').

# Chapter 4

1.  Georges Bataille, *Oeuvres Complètes*, vol. I (Paris: Gallimard, 1970; J.-J. Pauvert, 1967 for *Histoire de l'œil*), p. 5.

2.  Bataille, 'Le Petit', *Oeuvres Complètes*, vol. VII (Paris: Gallimard, 1974), p. 234: 'Le nom de Lord Auch se rapporte à l'habitude d'un de mes amis: irrité, il ne disait plus «aux chiottes», abrégeait, disait «aux ch'». Lord en anglais veut dire Dieu (dans les textes saints): Lord Auch est Dieu se soulageant.' ('The name Lord Auch refers to a habit of a friend of mine; when vexed, instead of saying 'aux chiottes!' (to the shithouse), he would shorten it to 'aux ch''. *Lord* is English for God (in the Scriptures): Lord Auch is God relieving himself. ('W. C. Preface to *Story of the Eye*' in the Penguin translation, p. 76)).

3.  The first edition (1928) differs markedly from the other three, known as the 'new version', to the extent that they have to be regarded as constituting two distinct texts, which is why the Gallimard edition of Bataille's complete works, volume I, includes both. My analysis here is based on the first

edition (1928), which is also the basis of the Penguin translation.

4.  *Madame Edwarda* was published secretly under the pseudonym of Pierre Angélique in 1941 and 1945 (an English edition was put out by the Paris-based Olympia Press in 1955), while *Ma Mère* and *Le Mort* were not published at all until after the author's death. The only novels published under his own name during his lifetime were *Le Bleu du ciel*, written in 1935, published in 1957, and *L'Abbé C*, which appeared in 1950.

5.  Michael Richardson, *Georges Bataille* (London and New York: Routledge, 1994), p. 138, n. 36.

6.  Jean-Jacques Pauvert, *Anthologie Historique des lectures érotiques, De Guillaume Apollinaire à Philippe Pétain 1905–1944* (Paris: Stock/Spengler, 1995), p. 574.

7.  Susan Rubin Suleiman, 'Pornography, Transgression and the Avant-Garde: Bataille's *Story of the Eye*' in Nancy K. Miller (ed.), *The Poetics of Gender* (New York: Columbia University Press, 1986), pp. 117–36; this reference, p. 118.

8.  Susan Sontag, 'The Pornographic Imagination' in *Story of the Eye* (London: Penguin, 1982), pp. 83–118; these references, pp. 106 and 111 respectively; also, in Douglas A. Hughes (ed.), *Perspectives on Pornography* (New York: Macmillan, St Martins Press, 1970), pp. 131–69.

9.  Richardson, *Bataille*, p. 3.

10. Bataille never held a university post.

11. Richardson refers to the 'violent swings of his personality'; for this critic, the author's surreal and perplexing compositions, 'L'Anus solaire' and 'L'Œil pinéal', 'bear witness to his disturbed state, which caused him to seek treatment with the psychoanalyst, Adrian Borel.' (Richardson, *Bataille*, p. 20). He certainly liked to live life on the edge, experimenting with Russian roulette and blood sacrifice. In the 1930s, he founded the magazine, *Acéphale*, which gave rise to a secret society of the same name. It was rumoured that the members planned human sacrifices, though there is no evidence that any were actually performed (see Alain Arnaud and Gisèle Excoffon-Lafarge, *Bataille*, Écrivains de toujours series (Paris: Éditions du Seuil, 1978), p. 18).

12. Georges Bataille, *L'Érotisme* (Paris: Éditions de Minuit, 1957), p. 48.

13. Suleiman, 'Pornography', p. 123.

14. Philippe Sollers, 'Le toit' in *L'Écriture et l'expérience des limites* (Paris: Éditions du Seuil, 1968), pp. 105–38.

15. Typical in this regard is the otherwise very helpful book by Michael Richardson. Peter Michelson, too, sees *Story of the Eye* as 'clearly illustrating' Bataille's major theoretical work, *L'Érotisme*, a curious observation, given that the latter was written much later: see Michelson's *Speaking the Unspeakable. A Poetics of Obscenity* (New York: State University of New York Press, 1993), p. 146.

16. Roland Barthes, 'La Métaphore de l'œil' in *Essais critiques* (Paris: Éditions du Seuil, 1964), pp. 238–45; English translation 'The Metaphor of the Eye', in the Penguin translation, pp. 119–27.

17. See, for instance, Sigmund Freud, *Three Essays on Sexuality* (London: The Pelican Freud Library, vol. 7, 1977), p. 73.

18. Gilles Deleuze, *Présentation de Sacher-Masoch. Le Froid et le Cruel* (Paris: Éditions de Minuit, 1967), pp. 51–2.

19. Linda Williams, *Hard Core. Power, Pleasure and the Frenzy of the Visible* (London: Pandora Press, 1990), p. 213.

20. Ibid., p. 215.

21. Deleuze, *Sacher-Masoch*, p. 108.

22. See Barthes, 'La Métaphore'.

23. Deleuze, *Sacher-Masoch*, p. 93.

24. Ibid., pp. 79 and 91.

25. Ibid., p. 63.

26. Ibid., pp. 29–30.

27. Barthes, 'La Métaphore', p. 240.

28. Other fictions by Bataille also return obsessively to the evacuation of the body: see *Madame Edwarda* and, especially, *Le Bleu du ciel* and *Le Mort*. In *Le Bleu du ciel*, the main female character, Dirty, urinates and defecates in public in the opening scene. In this text, there are also numerous references to bodily liquids (sweat, urine, semen) and images linking the sun and blood. In *Le Mort*, there is a similar insistence on evacuation: after the death of a man we assume to have been her lover (or, perhaps, client), Marie runs out into the rainy night, lies on the ground and urinates down her legs. Later, she urinates on to a dwarf she has met in a bar; the dwarf, who is simultaneously masturbated by a clown, comes soaked in urine. Marie, who is still urinating, proceeds to wash her face and body in her own urine.

29. Bataille, *L'Érotisme*, p. 65.

30. Ibid., p. 295.

31. Jean de Berg's *L'Image* is perhaps less palatable to female readers because the treatment of the female victim, Claire, including her forced urination, is predominantly sadistic: see

Williams's interesting discussion of the film adaptation of this novel, *Hard Core*, p. 200.

32. Andrea Dworkin, *Pornography: Men Possessing Women* (London: The Women's Press Ltd, 1981), p. 175.

33. We remember that, for Freud, blindness and castration are metaphorically linked. See discussion of the 'primal scene' below.

34. The Penguin translator regrettably avoided rendering the word directly.

35. See Pierre Guiraud, *Dictionnaire érotique* (Paris: Éditions Payot & Rivages, 1993), p. 195.

36. The 'femme castratrice' can be found elsewhere in Bataille's fiction. See, for instance, *Madame Edwarda* (Paris: Jean-Jacques Pauvert, 10/18, 1989), which contains a number of negative images of women: 'la nudité du bordel appelle le couteau du boucher' (p. 35) ('the nakedness of the brothel invites the butcher's knife'), 'le loup qui la masquait la faisait animale' (p. 39) ('the wolf that clothed her made her into an animal'), 'Elle était noire [...] angoissante comme un trou' ('She was black [...] as distressing as a hole').

37. Williams, *Hard Core*, p. 116.

38. Sigmund Freud, 'Fetishism' in *On Sexuality*, vol. 7 (London: The Pelican Freud Library, 1977), pp. 345–57.

39. Chris Straayer, 'The Seduction of Boundaries: Feminist Fluidity in Annie Sprinkle's Art/Education/Sex' in Gibson and Gibson (eds), *Dirty Looks. Women, Pornography, Power* (London: BFI, 1993), p. 172.

40. Deleuze, *Sacher-Masoch*, p. 87.

41. Ibid., p. 84.

42. Ibid., p. 79.

43. Ibid., p. 53.

44. Ibid., p. 88.

45. Andrew Hussey, 'Bull-fighting in Georges Bataille', *Manchester Working Papers in French*, no. 1 (Spring 1994), pp. 53–69. Hussey argues against a Freudian reading of *Histoire de l'œil*, proposing instead that images of the sun, eye and body orifices are linked to a 'Dionysian' celebration of the bullfight, a tragic ritual of waste. Hussey is right, in my view, to see the bullfight as a 'transgressive act, which goes beyond the limits of the possible', but the transgression seems to me to be more oedipal than metaphysical. What the author is ultimately destroying in *Histoire de l'œil* is not, of course, his real father, but the syphilitic father and his suffering, so vividly fixated and condensed in that horrible memory.

46. The father appeared to be laughing sardonically during an act that exposed his genitals to the son and so must have forcefully reminded the latter of his syphilitic condition. The text of 'Coïncidences' shows no conscious awareness on Bataille's part of this association between urination and the excruciating pain that his syphilitic father had to endure.

47. This is precisely the scenario of another of Bataille's 'oedipal' narratives, *Ma mère*, in which the narrator's mother actively seduces her adoring but guilt-ridden son.

48. Interestingly, in *Madame Edwarda*, 'white eyes' are actually a signifier of the male orgasm: in this narrative, a carriage-driver's eyes turn white as he is seduced by the eponymous heroine.

49. Richardson, *Bataille*, p. 95.

50. According to standard psychoanalytic findings, female fetishism of any kind is extremely rare: see Nancy Friday, *My Secret Garden* (London: Quartet Books, 1994; first published by Virago, 1975), pp. 171–3. This is not the case with female masochism, however, which, as I pointed out at the beginning of this chapter, is regrettably not considered by Deleuze.

51. Williams, *Hard Core*, pp. 259 and 266.

52. Deleuze, *Sacher-Masoch*, p. 109.

53. We saw earlier how, for Parveen Adams, the female spectator of SM films may similarly oscillate between different identificatory positions: see Williams, *Hard Core*, p. 215.

54. Laura Kipnis, *Bound and Gagged. Pornography and the Politics of Fantasy in America* (New York: Grove Press, 1996), pp. 196–7.

55. Williams, *Hard Core*, p. 228.

56. Julia Kristeva, 'Bataille solaire, ou le texte coupable' in *Histoires d'amour* (Paris: Denoël, 1983), pp. 341–6; this reference, p. 346.

# Chapter 5

1. John de St. Jorre, 'The Unmasking of O' in *The New Yorker*, 4 August 1994, pp. 42–50. The enigma of the author's identity is not, however, completely resolved, since, according to the St. Jorre interview, 'Dominique Aury' is not her real name either, the writer having adopted this earlier pseudonym during the war years.

2. Quoted by Régine Deforges in her *O m'a dit: entretiens avec Pauline Réage* (Paris: Jean-Jacques Pauvert, 1975), p. 33.

3. Quoted by Deforges, ibid., p. 16. In conversation with Deforges, Pauline Réage's response to these charges was simply that 'les camps de concentration offensent les bonnes mœurs, et la bombe atomique et la torture – la vie tout court offense les bonnes mœurs – et non pas spécifiquement les diverses manières de faire l'amour.' ('concentration camps offend against public decency, and the atom bomb and torture – life itself offends against public decency – not especially, the different ways of making love.') (ibid.).

4. John de St. Jorre, *The Good Ship Venus. The Erotic Voyages of the Olympia Press* (London: Pimlico, 1994), p. 210. Ch. 8, 'Une Lettre d'Amour: *the True Story of* Story of O', pp. 209–40, provides a useful and detailed account of the novel's publication and of attempts by the authorities to censor it and, together with *The New Yorker* article, is the source of much of my information in this area.

5. Andrea Dworkin, *Pornography. Men Possessing Women* (London: The Women's Press Ltd, 1981), p. 34.

6. St. Jorre, 'The Unmasking of O', p. 45.

7. Deforges, *O m'a dit,* p. 110.

8. Ibid., pp. 219–20.

9. Michel Butor, *Les Mots dans la peinture* (Genève: Éditions Skira, 1980), p. 17.

10. Deforges, *O m'a dit,* p. 105.

11. This line does not appear in the English version: 'In a final chapter, which was left out, O returned to Roissy, where Sir Stephen abandoned her.' (my translation)

12. St. Jorre, 'The Unmasking of O', p. 47.

13. See Gérard Genette, *Figures III* (Paris: Éditions du Seuil, 1972), pp. 238–40 and 252–4, for a fuller explanation of these narratological terms.

14. It seems that, on a conscious level, the use of this letter was not intended to be symbolic; O began as Odile, a friend of the author's: 'She was one of the North African group who came to Paris after the Liberation, and she was very much in love with Albert Camus at one time [...] We worked together, and she later married a Royal Air Force pilot and went to England. She knew all about the name and was enchanted. But after a few pages I decided that I couldn't do all those things to poor Odile, so I just kept the first letter. It has nothing to do with erotic symbolism or the shape of the female sex.' (St. Jorre, 'The Unmasking of O', pp. 45–6). This disclaimer does not, of course, explain why Aury chose Odile in the first place, nor does it preclude the possibility that the choice of both name and letter were *unconsciously* motivated.

15. See, for example, p. 265: 'Le plaisir qu'O prenait, elle, à tenir Jacqueline pareillement moite et brûlante resserrée sur sa main, lui était témoin et garant du plaisir de Sir Stephen.' ('O's own pleasure in grasping a similarly wet and burning Jacqueline in her contracting fingers was a constant reminder of the pleasure Sir Stephen took in doing the same thing to her.' (p. 219)).

16. O is watched by Sir Stephen: 'Elle savait qu'il pouvait la voir, cependant qu'elle ne le voyait pas, et une fois de plus elle sentit qu'elle était heureuse de cette exposition constante, de cette constante prison de ses regards où elle était enfermée' (p. 301) ('She knew he could see her, even though she could not see him, and once again she felt that she was fortunate to be exposed thus, openly, constantly, fortunate in this prison wherein his constant gaze enclosed her' (p. 253)) and by Natalie: 'Blottie sur le tapis dans l'alcôve au pied du lit d'O [...] elle regarda chaque fois O liée à la balustrade de bois se tordre sous la cravache, O à genoux recevoir humblement dans sa bouche l'épais sexe dressé de Sir Stephen, O prosternée écarter elle-même ses fesses à deux mains pour lui offrir le chemin de ses reins, sans autres sentiments que l'admiration, l'impatience et l'envie.' (p. 285) ('Cowering on the rug in the alcove at the foot of O's bed [...] she watched every time O was tied to the wooden bedstead, watched her writhe under the riding-crop, watched the kneeling O humbly receive the thick, uprisen sex of Sir Stephen in her mouth, watched the prostrate O spread her own buttocks with her own hands to open the passage into her behind, watched all that with no other emotions save admiration, impatience, and envy.' (pp. 237–8)).

17. See the discussion earlier of the alternative endings offered to the reader. It is perplexing that even critics who are in the main sympathetic to the novel choose to ignore the less than definitive status of O's suicide: see, for example, Peter Michelson, *Speaking the Unspeakable. A Poetics of Obscenity* (Albany: State University of New York Press, 1993), p. 58.

18. Andrea Dworkin, *Woman Hating* (New York: E.P. Dutton & Co., 1974), p. 56.

19. Dworkin, *Pornography*, pp. 167–78.

20. Susan Sontag, 'The Pornographic Imagination' in Douglas A. Hughes (ed.), *Perspectives on Pornography* (New York: Macmillan, St Martins Press, 1970), pp. 131–69; this reference, pp. 152–3.

21. Ibid., p. 164.

22. Luce Irigaray, *Spéculum de l'autre femme* (Paris: Éditions de Minuit, 1974), p. 238.

23. See Luce Irigaray, 'Ce Sexe qui n'en est pas un' in *Ce Sexe qui n'en est pas un* (Paris: Éditions de Minuit, 1977), p. 28.

24. Quoted by Deforges, *O m'a dit*, pp. 133–4.

25. Michelson, *Speaking the Unspeakable*, p. 63.

26. Deforges, *O m'a dit*, pp. 211–14.

27. St. Jorre, 'The Unmasking of O', p. 46.

28. 'ce qu'elle demandait aux femmes (et ne leur rendait pas, ou si peu), elle était heureuse et trouvait naturel que les hommes fussent acharnés à le lui demander. Ainsi était-elle à la fois et constamment complice des unes et des autres, et gagnait sur les deux tableaux.' (p. 171) ('what she asked of women (and didn't repay them, save in such small measure), she was happy, and found entirely natural, that men imperiously demand of her. Thus was she simultaneously and at all times the accomplice of both women and men, and stood only to gain with each.' (p. 136)).

29. Michelson, *Speaking the Unspeakable*, p. 62.

30. Stephen Marcus, *The Other Victorians*, quoted by Michelson, ibid., p. 56; also published as 'An Apology for Pornography' in Hughes (ed.), *Perspectives*, p. 65.

31. 'C'est que René la laissait libre, et qu'elle détestait sa liberté' (p. 175) ('It was that René was leaving her free, and that she abhorred this freedom' (p. 139)).

32. See Roland Barthes, *Le Degré zéro de l'écriture* (Paris: Éditions du Seuil, 1953 and 1972).

33. Pauline Réage, quoted by Deforges, *O m'a dit*, p. 209.

34. The owl symbolised wisdom in Greek antiquity. The owl mask therefore carries an appropriate symbolism, in the context of O's Zen-like quest for the absolute.

35. See, for example, p. 300: 'Il lui semblait en outre que les filles qu'elle caressait appartenaient de droit à l'homme à qui elle-même appartenait, et qu'elle n'était là que par procuration' ('It also seemed to her, furthermore, that the girls she caressed belonged by all rights to the man to whom she herself belonged, and that she was there in a role, and that this role was a procuress' (p. 252)). The reader will note that 'par procuration', meaning 'by proxy', is mistranslated in the English version.

36. J. E. Cirlot, *A Dictionary of Symbols* (London: Routledge, 1962; this edition, 1993), pp. 231–2.

# Chapter 6

1. In his *Anthologie historique des lectures érotiques. De Eisenhower à Emmanuelle, 1945–85* (Paris: Stock/Spengler, 1995), p. 506, Jean-Jacques Pauvert points out that, in the late 1950s, eroticism became one of the main subjects of conversation and that the cinema of the period reflected this preoccupation, with the appearance of films such as *Baby Doll* in the United States, and in Europe, Vadim's *And God Created Woman* , Buñuel's *Viridiana*, Fellini's *La Dolce Vita*, and the enormous popularity on both continents of sex symbols, like Brigitte Bardot and Marilyn Monroe.

2. A law passed on 23 December, 1958, the same year that *Emmanuelle* was published, strengthened penalties for 'books that offended public decency' and granted powers to force publishers to cease trading. Under the influence of Mme de Gaulle and a number of Christian ministers in the government, the early years of de Gaulle's return to power in 1959 were notable for the number and severity of legal actions against the book trade: see Pauvert, *Anthologie*, p. 507.

3. Quoted by Jean-Jacques Pauvert in his postface to the novel.

4. While the MLA Bibliography lists only one article dealing with Arsan's novel (Judith Roof, 'The Erotic Travelogue: The Scopophilic Pleasure of Race vs. Gender', *Arizona Quarterly*, 47:4 (Tucson, AZ.: Winter, 1991), pp. 119–35), the films, particularly the first one, are often cited as examples of 1970s' popular culture, usually in negative terms in the context of the debate surrounding censorship; see, for instance, Andrea Dworkin, *Pornography: Men Possessing Women* (London: The Women's Press Ltd, 1981), p. 128. It is not my intention in this brief discussion to consider the *Emmanuelle* films, which differ greatly from the novel and in which Emmanuelle Arsan had no creative involvement.

5. See Gaëtan Brulotte, 'Le Thème du dépaysement dans la littérature érotique d'expression française', *Revue francophone de louisiane*, vol. 1, no. 2 (1986), pp. 20–32.

6. See Peter Cryle, *Geometry in the Boudoir. Configurations of French Erotic Narrative* (Ithaca and London: Cornell University Press, 1994), Ch. 4: 'Toward the Learner-Centred Boudoir'.

7. The depiction of women and women's sexuality by pornographic writers and film-makers has been much debated by feminist commentators. See Chapter 1 for a detailed summary of the pro- and anti-censorship positions.

8. It is perhaps to be regretted that Arsan did not stick to her original plan of having a woman and not a man play the part

of Emmanuelle's educator. The author felt that, given the part played by other female characters in the heroine's instruction, there was a risk of men being completely excluded from the novel (source: personal letter from Emmanuelle Arsan to the author, dated 21 September 1994; referred to hereafter as 'Interview with E. A.'). Readers will judge for themselves whether Arsan was justified in putting a man into this key role.

9. Sade's *Juliette* and *Justine* provide well-known examples of this tactic.

10. Arsan has never given public interviews, consequently there has been much speculation about the author's real gender. If 'Emmanuelle Arsan' is indeed the pseudonym of a male writer, some would argue that this knowledge should inform our reading of a narrative the subject matter of which is female sexuality. In fact, there is no decisive evidence concerning the author's sexual identity and, even if there were, I see no reason on this or any other occasion to disinter the author from the grave dug by Roland Barthes in 1968: see his 'La mort de l'auteur' in *Le bruissement de la langue. Essais critiques IV* (Paris: Éditions du Seuil, 1984), pp. 63–9. It is not the voice of the author, but the voices of the text which are accessible to analysis.

11. Interview with E. A.

12. For Sade, the pleasure of sodomy derives in large part from the knowledge that it is a transgression of norms, the existence of which it presupposes. As Pierre Klossowski puts it, 'Pour Sade, l'acte sodomite est le mode par excellence de la transgression des normes – (ce qui suppose leur maintien paradoxal)' ('For Sade, the act of sodomy is the transgression of norms par excellence – which paradoxically presupposes their preservation') ('Le Philosophe scélérat' in *Sade mon prochain* (Paris: Éditions du Seuil, 1967), p. 37.)

13. Georges Bataille, *L'Érotisme* (Paris: Éditions de Minuit, 1957), p. 42.

14. For instance, Emmanuelle's and Mario's 'homosexual' desires are not labelled as such in the novel, which presents them rather as the expression of an excessive sexuality.

15. For psychoanalysis, the association between pleasure and transgression is essentially an unconscious one: it is at unconscious levels that prohibition stimulates desire. For an accessible and convincing discussion of the relationship that psychoanalysis identifies between prohibition and desire, see Catherine Belsey, 'Desire in Theory: Freud, Lacan,

Derrida', *Textual Practice*, vol. 7, no. 3 (Winter 1993), pp. 384–411.

16. See Chapter 1 for further discussion of the desirability of the taboo in eroticism.

17. For Jacques Lacan, women want to *be* the phallus, the object of desire, whereas men want to *have* it: see 'La signification du phallus' in *Écrits* (Paris: Éditions du Seuil, 1966), pp. 685–95. Like Freud and psychoanalysis in general, it is hardly surprising that Lacan has been criticised by some Anglo-American feminists for representing what they see as cultural stereotypes as universal sexual differences.

18. Gertrude Koch, 'The Body's Shadow Realm' in Pamela Church Gibson and Roma Gibson (eds), *Dirty Looks. Women, Pornography, Power* (London: BFI Publishing, 1993), pp. 22–45; this reference p. 40.

19. Ibid., p. 42.

20. See my discussion, in Chapter 4, of female urination as serving a similar function.

21. Those French feminists whose thinking is psychoanalytically informed might, however, find such metaphors unavoidable in any expression of the erotic. Julia Kristeva, for instance, closely follows Freud in her belief that the nature of the libido and therefore of the erotic in general is exclusively phallic and that there is no such thing as a purely feminine sexuality: see Freud, 'The transformations of puberty' in *Three Essays on Sexuality* (London: The Pelican Freud Library, vol. 7, 1977) and Kristeva, *Histoires d'amour* (Paris: Denoël, 1983), p. 80. Françoise Dolto has also argued that the libido of both men and women is essentially phallic: see her *Sexualité féminine* (Paris: Scarabée & Co, 1982), pp. 201–05. See also my conclusion to Chapter 4.

22. Gérard Genette, *Figures III* (Paris: Éditions du Seuil, 1972), p. 203.

23. Ibid., p. 203.

24. Gaëtan Brulotte, 'Petite narratologie du récit dit "érotique"', *Poétique*, no. 85 (Paris: Éditions du Seuil, 1991), pp. 3–16. Brulotte notes the preponderance of extradiegetic narration in the erotic genre – hence, he observes, the apparent simplicity of these narratives (though he adds that this innocence of form is, in fact, deceptive).

25. Genette, *Figures III*, p. 206.

26. Ibid., p. 210.

27. Claude Lévi-Strauss, *Les Structures Élémentaires de la parenté* (Paris: Plon, 1949).

28. Even in this part of the novel, there is a privileging of Emmanuelle's point of view: as elsewhere, we are frequently admitted, via direct narration or *style indirect libre*, to the heroine's unspoken thoughts and feelings, never to those of Quentin or Mario. Although Mario's is the dominant *voice* in Chapter 5, the *focalisation* is that of the female protagonist, as indeed it is in most scenes of the novel.

29. Jean-Marie Goulemot, *Forbidden Texts* (London: Polity Press, 1994), Chapter 2.

30. The very notion of women or men as sex objects or possessions is in fact explicitly attacked in the novel by Mario, together with the institution of the 'couple', whether married or unmarried.

31. The effect of this act of voyeurism is seen from the perspective of the viewed rather than the viewer.

32. Many have seen women's pleasure in being looked at as simply part of a positioning as object of the male gaze: see, for example, Laura Mulvey, 'Visual Pleasure and Narrative Cinema' (1975) in Robyn R. Warhol and Diane Price Herndl (eds), *Feminisms* (New Brunswick, New Jersey: Rutgers University Press, 1991), pp. 432–42; E. Ann Kaplan, 'Is the gaze male?' in *Women and Film: Both Sides of the Camera* (London: Methuen, 1983), pp. 23–35. More recently, however, some feminists have recognised that women, too, can enjoy being both exhibitionists and voyeurs: see, for instance, Grace Lau, 'Confessions of a Complete Scopophiliac' in Gibson and Gibson, *Dirty Looks*, pp. 192–206; this reference, p. 200. Female critics are beginning to accept the possibility of a female gaze in erotica written by women. For instance, Diana Holmes argues that in Rachilde's *Monsieur Vénus*, 'The gaze of the desiring subject can be transferred to the female protagonist, which in turn means that the reader is positioned to view the male body as object.' ('Monstrous Women: Rachilde's Erotic Fiction' in Alex Hughes and Kate Ince (eds), *French Erotic Fiction. Women's Desiring Writing, 1880–1990* (Oxford: Berg, 1996), pp. 27–48; this reference pp. 33–4.)

33. Linda Williams, *Hard Core. Power, Pleasure and the 'Frenzy of the Visible'* (London: Pandora Press, 1990), p. 205. For a female photographer's point of view questioning Laura Mulvey's somewhat polarised argument concerning the nature and gender of the gaze, see Lau, 'Confessions'.

34. The final line of this passage does not appear in the published translation.

35. The *Bildungsroman* or 'formation-novel', which began to appear in the eighteenth century, typically describes the protagonist's development from naïveté to knowledge. Voltaire's *Candide* (1759), Goethe's *Wilhelm Meister's Apprenticeship* (1795–96) and James Joyce's *Portrait of the Artist as a Young Man* (1916) are notable examples.

36. Both of Sade's best-known novels, which represent the adventures over time of female protagonists, may, in any case, be regarded as parodies of the *Bildungsroman*, rather than typical examples of the genre: while Juliette learns to do evil, not good, Justine learns nothing at all from her numerous predicaments.

37. Nancy K. Miller, 'Gender and narrative possibilities' in Allison, Roberts and Weiss (eds), *Sade and the Narrative of Transgression* (Cambridge: Cambridge University Press, 1995), pp. 213–27; this reference, p. 213, quoting Ellen Morgan, 'Human becoming: form and focus in the neo-feminist novel' in S. K. Cornillon (ed.), *Images of Women in Fiction: Feminist Perspectives* (Bowling Green: Popular Press, 1972), p. 184.

38. Miller, discussing Juliette, ibid., p. 214.

39. Ibid., p. 215.

40. The last two sentences do not appear in the published translation.

41. Arsan has unambiguously indicated that she is not an aficionado of 'happiness in slavery', ironically echoing the title of Jean Paulhan's preface to *Histoire d'O* (Interview with E. A.). On the other hand, she has acknowledged the debt of inspiration and example she feels she owes to Pauline Réage: see Emmanuelle Arsan, 'Le Creux du Rêve' in *Plexus* no. 29 (Paris: November 1969); republished as Appendix to Emmanuelle Arsan, *L'Hypothèse d'Eros* (Paris: Éditions Filipacchi, 1974), pp. 261–71.

42. According to the *Petit Robert*, for example, the very term, 'phallocentricisme' did not enter the French language until 1957.

43. Eric Losfeld, *Endetté comme une mule* (Paris: Losfield, 1979).

# Chapter 7

1. John de St. Jorre, *The Good Ship Venus* (London: Pimlico, 1994), p. 260.

2. Marguerite Duras's writing frequently contains an implied eroticism but rarely deals explicitly with sexuality. *L'homme assis dans le couloir* (Paris: Éditions de Minuit, 1980) is perhaps a notable exception.

3. The author tells us that when his 1974 film, *Glissements progressifs du plaisir* (*Progressive Slidings of Pleasure*), was released in Italy, there were public disturbances bordering on riots in some cinemas among audiences who had been led by the title and by poster images to expect conventional soft porn.

4. See note 3.

5. In the second volume of his autobiographical trilogy, Robbe-Grillet regales his readers with the background to the pseudonymously published *Histoire d'O* and *L'Image*, which we now know to have been the work of Dominique Aury and Catherine Robbe-Grillet respectively. He tells us, *inter alia*, that a German academic had proven by detailed textual analysis that both novels were written by him. Though admitting later in this text that *L'Image* was written by his wife, Catherine, we note that he studiously avoids denying the allegation that he was the author of *Histoire d'O*. (See *Angélique ou l'enchantement* (Paris: Éditions de Minuit, 1987), pp. 169–73.)

6. 'Glissements' is indeed the term preferred by Robbe-Grillet in descriptions of his approach to narrative: see Bruce Morrissette's interview with the author, 'Order and Disorder in Film and Fiction', *Critical Inquiry*, vol. 4, no. 1 (Autumn 1977), pp. 1–20; this reference, p. 16.

7. See especially Jean Ricardou, 'La Fiction flamboyante' in *Pour une théorie du nouveau roman* (Paris: Éditions du Seuil, 1971), pp. 211–33; Bruce Morrissette, 'Robbe-Grillet's "Project For a Revolution in New York"', *American Society Legion of Honor Magazine*, 42 (1971), pp. 73–88; Raylene Ramsay, *Robbe-Grillet and Modernity. Science, Sexuality and Subversion* (University Press of Florida, 1992); B. F. Stoltzfus, *Alain Robbe-Grillet and the New French Novel* (Carbondale: Southern Illinois University Press, 1964) and B. F. Stoltzfus, *Alain Robbe-Grillet: The Body of the Text* (Associated University Presses, 1985).

8. *Le Miroir qui revient* (Paris: Éditions de Minuit, 1984), *Angélique ou l'enchantement* (Paris: Éditions de Minuit, 1987), and *Les Derniers jours de Corinthe* (Paris: Éditions de Minuit, 1994).

9. Jean-Jacques Pauvert chooses for his *Anthologie historique des lectures érotiques. De Eisenhower à Emmanuelle, 1945–85* (Paris: Stock/Spengler, 1995). Robbe-Grillet's previous novel, *La Maison de rendez-vous*, which, though certainly redolent with erotic themes and motifs, is not as explicitly erotic as *Projet pour une révolution à New York*.

10. See Morrissette, 'Robbe-Grillet's "Project"', and Ricardou, 'La Fiction flamboyante'. Ricardou emphasises the role of

signifiers in generating the structure of the novel, an essentially non-mimetic process.

11. John Fletcher, *Alain Robbe-Grillet* (London and New York: Methuen, 1983), p. 64.

12. Morrissette, 'Robbe-Grillet's "Project"'. Morrissette goes on for seven pages or so to summarise the extremely dense fictional construction of the novel, and the reader who requires a detailed exegesis of the text is referred to this meticulous and very accurate summary, occupying the greater part of his article.

13. Daniel P. Deneau, 'Bits and Pieces Concerning One of Robbe-Grillet's Latest Verbal Happenings: The "Sado-Erotic" *Project*', *Twentieth Century Literature*, vol. XXV (1979), pp. 37–53; this reference, p. 37.

14. Ibid.

15. Susan Rubin Suleiman, 'Reading Robbe-Grillet: Sadism and Text in *Projet pour une révolution à New York*', *Romanic Review* (January 1977), 68 (1), pp. 43–62.

16. For instance, at a recent talk given at the Institut Français de Londres, South Kensington, September 1996.

17. Suleiman, 'Reading Robbe-Grillet', p. 63.

18. Ibid., p. 61.

19. Ibid., p. 62.

20. Ibid., pp. 66–9.

21. Deneau, 'Bits and Pieces', p. 42.

22. Ibid., p. 41.

23. Suleiman, 'Reading Robbe-Grillet', p. 64.

24. Ibid, p. 65.

25. See Chapter 1 for a discussion of definitions of pornography and eroticism, and of the history of the use of these terms.

26. Read metaphorically rather than literally, this line might be taken to refer to the processes of avant-garde art itself. For John Fraser, 'All change begins with a rape' (*Violence in the Arts* (New York: Cambridge University Press, 1974), p. 168). Such a reading does not seem inappropriate in a genre, the *nouveau roman*, which does violence to traditional narrative forms. In the case of Robbe-Grillet, this artistic violence is, for some commentators, more shocking than the violence represented in his texts.

27. This deception of the voyeuristic male is of course intradiegetic as well as extradiegetic (that is, in *Projet*, the male narrator is also taken in, as is the police inspector in the film, *Glissements progressifs du plaisir*, who hears similar recorded noises emanating from within Alice's cell).

28. Morrissette, 'Robbe-Grillet's "Project"', pp. 87–8.

29. Suleiman, 'Reading Robbe-Grillet', p. 64 et seq.
30. Ibid., p. 65. Suleiman goes on to claim, erroneously in my view, that the Sadean victim never experiences pleasure in the course of his/her torture, and that 'Sade's texts must be called realist: the fictions they enact are never designated as fictions; the text never explicitly calls attention to itself as invention, as *text*; its origin, like its destination, is ostensibly the world of flesh and blood' (p. 70). I have argued that, on the contrary, there are strong elements of self-referentiality in the Sadean text: see my "Laugh? I nearly died!' Humour in Sade's Fiction' in *The Eighteenth Century: Theory and Interpretation*, forthcoming.
31. See, for instance, Dolmancé's ironic pamphlet, 'Français, encore un effort, si vous voulez être républicains' ('Frenchmen, one more effort if you want to be republicans') in Sade's *La Philosophie dans le boudoir* (*Philosophy in the Bedroom*).
32. Cp. twelve apostles, twelve hours of the clock, twelve months in the year, etc. For J.E. Cirlot, 'systems or patterns based upon the circle or the cycle tend to have twelve as the end-limit' (J. E. Cirlot, *A Dictionary of Symbols* (London: Routledge & Kegan Paul Ltd, 1993, p. 354).
33. Suleiman, 'Reading Robbe-Grillet', p. 66.
34. Ibid., p. 67.
35. Emma Kafalenos, 'From the Comic to the Ludic: Postmodern Fiction', *International Fiction Review*, 12.1 (Fredericton, NB, Canada, Winter 1985), pp. 28–31; this reference, p. 31.
36. The need for control can be seen as a dominant characteristic of the author's personality: 'Je tiens à contrôler le hasard,' ('I like to control chance') says Robbe-Grillet in an interview about his film, *L'Éden et après*. He was, for example, against the idea of showing the reels of the film in a different order for every screening.

## Chapter 8

1. Christopher Robinson, *Scandal in the Ink. Male and Female Homosexuality in Twentieth-century French Literature* (London: Cassell, 1995), p. 70.
2. Ibid., p. 78.
3. It appears that public opinion was more hostile in 1975 than in 1968: see ibid., p. 30.
4. The homosexual text is perhaps the best example of writing censored by critical authority in France during the latter half of this century. Robinson argues that critics have either

played down or ignored homosexual elements in the life and work of writers like Proust and Gide or, if they have acknowledged them, have linked them to perversion and criminality: see ibid., p. vii. Indeed, Robinson suggests that gay Catholic writers such as Julien Green and Marcel Jouhandeau have been critically marginalised in favour of straight Catholic writers like Bernanos and Mauriac, whom Robinson considers much less interesting from an aesthetic point of view (ibid., p. 92, n. 7). This is less surprising when placed in the wider context of societal attitudes to the homosexual in general: as late as the 1960s, for instance, homosexuality was considered an illness that medecine could cure (cf. Porot, *Manuel alphabétique de psychiatrie* (1960), cited by Robinson, ibid., p. 20).

5.  For Robinson, 'Proust, Cocteau and Genet all work to the same stereotype of maleness, one which by definition consigns the homosexual to an inferior "feminine" role.' (ibid., p. 71).

6.  See E. Apter, *André Gide and the Codes of Homotextuality* (Stanford: Anma Libri, 1987) and Owen Heathcote, 'Masochism, sadism and homotextuality: the examples of Yukio Mishima and Eric Jourdan', *Paragraph*, vol. 17, no. 2 (1994), pp. 174–89.

7.  I am referring in particular to the work of Butler and Sedgwick: see, for example, Judith Butler, *Bodies that Matter: On the Discursive Limits of Sex* (London: Routledge, 1993) and Eve Kosofsky Sedgwick, *Tendencies* (London: Routledge, 1994).

8.  Jean-François Lyotard, *The Postmodern Condition* (Manchester: Manchester University Press, 1984).

9.  The second (1976) edition of *Récidive* is currently the only one available, so it is this version that I shall be discussing here.

10. Total sales to date (March 1998) amount to no more than 5000 copies: 'I don't remember the book being the object, at the time, of any kind of ban. Admittedly, it didn't make much of an impact when it came out.' (Jérôme Lindon of Éditions de Minuit, personal fax from JL to JP, 31 March 1998).

11. The MLA catalogue contains no reference whatsoever to any journal or book article on *Récidive* since its appearance until the time of writing.

12. Manuscripts were posted to the editor, Jérôme Lindon, who had no other contact with Duvert (source: personal letter from JL to JP, 30 March 1998).

13. Jean-Jacques Pauvert, *Anthologie historique des lectures érotiques. D'Eisenhower à Emmanuelle 1945–1985* (Paris: Stock/Spengler,

1995). Pauvert does, however, include an extract from Duvert's first polemic, *Le Bon sexe illustré*, which he describes, somewhat ambiguously, as 'appreciated in some quarters, ignored in others' (ibid., p. 842). Pauvert quotes a relatively anodine passage from this book, in which the author reproduces a conventional sex education entry from a contemporary encyclopedia, the 1973 five-volume Hachette *Encyclopédie de la vie sexuelle*.

14. See Chapter 1.
15. A repressive form of book censorship was still being practised in the last years of the 1960s in France, despite the fall of the Gaullist régime in 1968: in 1968 and 1969, for example, there were more than 60 prosecutions: see Robert Netz, *Histoire de la censure dans l'édition* (Paris: PUF, 1997), p. 117.
16. Pierre Guyotat's *Éden, Éden, Éden*, Bernard Noël's *Le Château de Cène* and, notwithstanding the legal victories won by Jean-Jacques Pauvert, the works of the Marquis de Sade were all subject to forms of legal control in the 1970s: see Chapter 1.
17. Until Robinson's *Scandal in the Ink*, published in 1995, there was only one extensive study of French homosexual writing in English: Stambolian and Marks (eds), *Homosexualities and French Literature. Cultural Contexts/Critical Texts* (Ithaca and London: Cornell University Press, 1979). In France, F. Martel, *Le Rose et le noir. Les homosexuels en France* (Paris: Éditions du Seuil, 1986) was a welcome addition to the field and, within the last few years, three more excellent studies have appeared in English: Jeffrey Merrick and Bryant T. Ragan, Jr. (eds), *Homosexuality in Modern France* (New York: Oxford University Press, 1996), Vernon Rosario (ed.), *Science and Homosexualities* (New York: Routledge, 1997) and A. Hughes, O. Heathcote and James Williams (eds), *Gay Signatures. Gay and Lesbian Theory, Fiction and Film in France, 1945–1995* (Oxford: Berg, 1998).
18. Hughes *et al*, *Gay Signatures*, p. 15.
19. Robinson, *Scandal in the Ink*, p. 259.
20. *Le Petit Robert*.
21. In contrast, Steven Smith sees Duvert's fourth novel, *Le Voyageur*, as innovative in form and as presenting a liberated and positive view of homosexuality. Smith argues, in relation to a corpus of five novels by Duvert and other homosexual writers, that there is a high correlation between form and socio-psychological content, so that traditional mimetic writing is more likely to portray traditional, negative attitudes towards homosexuality, whereas in writing, like Duvert's,

which acknowledges its own fictionality, 'homosexuality is accepted as a manner of authentic self-expression, a legitimate pathway to genuine pleasure and fulfillment' (Stephen Smith, 'Toward a Literature of Utopia' in Stambolian and Marks, *Homosexualities and French Literature*, p. 349). Smith, therefore, clearly views the disharmonies of form of Duvert's writing as 'liberated', rather than as expressing the existential crisis of the homosexual subject.

22. For Roland Barthes, homosexual 'cruising' means inhabiting an unattractive world: see *The Grain of the Voice: Interviews 1962–80* (London: Jonathan Cape, 1985), p. 299; cited by Michael Worton, 'Cruising (Through) Encounters' in Hughes *et al*, *Gay Signatures*, pp. 29–49; this reference p. 37.

23. The French word 'pédéraste' is defined as 'an adult male who has a taste for pre-pubescent boys' (Dominique Fernandez, *L'Étoile Rose* (Paris: Grasset, 1978), p. 89; cited by Robinson, *Scandal in the Ink*, p. 172, n. 2). Though the term 'pédé' has recently been recuperated by Queer Theory, it was still a term of abuse in the 1960s, except perhaps when used ironically by homosexuals themselves. In an article on Robert Pinget's novel, *Le Libera*, for example, Duvert himself uses the term pejoratively to draw attention to the sexuality of the characters: see Tony Duvert, 'La Parole et la fiction', *Critique*, no. 252 (May 1968), pp. 443–61; this reference, p. 448.

24. *L'Enfant au masculin* (Paris: Éditions de Minuit, 1980), p. 21. Despite the linguistic proximity of this word to 'paedophile' (defined as an adult person who has sexual desires for, and possibly relations with, children), commentators like Heathcote and Robinson, who are concerned to emphasise the more positive dimensions of French homosexual writing, not surprisingly seem reluctant to use a word that is currently highly emotive in Britain and the USA, if not in France.

25. Ibid., p. 21.

26. For Duvert, it is not from homosexuals that children need to be protected, but from what he calls the dictatorship of heterosexuals: see ibid., p. 120.

27. For a detailed discussion of the legal status of homosexuals or pederasts in France since the *ancien régime*, see Robinson, *Scandal in the Ink*, pp. 2–6.

28. *L'Enfant au masculin*, p. 23.

29. The images of pederasty found in the work of André Gide, for example, are conveyed in a far more euphemistic manner, and 'Apart from Gide, none of the main texts prior to the

1960s acknowledges sex acts between adult males and boys under seventeen' (Robinson, *Scandal in the Ink*, p. 155).

30. Owen Heathcote links the 'uncertainty' of the narrative to a sexual uncertainty in Duvert, a blurring of the labels of maleness and masculinity: see Owen Heathcote, 'Jobs for the Boys? Or: What's New About the Male Hunter in Duvert, Guibert and Jourdan?' in Hughes *et al*, *Gay Signatures*, pp. 173–192; this reference p. 176.

31. Worton, 'Cruising', p. 31.

32. The denial of a fixed identity is, moreover, part of a more general campaign by Duvert against the normalising influence of families in particular and the institutions of a control-obsessed society in general. However, the liberal character of this campaign is very much diminished by the author's misogyny. Queer Theory places similar emphasis on fluid identity, especially with regard to gender boundaries, but there is no attempt in Duvert to dismantle the heterosexual/homosexual binary division. On the contrary, the near absence of women from his fiction helps to perpetuate it. In *Récidive* sex with a woman is represented, in the only scene in which it occurs, as a sordid and unplea- surable affair: a fat prostitute, who enjoys deflowering boys, does the business in a deserted building; the bleakness of the location prepares the reader for the repulsiveness of the act itself.

33. Worton, 'Cruising', p. 33.

34. Roland Barthes, in *S/Z* (Paris: Éditions du Seuil, 1970), argued that the literary text was constituted by a plurality of voices, and that the fragment was in itself erotic.

35. The plurality of narrative voices within the narrative and the denial of fixed identity that this connotes are paralleled by slidings of authorial identity outside it. It has been suggested that the elusive Tony Duvert may be an avatar of the gay activist and writer, Renaud Camus: see Lawrence Schehr, *The Shock of Men: Homosexual Hermeneutics in French Writing* (Stanford, CA: Stanford University Press, 1995), p. 140, n. 2. I am grateful to Alex Hughes for drawing my attention to this possibility. Schehr leaves the matter unresolved, so we must form our own conclusions according to the evidence of the text. There are certainly many close thematic and formal similarities between the work of both – the avoidance of a fixed homosexual identity, for example, or the blending of sexual and textual experience (for a summary of Renaud Camus's approach to writing, see Robinson, *Scandal in the Ink*, pp. 99–100). On the other hand, unlike Duvert's, Camus's

fiction does not display any predilection for young boys. On balance, then, I think it unlikely that they are the same writer.

36.  Jean-Marie Goulemot, *Forbidden Texts. Erotic Literature and its Readers in Eighteenth Century France* (London: Polity Press, 1994), pp. 42–50.

37.  For Freud, narcissism is an important component of homosexual desire and the anxiety that accompanies it. Julia Kristeva reiterates Freud's negative view of homosexuality when she associates the narcissism of the homosexual with 'emptiness': see Julia Kristeva, *Tales of Love* (New York: Columbia University Press, 1987), p. 43; cited by Worton, 'Cruising', p. 37. Michael Worton, however, suggests that terms like narcissism can be recoded positively, arguing that one needs to love oneself to survive as an individual in society (ibid.).

38.  Smith sees striking similarities between Duvert's *Le Voyageur* and Robbe-Grillet's *Projet pour une révolution à New York*, especially with regard to the emphasis on fictionality and the essentially comic exploration of eroticism: see Smith, 'Utopia', p. 349.

39.  The novel's important intertextual dimension also establishes it as part of an existing literary tradition and so validates it as literature. For Robinson, this is a common technique in homosexual writing: see Robinson, *Scandal in the Ink*, p. 132.

40.  Michael Worton, 'You know what I mean? The operability of codes in gay men's fiction', *Paragraph*, 17 (1994), pp. 49–59; this reference, p. 58; cited by Christopher Robinson in 'Sexuality and Textuality in Contemporary French Gay Fiction', *French Studies*, vol. LII, no. 2 (April 1998), pp. 176–86.

41.  Duvert defines 'heterocracy' as the system in which heterosexuals consider themselves sufficient and universal: see *L'Enfant au masculin*, p. 51.

42.  Worton, 'Cruising', p. 38.

43.  Michel Foucault, *Dits et écrits: 1954–88, vol. 4 (1980–8)* (Paris: Gallimard, 1994), cited by Worton, ibid., p. 38.

44.  Gilles Deleuze and Félix Guattari, *Anti-Oedipus. Capitalism and Schizophrenia* (London: The Athlone Press, 1984).

45.  Deleuze and Parnet, *Dialogues* (Paris: Flammarion, 1996), pp. 96–7, cited by Worton, 'Cruising', p. 39.

46.  See Guy Hocquenghem, *Homosexual Desire* (Durham NH and London: Duke University Press, 1993) and Worton's commentary on it, 'Cruising', p. 39.

47.  Worton, 'Cruising', pp. 39–40.

48.  Robinson, *Scandal in the Ink*, p. 157.

49. Ibid., pp. 248–9.
50. Hughes *et al*, *Gay Signatures*, Introduction, p. 3.
51. Ibid., p. 14.
52. Heathcote, 'Jobs for the Boys', p. 173.
53. Ibid., p. 175.
54. There is, perhaps, an implication here that the fifth child, who sees all, is doomed to enter the cycle of abuse himself, first as victim, then later as abuser. This notion of sexuality as learnt behaviour is acknowledged, somewhat resignedly, as an unhappy ending to the *Grand Meaulnes* fairy tale: 'Il quitterait le parc la forêt la campagne il rentrerait à la ville dirait c'est moi et s'engagerait dans l'armée où des vétérans qui auraient des muscles énormes une mâchoire carrée et une très grosse bite le choisiraient pour mascotte et le baiseraient à dix ou vingt par nuit et à la fin il deviendrait comme eux, voilà' (p. 50) ('He would leave the grounds the forest the countryside he would go back to town would say it's me and would sign up with the army where veterans with enormous muscles square jaws and very large pricks would choose him as their mascot and between ten and twenty of them would fuck him every night and in the end he would become like them, there you are').
55. The terms *incipit* and *excipit* respectively denote the opening and closing passages of a text.
56. Robinson, *Scandal in the Ink*, p. 161.
57. Ibid.

## Chapter 9

1. See Chapter 6, n. 35.
2. Especially in the eighteenth and nineteenth centuries: cf. works by Sade, Laclos, Richardson, Fielding and others.
3. The 'paratexte' is the term, coined by Gérard Genette, to denote the borders of a text, such as the title, book cover, epigraphs, dedications and any other material surrounding or introducing the main narrative: see Gérard Genette, *Seuils* (Paris: Éditions du Seuil, 1987).
4. This epigraph does not appear in the English translation.
5. Roland Barthes, *La Chambre claire: Note sur la photographie* (Paris: 'Cahiers du cinéma'/Gallimard/Éditions du Seuil, 1980), p. 18.
6. Ibid., p. 165.
7. The word used by Barthes is 'intègre' (ibid., p. 139).
8. For Élise, the objectifying photographic image is therefore less 'true' than the ego's subjective self-image, which, Barthes

argues, gives rise to a 'méconnaissance que le sujet a de lui-même au moment où il assume de dire et de remplir son *je*' ('misrecognition of the self by the subject at the time when he takes it upon himself to say and to fulfil his ego') (*Sade, Fourier, Loyola* (Paris: Collection 'Points Essais', 1980), p. 55).

9. In the *Commedia dell'arte* of the sixteenth century in Italy, troops of actors travelled around Europe, improvising comic plays, whose characters and plots belonged to a well-known repertoire. One of these stock characters is Pantaloon, an old, rich father, who is tricked by the daughter's young lover, Inamorato, into giving her to him. The text obviously exploits the polysemy of the word, 'pantalon' ('comic mask' and 'trousers') to create a new metaphorical meaning: cheeks grotesquely swollen by an erect penis.

10. Hélène Cixous, 'La Venue à l'écriture' in *Entre L'Écriture* (Paris: des femmes, 1986), pp. 9–69; this reference., pp. 60–1.

11. Julia Kristeva, 'Women's Time' in Toril Moi (ed.), *The Kristeva Reader* (Oxford: Basil Blackwell, 1986), pp. 187–213; originally published in French as 'Le temps des femmes' in *33/44: Cahiers de recherche de sciences des textes et documents*, 5 (Winter 1979), pp. 5–19.

12. 'eau de rose' in French.

13. Colette's *Gigi*, for example.

14. For Barthes, as for Sade, subjectivity is rooted essentially in the body: see his *Le Grain de la voix: Entretiens 1962–1980* (Paris: Éditions du Seuil, 1981), p. 184.

15. *Le Figaro-Magazine*, 21 September 1996.

16. *Valeurs Actuelles*, 21 September 1996.

17. Nicholas Harrison, *Circles of Censorship. Censorship and its Metaphors In French History, Literature, and Theory* (Oxford: Clarendon Press, 1995).

18. *La Semaine du Pays Basque*, no. 162, 11–17 October 1996.

19. 'Les vérités de Marie' in *Sud Ouest*, 5 September 1996.

20. *Le Devoir*, 9–10 November 1996.

21. 'Vite, avant l'an 2000', *Les Inrockuptibles*, 4 September 1996.

22. The book itself has, in fact, been called 'millénariste' ('of the millennium').

23. Gérard Genette's term designates a first-person narrator who figures as the narrative's principal character: see Gérard Genette, *Figures III* (Paris: Éditions du Seuil, 1972), p. 253.

24. See Chapter 1.

25. 'Ils publient leur premier roman', *Lire*, September 1996.

26. Quoted in 'Darrieussecq: À quoi rêvent les jeunes femmes', *Le Figaro Magazine*, 21 September 1996.

27. 'Le phénomène Darrieussecq', *La Presse*, Montréal, 9 September 1996.

28. The reference here is to the popular feminist classic by Susie Orbach, *Fat is a Feminist Issue*.

29. Like their mainstream equivalents, French erotic novels seem to have become increasingly shorter.

30. 'Vite, avant l'an 2000', *Les Inrockuptibles*, 4 September, 1996.

# Select Bibliography

## 1. Primary Texts

Apollinaire, G. *Les Onze Mille Verges ou les Amours d'un hospodar* (Paris: Éditions *J'ai lu* (Jean-Jacques Pauvert, 1973))
—— *The Eleven Thousand Rods or, The Loves of a Hospodar, Flesh Unlimited* (London: Velvet Publications, Creation Books, 1995)
Arsan, E. *Emmanuelle* (Paris: Robert Laffont et Jean-Jacques Pauvert, 1988)
—— *Emmanuelle* (London: Grafton Books, 1975)
Barillé, E. *Corps de jeune fille* (Paris: Gallimard, 1986)
—— *Body of a Girl* (London: Quartet Books, 1989)
Bataille, G. *Histoire de l'œil* in Oeuvres Complètes, vol. 1 (Paris: Gallimard, 1970; ©J.-J. Pauvert)
—— *Story of the Eye* (London: Penguin Books, 1982)
Darrieussecq, M. *Truismes* (Paris: P.O.L., 1996)
—— *Pig Tales* (London: Faber & Faber, 1998)
Duvert, T. *Récidive* (Paris: Éditions de Minuit, 1976)
Louÿs, P. *Trois Filles de leur mère* (Paris: Éditions Allia, 1993)
—— *The She Devils* (London: Creation Books, 1995)
Réage, P. *Histoire d'O* (Paris: Le Livre de Poche, 1991; © Société Nouvelle des Éditions Pauvert 1954–1972)
—— *Story of O* (London: Corgi Books, 1998)
Robbe-Grillet, A. *Projet pour une révolution à New York* (Paris: Éditions de Minuit, 1970)
—— *Project for a Revolution in New York* (London: Calder & Boyars Ltd, 1973)

## 2. Secondary and Critical Reading

Amelinckx, F. 'Apollinaire's *Les Onze Mille Verges*: Humor and Pornography', *West Virginia Philological Papers*, vol. 29 (1983).
Apollinaire, G. *Alcools* (Berkeley and Los Angeles: University of California Press, 1965).
Apollinaire, G., Fleuret, F., and Perceau, L. *L'Enfer de la Bibliothèque Nationale* (Paris: Mercure de France, 1913).

Apter, E. *André Gide and the Codes of Homotextuality* (Stanford: Anma Libri, 1987).

Arnaud, A. and Excoffon-Lafarge, G. *Bataille*, 'Écrivains de toujours' series (Paris: Éditions du Seuil, 1978).

Arsan, E. 'Le Creux du Rêve' in *Plexus* no. 29 (Paris: November 1969); republished as Appendix to Emmanuelle Arsan, *L'Hypothèse d'Eros* (Paris: Éditions Filipacchi, 1974).

Assiter, A. and Carol, A. (eds), *Bad Girls & Dirty Pictures. The Challenge to Reclaim Feminism* (London and Boulder, Colorado: Pluto Press, 1993).

Bakhtine, M. *L'œuvre de François Rabelais* (Paris: Gallimard, 1970).

Bakhtin, M. M. 'Discourse in the Novel' in Michael Holquist (ed.), M. M. Bakhtin, *The Dialogic Imagination* (Austin: University of Texas Press, 1981).

Barthes, R. *le Degré zéro de l'écriture* (Paris: Éditions du Seuil, 1953 and 1972).

—— 'La Métaphore de l'œil' in *Essais critiques* (Paris: Éditions du Seuil, 1964); Eng. transl. 'The Metaphor of the Eye' in *Story of the Eye* (London: Penguin Books, 1982).

—— *S/Z* (Paris: Éditions du Seuil, 1970).

—— *Sade, Fourier, Loyola* (Paris: Collection 'Points Essais', 1980).

—— *La Chambre claire: Note sur la photographie* (Paris: 'Cahiers du cinéma'/Gallimard/Éditions du Seuil, 1980).

—— 'La mort de l'auteur' in *Le Bruissement de la langue. Essais critiques IV* (Paris: Éditions du Seuil, 1984).

—— *The Grain of the Voice: Interviews 1962–80* (London: Jonathan Cape, 1985); originally published in French as *Le Grain de la voix: Entretiens 1962–1980* (Paris: Éditions du Seuil, 1981).

Bataille, G. *L'Érotisme* (Paris: Éditions de Minuit, 1957).

—— 'Le Petit', *Oeuvres Complètes*, vol. VII (Paris: Gallimard, 1974).

—— *Le Bleu du ciel* (Paris: Jean-Jacques Pauvert, 10/18, 1988).

—— *Madame Edwarda, Le Mort, Histoire de l'œil* (Paris: Jean-Jacques Pauvert, 10/18, 1989).

—— *Ma mère* (Paris: Jean-Jacques Pauvert, 10/18, 1996).

Belsey, C. 'Desire in Theory: Freud, Lacan, Derrida', *Textual Practice*, vol. 7, no. 3 (Winter 1993).

Brulotte, G. 'Petite narratologie du récit dit "érotique"' in *Poétique* no. 85 (Paris: Éditions du Seuil, 1991).

—— 'Le Thème du dépaysement dans la littérature érotique d'expression française', *Revue Francophone de Louisiane*, vol. 1, no. 2 (1986).

Butler, J. *Bodies that Matter: On the Discursive Limits of Sex* (London: Routledge, 1993).

Butor, M. *Les Mots dans la peinture* (Genève: Éditions Skira, 1980).

Carol, A. *Nudes, Prudes and Attitudes* (Cheltenham: New Clarion Press, 1994).

Carter, A. *The Sadeian Woman. An Exercise in Cultural History* (London: Virago Press, 1979).

Cirlot, J.E. *A Dictionary of Symbols* (London: Routledge, 1962; this edition, 1993).

Cixous, H. 'La Venue à l'écriture' in *Entre L'Écriture* (Paris: des femmes, 1986).

Cryle, P. *Geometry in the Boudoir. Configurations of French Erotic Narrative* (Ithaca and London: Cornell University Press, 1994).

Darnton, R. *The Forbidden Best-Sellers of Pre-Revolutionary France* (London: HarperCollins, 1996).

Dauncey, H. 'Publishing, pornography and personal freedom: l'Affaire Dreyfus, l'Affaire Miller, l'Affaire Lolita and l'Affaire Kissinger', *French Cultural Studies*, iii (1992).

Deforges, R. *O m'a dit: entretiens avec Pauline Réage* (Paris: Jean-Jacques Pauvert, 1975).

Deleuze, G. *Présentation de Sacher-Masoch. Le Froid et le Cruel* (Paris: Éditions de Minuit, 1967). English translation: *Masochism: Coldness and Cruelty* (New York: Zone Books, 1991).

Deleuze, G. and Guattari, F. *Anti-Oedipus. Capitalism and Schizophrenia* (London: The Athlone Press, 1984); originally published in French as *L'Anti-Oedipe* (Paris: Éditions de Minuit, 1972).

Deneau, D. P. 'Bits and Pieces Concerning One of Robbe-Grillet's Latest Verbal Happenings: The "Sado-Erotic" *Project*', *Twentieth Century Literature*, vol. XXV (1979).

Diderot, D. *Les Bijoux indiscrets* (Paris: Actes Sud, 1995).

Dolto, F. *Sexualité féminine* (Paris: Scarabée & Co, 1982).

Duvert, T. 'La Parole et la fiction', *Critique*, no. 252 (May 1968).

—— *Le Bon sexe illustré* (Paris: Éditions de Minuit, 1974).

—— *L'Enfant au masculin* (Paris: Éditions de Minuit, 1980).

Dworkin, A. *Woman Hating* (New York: E. P. Dutton & Co, 1974).

—— *Pornography: Men Possessing Women* (London: The Women's Press Ltd, 1981).

—— *Intercourse* (London: Secker & Warburg, 1987).

Eco, U. *The Role of the Reader. Explorations in the Semiotics of Texts* (London: Hutchinson, 1981).

Fletcher, J. *Alain Robbe-Grillet* (London and New York: Methuen, 1983).

Foucault, M. *Histoires de la sexualité, vol. 1: La volonté de savoir* (Paris: Gallimard, 1976).

Frappier-Mazur, L. 'Marginal Canons: Rewriting the Erotic', *Yale French Studies*, vol. 75 (1988).

Fraser, J. *Violence in the Arts* (New York: Cambridge University Press, 1974).

Freud, S. *Three Essays on Sexuality* (London: The Pelican Freud Library, vol. 7, 1977).

Friday, N. *My Secret Garden* (London: Quartet Books, 1994).

Genette, G. *Figures III* (Paris: Éditions du Seuil, 1972).

Goujon, J-P. (ed.), *Pierre Louÿs: L'Oeuvre érotique* (Paris: Sortilèges, 1994).

Goulemot, J-M. *Forbidden Texts. Erotic Literature and its Readers in Eighteenth-Century France* (London: Polity Press, 1994); originally published as *Ces livres qu'on ne lit que d'une main* (Paris: Éditions Alinea, 1991).

Guiraud, P. *Dictionnaire érotique* (Paris: Éditions Payot & Rivages, 1993).

Guyotat, P. *Littérature interdite* (Paris: Gallimard, 1972).

Harrison, N. *Circles of Censorship. Censorship and its Metaphors in French History, Literature, and Theory* (Oxford: Clarendon Press, 1995).

Hartwig, J. *Apollinaire* (Paris: Mercure de France, 1972).

Heath, S. *The Sexual Fix* (London and Basingstoke: Macmillan, 1982).

Heathcote, O. 'Masochism, sadism and homotextuality: the examples of Yukio Mishima and Eric Jourdan', *Paragraph*, vol. 17, no. 2 (1994).

—— 'Jobs for the Boys? Or: What's New About the Male Hunter in Duvert, Guibert and Jourdan?' in A. Hughes, O. Heathcote and James Williams (eds), *Gay Signatures. Gay and Lesbian Theory, Fiction and Film in France, 1945–1995* (Oxford: Berg, 1998).

Hocquenghem, G. *Homosexual Desire* (Durham NH and London: Duke University Press, 1993).

Holmes, D. 'Monstrous Women: Rachilde's Erotic Fiction' in Alex Hughes and Kate Ince (eds), *French Erotic Fiction. Women's Desiring Writing, 1880–1990* (Oxford: Berg, 1996).

Hughes, A. and Ince, K. (eds), *French Erotic Fiction. Women's Desiring Writing, 1880–1990* (Oxford: Berg, 1996).

Hussey, A. 'Bull-fighting in Georges Bataille', *Manchester Working Papers in French*, no. 1 (Spring 1994).

Irigaray, L. *Spéculum de l'autre femme* (Paris: Éditions de Minuit, 1974).

—— 'Ce sexe qui n'en est pas un' in *Ce sexe qui n'en est pas un* (Paris: Éditions de Minuit, 1977).

Itzin, C. (ed.), *Pornography. Women, Violence and Civil Liberties* (Oxford: Oxford University Press, 1992).

—— 'Harm in Porn', *The Law* (June, July, August 1995).

Kafalenos, E. 'From the Comic to the Ludic: Postmodern Fiction', *International Fiction Review*, 12.1 (Winter 1985).

Kaplan, E. A. *Women and Film: Both Sides of the Camera* (London: Methuen, 1983).

Kipnis, L. 'She-Male Fantasies and the Aesthetics of Pornography' in Gibson and Gibson (eds), *Dirty Looks. Women, Pornography, Power* (London: BFI Publishing, 1993).

—— *Bound and Gagged. Pornography and the Politics of Fantasy in America* (New York: Grove Press, 1996).

Klossowski, P. *Sade mon prochain* (Paris: Éditions du Seuil, 1967).

Koch, G. 'The Body's Shadow Realm' in Gibson and Gibson (eds), *Dirty Looks. Women, Pornography, Power* (London: BFI Publishing, 1993).

Kristeva, J. *Histoires d'amour* (Paris: Denoël, 1983). English translation, *Tales of love* (New York: Columbia University Press, 1987).

—— 'Bataille solaire, ou le texte coupable' in *Histoires d'amour* (Paris: Denoël, 1983).

—— 'Word, Dialogue and Novel' in Toril Moi (ed.), *The Kristeva Reader* (Oxford: Basil Blackwell, 1986).

—— 'Women's Time' in Toril Moi (ed.), *The Kristeva Reader* (Oxford: Basil Blackwell, 1986); originally published in French as 'Le temps des femmes' in *33/44: Cahiers de recherche de sciences des textes et documents*, 5 (Winter 1979).

Lacan, J. 'La signification du phallus' in *Écrits* (Paris: Éditions du Seuil, 1966).

Lau, G. 'Confessions of a Complete Scopophiliac' in Gibson and Gibson (eds), *Dirty Looks. Women, Pornography, Power* (London: BFI Publishing, 1993).

Lévi-Strauss, C. *Les Structures Élémentaires de la parenté* (Paris: Plon, 1949).

Losfeld, E. *Endetté comme une mule* (Paris: Losfeld, 1979).

Lyotard, J-F *The Postmodern Condition* (Manchester: Manchester University Press, 1984).

MacKinnon, C. *Only Words* (London: HarperCollins, 1994).

Mainil, J. 'Érotisme carnavalesque dans un roman obscène de l'Ancien Régime', *La Chouette*, no. 26 (1995).

de Mandiargues, A. P. *Le Désordre de la mémoire: Entretiens avec Francine Mallet* (Paris: Gallimard, 1975).

Martel, F. *Le Rose et le noir. Les homosexuels en France* (Paris: Éditions du Seuil, 1986).

Merrick, J. and Ragan, Jr., B. T. (eds), *Homosexuality in Modern France* (New York: Oxford University Press, 1996).

Michelson, P. *Speaking the Unspeakable: A Poetics of Obscenity* (New York, Albany: State University of New York Press, 1993).

Miller, N. K. 'Gender and narrative possibilities' in Allison, Roberts and Weiss (eds), *Sade and the Narrative of Transgression* (Cambridge: Cambridge University Press, 1995).

Morgan, E. 'Human becoming: form and focus in the neo-feminist novel' in S.K. Cornillon (ed.), *Images of Women in Fiction: Feminist Perspectives* (Bowling Green: Popular Press, 1972).

Morrissette, B. 'Robbe-Grillet's "Project For a Revolution in New York"', *American Society Legion of Honor Magazine*, 42 (1971).

—— 'Order and Disorder in Film and Fiction', *Critical Inquiry*, vol. 4, no. 1 (Autumn 1977).

Mulvey, L. 'Visual Pleasure and Narrative Cinema' in Robyn R. Warhol and Diane Price Herndl (eds), *Feminisms* (New Brunswick, New Jersey: Rutgers University Press, 1991).

Netz, R. *Histoire de la censure dans l'édition* (Paris: PUF, 1997).

Pauvert, J-J. *Nouveaux Visages de la Censure* (Paris: Les Belles Lettres, 1994).

—— *Anthologie historique des lectures érotiques. De Guillaume Apollinaire à Philippe Pétain, 1905–1944* (Paris: Stock/Spengler, 1995).

—— *Anthologie historique des lectures érotiques. De Eisenhower à Emmanuelle, 1945–85* (Paris: Stock/Spengler, 1995).

—— 'Un pornographe ou les deux Guillaume', *Magazine Littéraire*, November 1996.

Perceau, L. *Bibliographie du roman érotique, II* (Paris: Fourdrivier, 1930).

Perkins, M. *The Secret Record: Modern Erotic Literature* (New York: William Morrow, 1976).

Pia, P. *Apollinaire*, 'Écrivains de toujours' (Paris: Éditions du Seuil, 1965).

Pierrot, J. *The Decadent Imagination 1800–1900* (Chicago and London: University of Chicago Press, 1981).

Porter, R. and Teich, M. (eds), *Sexual Knowledge, Sexual Science: The History of Attitudes to Sexuality* (Cambridge: Cambridge University Press, 1994).

Ramsay, R. *Robbe-Grillet and Modernity. Science, Sexuality and Subversion* (Gainesville, Fl.: University Press of Florida, 1992).

Ricardou, J. 'La Fiction flamboyante' in *Pour une théorie du nouveau roman* (Paris: Éditions du Seuil, 1971).

Richardson, M. *Georges Bataille* (London and New York: Routledge, 1994).

Ricoeur, P. *La métaphore vive* (Paris: Éditions du Seuil, 1975).

Robbe-Grillet, A. *Le Miroir qui revient* (Paris: Éditions de Minuit, 1984).

—— *Angélique ou l'enchantement* (Paris: Éditions de Minuit, 1987).

—— *Les Derniers jours de Corinthe* (Paris: Éditions de Minuit, 1994).

Robinson, C. *Scandal in the Ink. Male and Female Homosexuality in Twentieth-century French Literature* (London: Cassell, 1995).

—— 'Sexuality and Textuality in Contemporary French Gay Fiction', *French Studies*, vol. LII, no. 2 (April 1998).

Rosario, V. A. *The Erotic Imagination. French Histories of Perversity* (New York and Oxford: Oxford University Press, 1997).

—— (ed.), *Science and Homosexualities* (New York: Routledge, 1997).

Ross, A. 'The popularity of pornography' in Simon During (ed.), *The Cultural Studies Reader* (London: Routledge, 1993).

Sade, D.A.F. *Les 120 Journées de Sodom* (Paris: La Collection P.O.L., 1992).

Schehr, L. *The Shock of Men: Homosexual Hermeneutics in French Writing* (Stanford, CA: Stanford University Press, 1995).

Sedgwick, E. K. *Tendencies* (London: Routledge, 1994).

Smith, S. 'Toward a Literature of Utopia' in Stambolian, G. and Marks, E. (eds), *Homosexualities and French Literature. Cultural Contexts/Critical Texts* (Ithaca and London: Cornell University Press, 1979).

Sollers, P. 'Le toit' in *L'Écriture et l'expérience des limites* (Paris: Éditions du Seuil, 1968).

Sontag, S. 'The Pornographic Imagination' in *Story of the Eye* (London: Penguin, 1982); also, in Douglas A. Hughes (ed.), *Perspectives on Pornography* (New York: Macmillan, St Martins Press, 1970).

St. Jorre, J. de *The Good Ship Venus. The Erotic Voyage of the Olympia Press* (London: Pimlico, 1994).

—— 'The Unmasking of O' in *The New Yorker*, 4 August 1994.

Stoltzfus, B. F. *Alain Robbe-Grillet and the New French Novel* (Carbondale: Southern Illinois University Press, 1964).

—— *Alain Robbe-Grillet: The Body of the Text* (London: Associated University Presses, 1985).

Straayer, C. 'The Seduction of Boundaries: Feminist Fluidity in Annie Sprinkle's Art/Education/Sex' in Gibson and Gibson (eds), *Dirty Looks. Women, Pornography, Power* (London: BFI, 1993).

Strossen, N. *Defending Pornography. Free Speech, Sex and the Fight for Women's Rights* (London: Abacus, 1995).

Suleiman, S. R. 'Pornography, Transgression and the Avant-Garde: Bataille's *Story of the Eye*' in Nancy K. Miller (ed.), *The Poetics of Gender* (New York: Columbia University Press, 1986).

—— 'Reading Robbe-Grillet: Sadism and Text in *Projet pour une révolution à New York*', *Romanic Review* (January 1977), 68 (1).

Thompson, B. *Soft Core. Moral Crusades against Pornography in Britain and America* (London: Cassell, 1994).

Wallace, J. 'What does it take to be a woman?', *The Times Higher Educational Supplement*, 8 May 1998.

Williams, L. *Hard Core. Power, Pleasure and the Frenzy of the Visible* (London: Pandora Press, 1990).

—— 'A Provoking Agent. The Pornography and Performance Art of Annie Sprinkle' in Gibson and Gibson (eds), *Dirty Looks. Women, Pornography, Power* (London: BFI Publishing, 1993).

—— 'Second Thoughts on Hard Core. American Obscenity Law and the Scapegoating of Deviance' in *Dirty Looks. Women, Pornography, Power* (London: BFI Publishing, 1993).

Worton, M. 'Cruising (Through) Encounters' in A. Hughes, O. Heathcote and J. Williams (eds), *Gay Signatures. Gay and Lesbian Theory, Fiction and Film in France, 1945–1995* (Oxford: Berg, 1998).

Yaguello, M. *Les mots et les femmes* (Paris: Payot, 1978).

# Index